# DAILY LIFE IN CHINA

# DAILY LIFE IN
# CHINA

## ON *THE EVE OF THE*
## *MONGOL INVASION 1250-1276*

## Jacques Gernet

TRANSLATED FROM THE FRENCH BY
*H. M. Wright*

STANFORD UNIVERSITY PRESS
STANFORD, CALIFORNIA

Originally published as
*La vie quotidienne en Chine à la
veille de l'invasion mongole, 1250–1276*
(Paris: Hachette, 1959)


Stanford University Press
Stanford, California
English translation © 1962 by George Allen & Unwin Ltd
Originating publisher: George Allen & Unwin Ltd, London
First published in the United States by
The Macmillan Company, 1962
Paperback edition first published in 1970 by Stanford University Press
Printed in the United States of America
SBN 8047-0720-0
LC 73-110281
Last figure below indicates year of this printing:
89  88  87  86  85  84  83  82  81  80

# CONTENTS

# MAPS

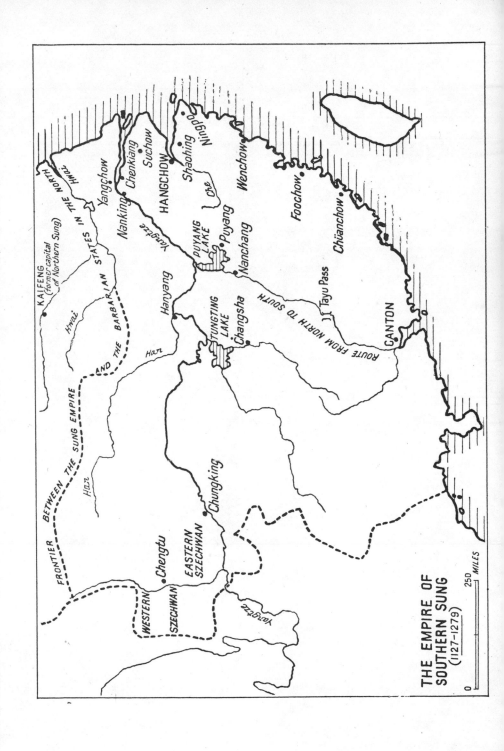

THE EMPIRE OF
SOUTHERN SUNG
(1127-1279)

KAIFENG
(former capital
of Northern Sung)

FRONTIER BETWEEN THE SUNG EMPIRE AND THE BARBARIAN STATES IN THE NORTH

Hwai

Hwai

Han

Han

Yangchow

Nanking

Chenkiang

Suchow

HANGCHOW

Shaohing

Ningpo

Che

Wenchow

Foochow

Chüanchow

CANTON

Yangtze

Hanyang

PUYANG
LAKE

Puyang

Nanchang

TUNGTING
LAKE

Changsha

Tayu Pass

ROUTE FROM NORTH TO SOUTH

Chungking

Chengtu

EASTERN
SZECHWAN

WESTERN
SZECHWAN

Yangtze

0        250        MILES

# DAILY LIFE IN CHINA

# INTRODUCTION

IT USED to be taken as a foregone conclusion that the civilization of China was a static one, or at any rate stress was continually laid on its extraordinary continuity. This continuity, however, is nothing but an optical illusion: anything seen indistinctly always appears featureless. If our own civilization had been as much neglected by historians, and if the complexity of its development from classical times onwards had been as little understood as has been the case with China, it, too, would run the risk of displaying the same majestic immobility, and a certain Chinese quality of permanence might be detected in some of its traditions and mental attitudes. Moreover, the illusion in this case might contain a measure of truth, at least in so far as it might bring home to us the fact that our civilization is just as strange and just as arbitrary in its choices as that of China. It is only lack of adequate comparisons that makes appreciation of its peculiarities difficult, although this has not prevented frequent exercises in self-contemplation.

It should again be stressed that our civilization is not unique in having gone through stages of development. As research progresses, the conventional picture of China which we have built up is vanishing, and the history of China, once the mists veiling its contours have dispersed, will be found to consist, not in continuity and immobility, but in a succession of violent shocks, upheavals and breaks in continuity. Thus, from the sixth to the tenth centuries A.D. China went through a period from which she emerged completely unrecognizable: the establishment of the nomads of the steppes in the northern provinces and the general triumph of Buddhism had left profound marks. Indeed, every period has its own characteristic traits and, so to speak, an atmosphere peculiar to it. Besides, the geographical immensity of China means that there are appreciable variations in climate, landscape, mode of life, customs and dialects. Each region has its own particular features. So that if any useful statements are to be made about this country, which is comparable in size to the whole of Europe and which has a recorded history of nearly 3,000 years, they must refer to a precise time and place. It is no longer permissible to talk of an 'eternal' China.

It was at first intended to give this book a general title; but owing to the vastness of the Chinese world, its regional diversity and unceasing historical development, some more precise delimitation of the field of study was found to be necessary. The particular period of time chosen for this description of life in China is that of the last years of the dynasty known as Southern Sung (1227-1279), the years that preceded the capture of the capital by the Mongols at the beginning of 1276. The place chosen is the region of Hangchow, and more specifically the city itself, the seat of the great prefecture which then had the name of Lin-an, and also the capital of China at that time. Now a place for tourists to visit, renowned for the charms of its scenery, Hangchow today is a small town of several hundred thousand inhabitants, situated some 120 miles south-west of Shanghai, at the head of the estuary of the river Che. About 1275, it was the largest and richest city in the world.

But before explaining the reasons for our choice, a brief historical summary is indispensable.

The differences are striking between the China of the twelfth and thirteenth centuries and the China of T'ang times, the most brilliant period of which occurred during the eighth century. During these four centuries a radical change had taken place. An uncouth, warlike, rather stiff and hieratical society had given place to one that was lively, mercantile, pleasure-seeking and corrupt.

Common to the whole period is the poverty-stricken and precarious life of the peasants which can be glimpsed in the background, and there was indeed a relative increase in their poverty; but the general atmosphere changed completely. The China of T'ang times owed its rather severe grandeur to the character of its climate and its people. Its centre of gravity lay in the dry, dusty plains of the Yellow River valley where they open out at the end of the Kansu corridor which led, through a jumble of mountains and valleys, to the garrisons established in the very heart of Central Asia. The China of the thirteenth century, the Mangi of Marco Polo—the contrast between the two Chinas is so sharp that they appeared as two separate worlds to the eyes of the Venetian traveller—is that of the fertile rice-plains, crisscrossed with canals, that lie between the valley of the Huai and the mountains of Chekiang, of the maritime provinces of the south-east (present-day Kiangsu, Chekiang and Fukien), and of the valley of the Yangtze.

In the eighth century, this China of the South, with its heavy, enervating climate, was no more than an undeveloped area of a vast empire. Interests lay elsewhere, and emotional ties too. For many people, the South was not the home of their ancestors, and they felt themselves exiles there. The great Chinese dynasties had always had their capitals in the North, in the region of present-day Si-an or further to the east of it.

However, with the passing of the centuries, the growing importance of South China had gradually been making itself felt. It had become more densely populated, richer, had developed its maritime and riverine communications, had given rise to a specifically urban mode of life which had been almost unknown in North China, and given birth to great scholar-families, until finally it had become aware of itself and of its dynamism. For this profound, yet barely perceptible process of change there is an explanation which is the first to come to mind and which in all probability is the correct one: it was the continuous pressure exerted, from the tenth to the thirteenth centuries, by the barbarian nomads of Central Asia and of present-day Mongolia that must be held to account mainly for the advance in the general economy of China in the region of the Yangtze valley and in the provinces of the south-east.

The cutting of the routes to Central Asia, in T'ang times, was the first stage in the forward thrust of the nomads. The establishment of powerful barbarian States (Hsi-hsia, Liao and Chin) to the north of the Great Wall, and the constant threat they brought to bear on the northern provinces from the end of the tenth to the beginning of the twelfth century, constituted the second. The final stage brought a more tragic turn of events, and the period of history in which these events occurred forms the background to this description of daily life in China. Two dates encompass it: 1126, the date of the fall of the capital of Northern Sung (960-1126)—the present-day Kaifeng, in Honan—which was followed by the invasion of the whole of North China as far as the Yangtze, and then by the stabilization of the frontier between Chinese and Barbarians along the valley of the Huai, when the Emperor and his court finally took up residence in Hangchow; and 1276, the date of the capture of Hangchow by the Mongols and of the occupation of the whole of China for the first time in her history. The complete subjection of China by barbarians who rebelled against all culture and who were rigidly attached to their warlike tribal traditions—those hordes whose prodigious conquests had been a source of wonder to the West— was a soul-shattering experience for the Chinese. The Mongol occupation dealt a profound blow to the great Chinese Empire, which at that time was the richest and most advanced country in the world. In many spheres, Chinese civilization was at its most brilliant on the eve of the Mongol conquest, and suffered a drastic break in its history as a result of that event.

Would it be correct to say that this period was a disturbed one? If so, it is tantamount to saying that great historical events have a direct repercussion on everyday life. But most people are not affected by the great catastrophes of history unless and until they are personally involved in them. No doubt this was a disquieting period for those in power with a sense of patriotism strong enough to make them aware of the dangers. But it is clear that, until the siege of the town, life went on in Hangchow in the same old carefree way as before. As is well known, the Chinese take things with a good pinch of philosophy.

It must also be recognized that the upper classes were almost without exception irresponsible and avid in the pursuit of pleasure. Later Chinese historians did not fail to ascribe the defeat and subjection of China to this weakening of moral sense among her rulers. This echoes an old classical theme: when indulgence in pleasure and neglect of the rites characterize the sovereign, the empire is led to its ruin. The last emperor of Northern Sung was an aesthete with a passion for painting and for art-collecting. The last emperors of Southern Sung were as lacking in 'virtue' as they were in realism. Yet defence was solidly organized, and the State devoted the major part of its resources to the upkeep of an army of over a million men. Doubtless further research will one day be able to show that the real causes of China's collapse had nothing to do with loose morals, and are more likely to have been of an economic and sociological nature. The impression of order and prosperity given by the South China of the thirteenth century is illusory. Behind it lie the continuous and tragic impoverishment of the State, destitution and disaffection in the countryside, and the struggle of factions within the ruling class. The edifice was fragile, and ready to collapse at the first vigorous push administered by the barbarians.

Yet, in spite of its fragility, it is impressive. The China of the thirteenth century, even with its northern provinces amputated, is still a great empire. It measured, from the westernmost province, Szechwan, to the plains of the lower Yangtze, over 1,200 miles; and from the southern coast to the northern frontier, over 600. It covered a total area of over 700,000 square miles, that is to say, almost four times the size of present-day France. It had a population of over 60,000,000*—an enormous figure for that time, and all the more astonishing in view of the fact that the mountainous regions covering three-quarters of the area were almost entirely unpopulated—which was concentrated in two areas of highest density: the Chengtu basin in western Szechwan, and the plains of the lower Yangtze valley (present-day Kiangsu and Chekiang provinces). The Yangtze, navigable as far up as the rich plains of the region around Chengtu, which could be reached by an affluent of the great river, was South China's principal commercial artery. A network of canals in the eastern part of the empire provided a link between the larger towns, and day and night carried an uninterrupted flow of traffic. A vast fleet of coastwise vessels kept the huge trading centres on the south-east coast in touch with those of the south coast as far as Canton; while the great sea-going junks plied each year, at the monsoons, between China and the main islands of the East Indies, India, the east coast of Africa, and the Middle East. In the interior, at the junction of the north-south roadways with the Yangtze river, permanent markets developed, where the volume of trade far surpassed that of the main commercial centres of Europe at the same epoch.

Thirteenth-century China is striking for its modernism: for its exclusively monetary economy, its paper money, its negotiable instruments, its highly-developed enterprises in tea and in salt, for the importance of its foreign trade (in silks and porcelains) and the specialization of its regional products. Large sections of commerce were in the hands of the omnipresent State,

* According to the official censuses, the total population of China seems to have doubled between 1060 and 1110, and had reached the figure of 100,000,000 persons on the eve of the barbarian invasions of 1126.

which derived the main part of its revenue from a system of State monopolies and indirect taxation. In the spheres of social life, art, amusements, institutions and technology, China was incontestably the most advanced country of the time. She had every right to consider the rest of the world as being peopled by mere barbarians.

Let us now give the reasons for our choice of the time and the place of our description.

The Mongol invasion put an end to a period of rapid progress which had already announced the beginning of modern times in China. This period was marked by an extraordinary development of urban centres and of commercial activity. In less than one century, the population of Hangchow had doubled, and it had gone beyond the million mark by 1275. But this increase is not peculiar to the capital. In directing attention to urban life, we are merely underlining a feature that was typical of the epoch.

There were other considerations which motivated our choice of locality and of period. It is undeniable that archaeological documents of the Sung era are rare, and not particularly revealing. Apart from the ceramics, the production of which was of great importance during the twelfth and thirteenth centuries, and of which countless specimens survive, nothing remains but a few small objects such as women's ornaments, glass cups, lacquer boxes or vases, pillows in painted *faïence*, copper coins . . . Not a single architectural monument has survived, due to the fragile and perishable nature of the materials used in Chinese buildings. It is chiefly the paintings that might furnish us with details of daily life. The Sung painters did in fact like to portray intimate scenes in the life of the rich, or street scenes. We could refer, among other documents of this kind, to the long scroll representing the city of Kaifeng at the beginning of the twelfth century, a scroll attributed to an artist who specialized in the painting of town walls and carts. Unfortunately, the number of these paintings in lively, realistic style which has survived is limited to a very few specimens (or, to be exact, copies), owing to the exclusive preference of collectors of the Ming period (1368-1644) for paintings of flowers, bamboos and landscapes.

However, the scarcity of archaeological documents is largely compensated for by the almost inexhaustible riches of the literary sources. It is in the Sung period that texts from which it is possible to extract information about everyday life begin to become more numerous: daily jottings, collections of anecdotes, tales, local gazeteers, supply us with a mass of precise and picturesque details. The explanation for this sudden increase in sources of information lies in the emergence of printing and the spread of its use from the beginning of the tenth century, in the advances in education, and, parallel with that, the rise of the merchant class, among whom there was not the same scorn for the trivial details of everyday life as there was on the part of the scholar-officials. And what, above all, contemporary documents provide us with an astonishing mass of information about, is the city of Hangchow itself, as it was around the year 1275. There is nothing concerning their city that its inhabitants have failed to note for us: its streets, its canals, its buildings, its administration, its markets and its commercial transactions, its festivals and its amusements—to such an extent, that it is possible today to reconstruct this capital in its minutest details, to find the exact place for each type of trade, for every temple. We even know the names of the most celebrated courtesans, the number of paving-stones in the principal street, the best addresses: it is near to such-and-such a bridge, at such-and-such an establishment, that the best honey-fritters are to be found; in such-and-such an alley that the best fans are sold.

The choice of this city has another advantage: Marco Polo stayed there for a considerable length of time during the years 1276-1292, between the time when Hangchow fell into the hands of the Mongols and that of his return to Europe. At this point in time, the city had not greatly changed. The description which Marco Polo has left of the capital of China is one of the longest and most detailed which occur in his memoirs. It is also one of the most lively. If, as is indicated in certain versions of his book, it was based on an official description supplied to the Mongol general who conducted the siege of Hangchow at the beginning of 1276, it is evident that he often made use of his own personal recollections as well. His astonishment and admiration are manifest. His descriptions, racy and naïve at the same time, merit confrontation with those furnished by Chinese texts. It will be seen that as often as not they agree in precise detail with the indications left to us by the inhabitants of Hangchow.

SUNG CHiNA
*at the beginning of the 12th. century*

0          300
MILES

THE CHIN EMPIRE
(*JU-CHEN*)

HSI-HSIA
KINGDOM

Part of the
Great Wall

SHANSI          HOPEH

SHAN-
TUNG

KANSU

S H E N S I
Wei
Sian
Loyang
Yellow R.
KAIFENG

H O N A N

KIANGSU

SZECHWAN          HUPEH
Chengtu          Yangtze          ANHUI

HANGCHOW

CHEKIANG

H U N A N   KIANGSI

FU-KIEN

Foochow
Chüan-
chow

KWANGSI          KWANGTUNG
Canton

M.

Canal

The version known as the Ramusio text, which has for long been suspect, and which is much more detailed in its account of Hangchow than the better-known versions of *The Book of Marco Polo*, is found to be for the most part confirmed in its details by comparison with Chinese sources. This is the text to which we have most frequently made reference.

We might add that this book has been written almost entirely on the basis of original Chinese texts, and on many points supplies entirely new information. There is still a great lack of secondary sources to draw upon, because the various aspects of everyday life have not yet attracted more than a very few research workers. Furthermore, Chinese is indubitably a difficult language. May these considerations serve as an excuse for the shortcomings of this book!

# CHAPTER I

# THE CITY

THE CHOICE OF HANGCHOW AS CAPITAL: *A provincial town. Its ramparts and its lay-out.* OVERPOPULATION AND SCARCITY OF ACCOMMODATION: *Censuses. Degree of urban concentration about 1275. Crowding-together of buildings and multi-storeyed houses. Rents.* OUTBREAKS OF FIRE AND FIRE-FIGHTING: *Frequency and seriousness of outbreaks. Warehouses surrounded by water. Fear of fire.* COMMUNICATIONS AND SUPPLIES: *Main thoroughfares and canals. The upkeep of roads. Cleanliness of the town. Provisioning by waterways. Main articles of consumption. Markets.* AMENITIES OF TOWN LIFE: *Luxury shops. Tea-houses, taverns and restaurants. Pleasure outings. The lake and the river. Amusements.*

## THE CHOICE OF HANGCHOW AS CAPITAL

THERE ARE times when chance arranges things nicely. When, in 1126, the barbarian Ju-chen horsemen took the Sung capital (present-day Kaifeng, in the Yellow River valley) by storm and the exodus to the south began, there was nothing to indicate that Hangchow was destined to become the seat of the new dynasty. It was then no more than the capital of a distant province, situated at the head of the estuary of the Che river, well off the main commercial highways. The Emperor and his court, more than three thousand prisoners in all, were led into captivity, beyond Mukden, by the barbarians. A prince who escaped proclaimed himself Emperor at Nanking in 1127, and was to be seen fleeing before the nomad invasions, sometimes in the towns of the middle Yangtze, and sometimes, further east, at Yangchou, where the Grand Canal joins up with the river Huai, at Chen-chiang on the right bank of the Yangtze downstream from Nanking, at Suchow, further south, or at Hangchow. None of these walled towns was safe from invasion. But Hangchow, where the Emperor made several halts, was comparatively better protected than the Yangtze towns. To reach it, a region had to be traversed which was riddled by innumerable lakes and by muddy rice-fields: difficult terrain for the deployment of cavalry.

Ten years after the fall of Kaifeng, when, with the return of peace, China had been divided out between the barbarians to the north of the Huai and the Chinese to the south, the Emperor had definitely fixed his choice on Hangchow.

It was neither the importance of the town nor even its past history which brought about this decision. Nanking alone, the one-time capital of the petty dynasties of the South between 317 and 590, would have been considered worthy of serving as the residence of the Son of Heaven. Hangchow, apart from its convenient distance from the areas threatened by invasion, had only one trump: the charm and attractiveness of its scenery. The lake which lies to the west of it and the graceful curves of the hills which surround it still make of it today one of the most breathtaking of China's beauty spots. Here is a thirteenth-century description of it, clumsy enough compared with the eloquence of a scholar, but perhaps sufficiently evocative for us. 'Green mountains surround on all sides the still waters of the lake. Pavilions and towers in hues of gold and azure rise here and there. One would say, a landscape composed by a painter. Only towards the east, where there are no hills, does the land open out, and there sparkle, like fishes' scales, the bright-coloured tiles of a thousand roofs.'[1]

Once the choice had been made—and it may well be that the charm of Hangchow had something to do with it—the advantages of the geographical situation of the town began to reveal themselves. Midway between the Yangtze and the south-east coast, where large trading-ports were growing up (chief of which were Fuchow and Chüanchow), Hangchow, as well as being the capital, was destined also to become the great economic centre of this new South China which was then in the full flood of development. Taking into account the realities of the time, Hangchow, an expanding town, was more suited to be the capital than ancient Nanking, a city in decay. But it was mere chance that decided its special destiny.

The fact of the matter was that there was no enthusiasm at all about the adoption of this town as the seat of the central government. Up until the middle of the twelfth century the Emperor and his court were still hesitating about settling permanently in their residences there. They grudged spending money on improving them; it was enough, they said, to make them secure

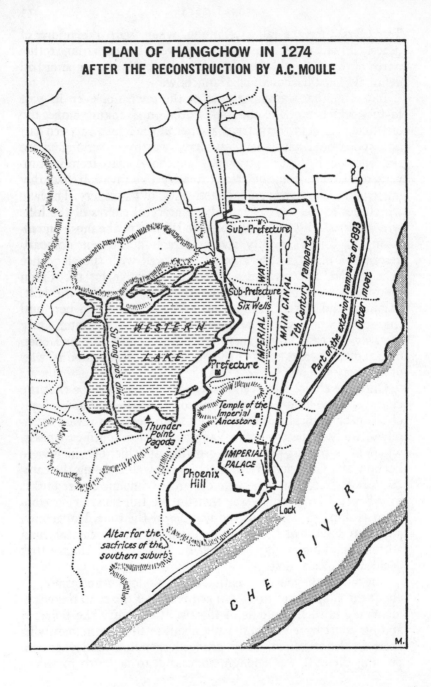

PLAN OF HANGCHOW IN 1274
AFTER THE RECONSTRUCTION BY A.C. MOULE

from the wind and the rain. And it was the prefectural buildings, transferred further to the north, that were used to house the Emperor and the chief administrative organs. The buildings of the improvised palace did not run to more than a hundred to two hundred spans between main columns.* In 1133 it was reluctantly decided to build covered alleyways at the south gate of the palace (the former citadel of the prefecture) so that officials would no longer have to wade through the mud in rainy weather. And it was not until 1148 that it was decided to extend the walls of the enclosure towards the south-east. Still the buildings remained sparse and meagrely decorated. The two principal ones were only 60 feet high, and no more than 80 feet in width. The whole was scarcely more imposing or more luxurious than the administrative quarters of a large prefectural city.[2]

All the evidence goes to show that the court, not used to provincial life, maintained for a long time an attitude of reserve. It was not that they had anything against Hangchow itself, but for more than a century the Emperor and his ministers retained the hope of re-conquering the northern provinces, and Hangchow never acquired the right to the title of capital. It was merely the temporary residence of the Emperor—in Chinese, Hsing-tsai, which is the term usually transcribed as Quinsai (Quinsay, Kinsay, etc.) in the various versions of The Book of Marco Polo (this term having clung to Hangchow in spite of its occupation by the Mongols). It was as a temporary arrangement, then, that the court took up residence there, but the consequences of this arrangement were prodigious: in less than two centuries, this town of medium size and provincial character was to become the richest and most populous city in the world. The animation, the luxury and the beauty of Hangchow at the end of the thirteenth century was a kind of revelation to Marco Polo. Little can he have realized that such a great city had had such modest beginnings, or that the Sung Emperors had been so half-hearted about making it their capital.

The town had not always been on the same site as that occupied by Hangchow in the Sung period, for early in its history, on account of the lack of fresh water for irrigation and supply, the idea had been hit upon of creating an artificial lake. This was

* See page 114.

formed by constructing a dyke which damned up the waters of the surrounding hills. By the seventh century the town had come to occupy its final site: a narrow strip of alluvial soil between one and two miles in width which lies between the left bank of the Che river, here approaching its estuary, and the lake, which bounds the town to the west for a distance of nearly two miles. The ramparts constructed at the beginning of the seventh century followed the outline of this area. Eleven miles long, they formed a rough rectangle orientated from north to south. It was these walls, extended to the south-west in Sung times, that formed the ramparts of the city in the thirteenth century. They were pierced by five gateways through which canals passed, and by thirteen monumental gates at which terminated the great thoroughfares of Hangchow. They delimited the city proper, and it was to these walls that the inhabitants still constantly referred in the thirteenth century in order to distinguish the city from the suburbs. At the points, to the north and to the south, where the walls were farthest apart, there was a distance of over four miles between them, but the east and west ramparts, running more or less parallel, enclosed the city within a space of half a mile to just over one mile at the most. These walls, built of tamped earth and stone, and probably faced with brick, were thirty feet high and about ten feet thick at the base. Ornamented with large crenellations, they were probably whitewashed every month, as was then the custom in several other towns.[3] The thirteen road-gates, with rounded or polyginal arches, were surmounted by towers, except for the three gates on the eastern ramparts, on the vulnerable side of the city, and these were fortified with advance defence-works.[4]

After 893 the plan was formed of building a further line of defence between the eastern ramparts and the river. Two hundred thousand peasants, requisitioned by order of the local potentate of the time, together with the local armies of thirteen districts, worked on the construction of this new rampart. Over eighteen miles long, and stretching well beyond the city to the north and to the south, its primary purpose was to protect Hangchow on the side where there was danger of surprise naval attack from the river, and it is unlikely that it completely encircled the whole town by running round the far side of the lake, as Marco Polo seems to suggest. On the side facing the river, it had an embankment along it and a huge moat which linked up with the canals of the city and which was closed by a sluice at high tide.⁵ As for the banks of the river, which were steep and inclined to crumble, an attempt was made towards the end of the eleventh century to shore them up with faggots and tree-trunks, and each inhabitant was obliged to supply a certain number of faggots. But later, because of the frequent breaches made by the current and the tides in these rather fragile defences, the river banks were paved with large slabs of stone.⁶

We still have a detailed plan of Hangchow as it was in 1274.⁷ The names of each district, each bridge, of its public buildings, its military camps and its temples, are marked there with the utmost precision. In the traditional manner, the city appears on it as a rectangle with each side corresponding to one of the cardinal points. But in spite of this convention which distorts the actual physical features of Hangchow, it is possible, owing to the numerous details of the plan, to our knowledge of the actual configuration of the terrain, and to the rare vestiges of the Sung period which still remained at the beginning of the twentieth century, to reconstruct the town as it was in 1274.

The lay-out was simple: a large thoroughfare, which became the Imperial Way after the court had installed itself at Hang-chow, traversed the city from north to south, terminating at the north gate of the Imperial Palace, and then, beyond the Palace, continuing southwards to the altar for the sacrifices to Heaven and Earth. This thoroughfare was crossed at right angles by others running east and west. In addition, several canals ran parallel to the Imperial Way. The suburbs that extended to the north, the east and the south of the city, between the ramparts and the wall constructed at the end of the eleventh century, were also traversed by numerous canals and by the continuation of the streets of the walled city. But it is not known how far these suburbs extended to the north and to the south; all that can be said is that it would appear that the whole built-up area must, by 1274, have covered a surface of between seven and eight square miles.

## OVERPOPULATION AND SCARCITY OF ACCOMMODATION

The space which nature had measured out to Hangchow in such niggardly fashion was occupied in the thirteenth century by the biggest urban concentration in the world at that time. The largest cities of Europe, with a population of several tens of thousands, were nothing but petty market-towns in comparison with the 'provisional capital' of China. The population of Hangchow had, by 1275, gone beyond the million mark. But how, it may be asked, can such a figure be arrived at? The answer is, that while statistics may be a modern phenomenon in Europe, they are not so in China. The picture of this country's recent past is one of such complete anarchy and disorder that it is hard to imagine how very different it was in former times. It is nevertheless the case that precision of vocabulary and of chronology was one of the earliest triumphs of Chinese civilization, and from the time when the empire was established, in the third century B.C., administrative necessities imposed the need for a similar precision in numerical calculations.

In T'ang and Sung times, the government, once every three years (theoretically, every year with an intercalary month), undertook a complete census of the population by district, by sub-prefecture, by prefecture, and by province; and if all the census registers compiled in China since the beginning of the Christian era were now in our possession, we should be able to follow, in the minutest detail, the demographic evolution of China through the centuries. The census registers which have been discovered in Kansu, near Tun-huang, bear witness to the extreme care with which these documents were drawn up. As well as the area of land cultivated and its exact location, they give us the name and age of the members of every peasant family. At the beginning of the Mongol occupation of Hangchow, after 1276, it became obligatory to post a list of the inmates at the doorway of every house. This law, so typical of the enemy in occupation, as was also the curfew imposed on Hangchow, must have been felt to be in the nature of a joke in bad taste. But China had long been accustomed to a police regime.

'There is another thing I must tell you,' says Marco Polo. 'It is the custom for every burgess in this city, and in fact for every description of person in it, to write over his door his own name, the name of his wife, and those of his children, his slaves, and all the inmates of his house, and also of the number of animals that he keeps. And if anyone dies in the house then the name of that

person is erased, and if any child is born its name is added. So in
this way the sovereign is able to know exactly the population of
the city. And this is the practice also throughout Manzi (South
China) and Cathay (North China).'⁸

The system of division into districts for administrative purposes bore no relation to the actual geography of the town. It was
only the ramparts that made the city proper a recognizable
entity, and it was this walled enclosure that contained the organs
of administration, affording them protection in the event of
rebellion, as it also provided protection for the peasantry of the
surrounding countryside in the event of war. At such times, the
population *intra muros* became vastly augmented. But commercial activities were to some extent independent of the walled city,
which was primarily the seat of the civil and of the military
authorities.

In the Hangchow of the thirteenth century there was a considerable overspill of population beyond the ramparts. Moreover,
as with the large permanent markets in the middle Yangtze
valley, the commercial centre, disregarding the walled city, established itself along the river bank at some distance from the ramparts. Hangchow itself was a city of multiple functions. It was
at once the capital, since it contained the Imperial Palace and the
offices of the central government, the seat of a large prefecture,
and also the seat of two sub-prefectures, the offices of which were
situated within the ramparts. In addition, it was an important
centre of trade. The territory of the two urban sub-prefectures
included the city, the suburbs and the surrounding countryside,
but the population of the rural areas enclosed within their
boundaries must have been negligible in comparison with that of
the urban areas.

Now it so happens that we know the number of inhabitants of
these two sub-prefectures according to censuses taken at three
different periods during the twelfth and thirteenth centuries.
Between 1165 and 1173, 104,669 families were counted, the
equivalent, that is, if the current average of four to five individuals per family is accepted, of a population of just below half a
million. Between 1241 and 1252, 111,336 families were regis-
tered, a figure corresponding to over 500,000 individual inhabitants. The final figure, about the year 1270, was 186,330 families,

that is to say, a total population of around 900,000.[9] These figures provide evidence of a sudden increase in population during the twenty or thirty years preceding 1270. 'Still, today,' says an inhabitant of Hangchow in 1275, 'the population of the town continues to increase year by year and month by month.' In point of fact, the figures given by the censuses must be regarded as a minimum, since neither visitors nor, probably, soldiers garrisoned in Hangchow, were included. It is, therefore, safe to assume that the whole area had over a million inhabitants about 1275, and this corresponds to the estimate frequently made by contemporary writers. 'At Hangchow,' says one of them, 'the buildings are close together, and the number of inhabitants, within and without the ramparts, is certainly more than several hundred thousand families, and over a million persons.'[10]

However, at the time when the court moved to Hangchow in the first half of the twelfth century, the city was probably similar in size to many other prefectural cities in that part of the country. Its population, then confined within the ramparts, must have been less than two hundred thousand individuals. The influx of emigrants from the northern provinces in 1126 and 1138 made a sudden increase in the number of inhabitants. These new arrivals, for the most part persons of high rank coming from Kaifeng and the north-western provinces, had to be housed as well as could be managed under the circumstances. They experienced the discomfort of temporary lodgings. Some were given quarters, with their wives and concubines, in the military camps. But these neighbourhoods, where prostitution flourished, were scarcely suitable for society ladies, and their husbands were sent off to search for accommodation in the city.[11] Other refugees were lodged in the Buddhist monasteries of Hangchow and its environs, and a special imperial edict authorized this transformation of religious establishments into temporary shelters.[12] Later, in spite of the very large number of new buildings, accommodation problems persisted on account of the incessant and extremely rapid growth of the population and also because of the fires which so frequently ravaged the city and its suburbs.

From the middle of the thirteenth century the entire area within the ramparts was built over, and the unbroken line of frontages along the streets and lanes seems to have impressed the Chinese themselves. For in most Chinese towns the buildings were usually rather sparse in the area within the ramparts, which often encircled quite considerable stretches of waste land, orchards, gardens, and even cultivated fields.[13] Such was the case with Ch'ang-an, the capital of the T'ang dynasty from the seventh to the tenth century. The area covered by that city was not much smaller than that of Paris today. So that Hangchow, with its buildings crowded together, presented quite an unusual spectacle. 'The city of Hangchow,' writes one of its inhabitants, 'is large, extensive and overpopulated. The houses are high and built close to each other. Their beams touch and their porches are continuous. There is not an inch of unoccupied ground anywhere.'[14] For his part, Oderic de Pordenone, who described Hangchow some years later than Marco Polo, expressed his admiration thus:

'This city is greater than any in the world, and is quite 100 miles round; nor is there any span of ground that is not well inhabited, and often there will be a house with ten or twelve families. This city has also great suburbs containing more people than the city itself contains. It has twelve principal gates; and at each of these gates at about eight miles are cities larger than Venice or Padua might be, so that one will go about one of those suburbs for six or eight days and yet will seem to have travelled but a little way.'[15]

There was a dearth of building land, and this, together with the increase in population, necessitated the construction of dwelling-houses of several storeys. This was a novelty at that time. Oderic mentions houses of eight or ten storeys, but various Arab travellers give the more modest and without doubt more probable figure of from three to five.

One passage from The Book of Marco Polo would seem to indicate that it was actually the court, beset by problems of accommodation in Hangchow, that by various measure incited the proprietors to add storeys to their houses or construct multi-storeyed ones.

'And again this king did another thing; that when he rides by any road in the city . . . and it happened that he found two beautiful great houses and between there might be a small one . . then the king asks why that house is so small . . . And one told him that that small house belongs to a poor man who has not the power to make it larger like the others. Then the king commands that that little house may be made as beautiful and as high as were those two others which were beside it, and he paid the cost. And if it happened that the little house belonged to a rich man, then he commanded him immediately to cause it to be taken away. And by his command there was not in his capital in the realms of Mangi, which was named Quinsai (Hangchow) any house which was not both beautiful and great, besides the great palaces and the great mansions of which there was great plenty about the city.'[16]

Western travellers so frequently mention multi-storeyed buildings in Hangchow that we cannot doubt their existence, despite the lack of information in Chinese sources, which only contain vague references.[17] It would, moreover, be difficult to understand how a town so circumscribed in area could house a population of over a million people in 1270 if the houses had mostly been single-storeyed, as in the other towns in China at that time. The multi-storeyed houses gave Hangchow a typically urban appearance, and they greatly increased the density of its population. In view of the latter factor, this mode of construction had important effects on the general style of life and on the intensity of social relations.

As has been seen, the suburbs in the urban area outside the walled city did not extend very far: the lake, the river and the hills were obstacles to the town's expansion. The average density of population seems to have been, about 1270, in the region of 200 persons per acre. But the density varied in different parts of the urban area. The hills to the south, where the Imperial Palace lay, were the residential area of the rich. The high officials lived on the hill of the Ten-thousand Pines,[18] and the merchants who had made their fortune in the maritime trade lived on Mount Phoenix, further to the south.[19] There, summer-houses and pavilions were scattered about amidst groves and gardens.

On the other hand, the low-lying part of the walled city, north of the palace, was overpopulated, and in the poorer districts off the Imperial way the density was probably 324 persons per acre. It was there that the multi-storeyed houses stood, giving on to alleyways which were narrow and congested. There is a striking

contrast between the spacious planning of the wide thoroughfares that cut right across the city, the monumental character of
the walls and the gates, the splendour of the official edifices and
of the temples, and the narrowness of the alleyways and chaotic
overcrowding of the poorer districts. True, this contrast was not
peculiar to Hangchow. It was common to all the towns of the
empire, and it seems to reflect the political state of affairs: to be
a symbol, as it were, of the juxtaposition of an omnipresent
government and a vast population living in its shadow, cheek-by-
jowl with those in power yet taking no part in the management
of affairs.

The houses in the poorer districts probably had a very narrow
frontage, and extended mainly in depth. The ground-floor was
usually occupied by a shop or by the workroom of an artisan.
The testimony of Oderic de Pordenone, who sometimes refers to
ten storeys and sometimes to ten families per house, seems to
indicate that these buildings housed one family on each floor,
whatever the actual number of storeys may have been. Rents
were probably paid monthly to the landlord, whether private
person or public authority. The houses belonging to the State
were managed by a special office called the Control of Shops and
Multi-storeyed Houses. 'This office', says one text, 'was to the
north of the Liu-fu Bridge. Its employees, appointed by the public
authorities, fixed rents according to the number of inhabitants,
and collected the annual payments of house-rent and of rent for
unbuilt land.'[20]

It is not known what the amounts paid in rent were, but the
scarcity of accommodation, and the liberal measures fairly frequently decreed by the court, lead one to suppose that rent must
have been a heavy burden on the townspeople. There were, says
one of them, three classes of rent: high, medium, and low. On
the occasion of ordinary ceremonies or of decrees of mercy following upon calamities (times of intense cold, excessive rains,
fires), the government and the private landlords published notices
announcing the remission of a certain number of days to be sub-
tracted from the rent. For the high class of rent, these exemptions ran from three to seven days, for the medium class, from
five to ten, and for the low class, from seven to fifteen. If the
rents had not been reduced for one or other of such reasons, a
remission of three-tenths of the rent was accorded on the occa-

sions of special ceremonies. In this case, on a rent of one thousand cash, the government and private landlords would receive only seven hundred.[21]

## FIRES AND FIRE-FIGHTING

The multi-storeyed houses, situated in the most crowded districts which were a mere network of alleyways, were built of wood and bamboo. This makes it easy to understand the frequency and gravity of the outbreaks of fire and the measures that were taken to fight them. In no other Chinese town had the danger ever been so great. Indeed, the ancient capitals in the northern plains had been traversed by vast avenues which crossed at right angles and divided off the various districts. The main ones were over a hundred yards wide, the lesser ones forty yards or more. Thus fires were generally confined within specified districts. However, at Kaifeng, capital of Northern Sung, fires had already become something of a menace. The population was dense, and, apart from the great Imperial Way which ran from the south gate of the palace to one of the gates on the outer ramparts, the streets seem to have been narrower than those of the capitals in T'ang times. So it is not surprising that it was in this city that for the first time a form of organization is to be found which is important with regard to the question of fire-fighting. It consisted of guard-stations placed every 500 yards and of watch-towers permanently manned by a hundred soldiers and furnished with all the necessary equipment (scythes, hatchets, buckets, etc.).[22]

This form of organization was somewhat tardily adopted in Hangchow. The first years after the court had installed itself there were a period of improvization, and a refugee from Kaifeng complains bitterly about the lack of foresight shown. In the 5th moon (that is, in June) of 1132, he only just escaped in time, with his mother and his wife, to the shores of the lake. Thirteen thousand houses were destroyed, and the only place he could find to live was in the neighbouring hills. They were still living there when, at the beginning of 1137, he was an eye-witness of another fire almost as bad as the previous one, in which 10,000 houses went up in flames.[23]

Hardly a year passed without an outbreak of fire, and sometimes several are noted as having occurred in the same year. Thus, in 1132 fire ravaged several parts of the town in the 5th,

8th, 10th and 12th moons, and the following year attention is drawn to the occurrence of fires in the 1st, 9th and 11th moons, and to two outbreaks in the 12th moon. In the case of the catastrophe in June 1132, to which our refugee from Kaifeng alludes, the fire, in one hour, had spread nearly two miles. In the 8th moon of the same year the victims of disaster were authorized to camp in the two Buddhist monasteries in the neighbourhood of the city. The sale of bamboo, waterproof rush-matting, and planks, was exempted from tax, and the payment of rents was suspended by government order. The court distributed 120 tons of rice among the poor. Similar measures were taken after each outbreak of fire, and taxes on wood and bamboo were lifted for a period varying from one year to several months.[24]

However, a few years after the great fire of 1137, more energetic measures had to be taken, and the organization which had formerly existed at Kaifeng was copied. A description of the city, dating from around 1275, reports that observation towers had been erected here and there in the most overcrowded districts. It was reckoned that there were eight of them within the ramparts, where the population was at its densest, and no more than two in the area beyond the ramparts. If smoke was sighted somewhere, the soldiers on guard in the towers gave warning of this first sign of fire by running up flags during the day, and by lighting lanterns at night. The number of flags or lanterns gave an approximate indication of the location of the disaster. Thus, should fire have broken out to the south of the Heavenly Gate (an old gateway no longer in use, through which the Imperial Way ran), the guards ran up three flags, if it was burning to the north of this gate, two, and only one if the telltale smoke had shown itself beyond the ramparts.

The town was divided into sectors for the purpose of fighting the flames: fourteen sectors within the ramparts, and eight outside. The squads of soldiers allocated to this rescue service numbered two thousand within the city and twelve hundred outside its walls. As at Kaifeng, they were equipped with buckets, ropes, flags, hatchets, scythes, lanterns and fireproof clothing. But these squads were not the only forces employed in defence against fire; as soon as an outbreak was discovered, a whole section of the troops garrisoned in Hangchow was mobilized immediately. In addition, the soldiers encharged with policing the streets had to give notice of any outbreak of fire. These soldiers, whose main duty was to prevent brawls and to form patrols at night against thieves, were quartered, four or five together, at intervals of three hundred yards or thereabouts.[25]

The information given by Marco Polo about fire-fighting precautions in Hangchow does not correspond exactly with the information given by Chinese texts of the Sung period. It must be supposed that the organization was changed in some respects after the Mongol occupation. Moreover, restrictions became more severe, and the curfew had to be strictly observed. 'Part of the watch', says Marco Polo, 'patrols the quarter, to see if any light or fire is burning after the lawful hours; if they find any they mark the door, and in the morning the owner is summoned before the magistrates, and unless he can plead a good excuse he is punished. Also if they find anyone going about the streets at unlawful hours they arrest him, and in the morning they bring him before the magistrates.'[26]

These severe measures must have seemed extremely harsh to the inhabitants of a town where the night life had always been very lively. Before the Mongol occupation, many districts of the town, particularly those bordering on the Imperial Way, remained in a state of animation until very late into the night. Multi-coloured lamps lit the entrances and courtyards of restaurants, taverns and tea-houses, and illumined shop displays. Probably, however, there was no public lighting of any kind, and where the streets were not lit by the lamps of nocturnal trades, no doubt it was necessary to make one's way by the light of a lantern.

Such a lack of regimentation may partly explain the serious fires which Hangchow still experienced in the thirteenth century in spite of the rapidity with which help could be organized. On the 28th of the 3rd moon, April 15, 1208, the fire that had broken out in the district where the government buildings were situated, to the north of the Imperial Palace, raged for four days and four nights and destroyed a large part of Hangchow. Fifty-eight thousand and ninety-seven houses were reduced to ashes over an area of more than three miles lying both within and without the ramparts. Fifty-nine persons perished in the flames, and numberless people were crushed to death in the rush for safety. Four months later the government decided to provide lodging for the victims of the disaster, 5,345 persons in all, of whom 4,077 were adults and 1,268 children, in the various religious establishments (Buddhist and Taoist monasteries, and the temples of the official cult). The alms distributed to the families of those who had succumbed amounted to 160,000 strings of cash and 400 tons of rice. The victims were allotted 500 cash and 2¼ bushels of rice per adult, 200 cash and 1 bushel of rice per child. Some officials who were left homeless hired boats on the lake.[27]

Three other great fires in the thirteenth century are recorded, one in 1229, scarcely less serious than that of 1208, another in 1237, in which 30,000 houses were consumed by the flames, and the last in 1275, just before the Mongols laid siege to the town.

Because of the frequency of fire, the big merchants of the town and those who did business in Hangchow found it prudent to store their goods in buildings specially constructed so as to be completely proof against fire. According to a contemporary account, this gave rise to an institution peculiar to Hangchow: in a part of the town, near the gate on the north-east ramparts, which was well channelled with water, rich families, empresses and eunuchs of the imperial harem had had a score of huge buildings constructed which they then rented out to visiting merchants and to shopkeepers in the town. Warehouses of this kind, surrounded by water on all sides, were completely protected against fire and against thieves, and their owners, who also employed watchmen whose duty it was to start making the rounds as soon as night fell, charged a large monthly sum for this protection and for the space hired.[28]

The townspeople were permanently haunted by the fear of fire. Panicking was frequent, and an imperial edict had to be issued forbidding the spreading of alarming reports of incidents which had occurred. The government also had to take precautions against pillage, for the dregs of the populace took advantage of the panics which accompanied outbreaks of fire to start looting. These 'fire followers', to use the Chinese expression, were tried under martial law.

Many superstitions arose due to the terror caused by the danger of fire. For instance, the numerous fires during the years 1132 and 1133 were attributed to the influence of the name of the first reign-period of Southern Sung: it was known as

'Foundation of Blazing (glory)'. In 1282, a whale over thirty yards long was stranded on the sandbanks of the Che river near the ramparts of Hangchow, and some rascals brought ladders and climbed on to its back to cut it up for meat. Not long after, fire broke out in the town. Notwithstanding the lack of factual evidence, there were people who declared that the fire had been caused by the whale. In the night between the 22nd and the 23rd days of the 12th moon, another and even bigger whale was found dead near the ramparts, and almost immediately afterwards fire destroyed several official buildings and several thousand houses, including the dwelling of the provost of the Arab merchants. 'One sees from this,' says the author who relates this anecdote, 'that the idle tales which circulate among the people are not always without foundation.'[29]

There were temples dedicated to the gods of the river and of streams as well as to the dragon-kings. The townspeople hoped that these divinities, flattered by the sacrifices offered to them, would protect the town from fire. Late sources also mention that in the middle of a pool in the north of the city there was a pavilion dedicated to Mercury, the water-star. This hexagonal building, over seventy feet high, must date from the end of the thirteenth century.[30]

## COMMUNICATIONS AND SUPPLIES

Within less than two centuries the population of Hangchow had increased phenomenally; as we have seen, from 200,000 at most at the beginning of the twelfth century it had reached nearly half a million about 1170, and numbered over a million individuals a century later. Yet the town had expanded very little beyond its ramparts. Owing to the construction of multi-storeyed houses and the occupation of all open spaces, more than two-thirds of its inhabitants, about 1270, dwelt within an enclosure which had been laid out at the beginning of the seventh century and built to shelter the population of a small town. The question therefore arises as to how it was possible to move about thirteenth-century Hangchow and how the transport problems involved in provisioning such a large number of people were solved. In fact, the great thoroughfares running east and west, as well as the Imperial Way, and, more important still, the numerous canals that traversed Hangchow, were sufficient for all requirements.

'The city,' says Marco Polo, 'is situated in such a way that it has on the one side a lake of fresh water which is very clear, and on the other an enormous river. The water (of the lake) feeds a number of canals of all sizes which run through the various districts of the city, taking away all impurities . . . The water then flows out and runs into the ocean, making the air very wholesome. One can go everywhere about the city by means of these canals, as well as by the streets. Streets and canals are so wide and spacious that carts on the one and boats on the other can easily come and go to transport the provisions required by the inhabitants.'[31]

In the eleventh century the canals of the town got periodically silted up with mud brought up by the strong tides, and their beds had to be re-dug every three to five years. The operations interfered with commercial activities and inconvenienced the whole population. All the petty employees and the soldiers engaged in the operation took advantage of every opportunity to put pressure on the townspeople in order to extract bribes from them. 'We shall have to dump earth here,' they might say, 'the outlet canal will have to run in that direction,' loud enough to be overheard by the neighbour on the right; and when a landlord, alarmed at the prospect of the navvying that was going to be done outside his property, had made a fat payment to the overseers, they would be off to make the same extortion from the landlord next door. Finally, more efficient repairs and the installation, during the years 1086-1093, of a big sluice which was closed at high tide, put an end to all these troubles.[32]

The canals that ran through the city and those which, after issuing from the ramparts, led to the big neighbouring prefectures, were of varying dimensions. The biggest must have been between eighteen and thirty feet wide, which allowed room for the biggest transport barges, carrying a load of six tons or more, to pass each other. Even the Grand Canal constructed by Emperor Yang of the Sui dynasty (605-617) as a link between the Huai basin and the Yangtze, which was one of China's main commercial arteries, was little more than eighteen feet wide, according to the Japanese pilgrim Jôjun, who went along it in 1072. As for the canals which in the eighth century ran through the T'ang capital (present-day Si-an), they were much narrower. One of them is described as being eight feet wide and about ten feet deep; presumably big barges could only use it with traffic going alternately one way and then the other.[33]

Boats of many different kinds, big and small, propelled either by a pole or by an oar fixed at the stern, passed along the canals of Hangchow. The ports to the north and to the south of the town, outside the ramparts, were filled with a host of picturesque craft: heavy barges loaded with rice hailing from Wu-hsing, boats loaded with wood, coal, bricks, tiles, sacks of salt, with their boatmen and their families living on board. Most of them were furnished with sails which were hoisted in open country. On a painting representing the streets, canals and bridges of Kaifeng, the former Sung capital, some boats can be seen to have sails made of pleated matting, folding up concertina fashion, and when thus rolled up, looking like long narrow benches.[34] Doubtless this type of sail was also to be found on boats at Hangchow. Some craft were exclusively reserved for passenger traffic: going by boat was a favourite way of getting from one part of the town to another, and it was easier and less expensive to hire a boat to go to one of the neighbouring towns than to go by road. Some rich families even had their own boats, both for pleasure outings and for transport of goods, and the Buddhist monasteries, too, had private fleets for provisioning them with vegetables and with firewood.[35]

Wherever possible, water transport was preferred by the people of Hangchow. In any case, the country round about was not suited for road transport. Lakes, marshes and quagmires were numerous, and the roads, made of beaten earth, did not stand up to heavy loads. 'Formerly, at Kaifeng, carts were used for bringing goods to the centre of the city,' says an inhabitant of Hangchow. 'But at Hangchow, where the streets are all paved with stones, carts have difficulty in getting along because of the uneven surface. That is why only boats are used, or else goods are carried by porters.'[36] It was in fact only on the Imperial Way that carts were to be seen; but then they were only light vehicles exclusively used for passengers.

'In the main street of the city,' says Marco Polo, 'you meet an infinite succession of these carriages passing to and fro. They are long covered vehicles, fitted with curtains and cushions, and affording room for six persons; and they are in constant request for ladies and gentlemen going on parties of pleasure. In these they drive to certain gardens, where they are entertained by the owners in pavilions erected on purpose, and there they divert themselves the livelong day, with their ladies, returning home in the evening in those same carriages.'[37]

Rich people also often went about on horseback or, if they were ladies, in chairs carried by porters. These chairs had a canopy and small folding doors. As well as the bearer-shafts, they had a third pole which rested on the shoulders of the porters.

In the streets and alleys the only method of getting goods transported was by means of porters, or, if the load was too great, donkeys and mules.[38] The Japanese pilgrim Jôjun, who visited Hangchow in 1072, asserts that he saw tiny horses which served as pack-horses, of which he gives the exact measurements: thirty-five inches high, about forty-seven inches in length, and the ears nearly ten inches long, which accounted for their being called 'rabbit-horses'.[39] Porterage by men, very general and cheap because of the abundance of manpower, was done by means of a bamboo pole from which suspended cloth bundles, wicker baskets, large earthenware jars or square wooden tubs.

The Imperial Way, the city's finest thoroughfare, stretched for more than three miles, from the north gate of the Imperial Palace to the gate on the north-west ramparts. It was sixty yards wide and is thus described by Marco Polo:

' . . . the main street of which we have spoken above, which runs from one end of the city to the other, is paved like this with stones and with bricks ten paces along either side, but in the middle it is all filled with small and fine gravel, with its vaulted conduits which lead the rain waters into the canals near by, so that it always stays dry.'[40]

This was certainly a magnificent thoroughfare compared with the streets of our towns in the Middle Ages. Yet Hangchow was far from attaining the splendour of Kaifeng, the former capital which had fallen into the hands of the barbarians. There, the Imperial Way was 300 yards wide! On each side there were

covered-in arcades where the merchants, up to the years 1111-
1117, were authorized to trade. Barriers, painted black, and a
double barrier painted red, partitioned the route from north to
south, leaving a central passage which was reserved for the
emperor and prohibited to people and horses. Traffic was confined to the arcades, beyond the barriers. Two narrow canals ran
alongside the arcades. They had lotuses planted in them, and
were bordered by flowering trees: plum, peach, pear and apricot;
so that in spring one got the impression of a brilliantly-coloured
embroidery.[41]

Almost all the streets in Hangchow seem to have been sur-
faced with large paving-stones such as can still be seen today on
the roads bordering the lake and in the environs of the town.
The dampness of the ground no doubt made this paving necessary, and, as it happened, the district was not lacking in good
quarries. In the thirteenth century one of the streets of Hangchow bore the name of Earth Street, which may indicate that it
was the only one of its kind. Marco Polo himself seems to have
been struck by the paving of the streets of the city, and no doubt
all the more so since the roads in North China, where he had
made such a long stay, were all made of beaten earth.

'And first you may know quite truly,' he says, 'that all the
ways in this town of Quinsai are paved with stones and with
baked bricks; and so are all the ways and causeways of all the
province of Mangi paved so that one can ride . . . both on
horseback and on foot through all the lands of it without soiling
the feet.'[42]

But it was on the upkeep of the Imperial Way that the greatest
cares were lavished. In 1271 the governor of the city received an
order from the court to repair a stretch of it south of the
Heavenly Gate, and another official was encharged with restoring it to a state of repair along its whole length north of this
gate. Originally, it was said, 35,300 stone slabs had been used
for its entire length and breadth; 20,000 slabs, either missing or
broken, were replaced during the repairs.[43]

There is further evidence to show what care was taken to keep
the roadways in order. In 1268, three years before the repairs to
the road-surface of the Imperial Way, the governor of the city
had been encharged with rebuilding the bridges of Hangchow.

In 1170 there were seventy-one of these bridges within the ramparts, in 1250 a hundred, and in 1271 as many as 117, not counting the 230 there were by that time in the suburbs. More than half of them were demolished and entirely rebuilt, and most of the rest were repaired. The low bridges, which interfered with traffic on the canals, were heightened, and the narrow ones widened, in order that boats, people and vehicles could circulate more freely and bottlenecks become less frequent. These rebuilding operations lasted from October 1268 until November 1269, and the cost reached a total of 466 million cash.[44]

It was probably when the court settled in Hangchow that attention began to be paid to the safety of pedestrians. Formerly, according to one author, the quays along the canals had no continuous railings, but only, here and there, parapets constructed by waterside landlords. Drunken revellers, confused by the lights and failing to notice the twists and turns of the canals, often used to fall in, and tens and hundreds of them were drowned every year, until the day came when the governor of the city had solid balustrades placed along the edge of the canals, with gates at the points of embarkation.[45]

Finally, a high standard of cleanliness was maintained in Hangchow. This was in any case essential, particularly at the hottest time of the year, in July and August, otherwise epidemics would have spread quickly and taken a heavy toll in such an overcrowded town. The streets were cleansed by the public authorities, who had the refuse removed by boat. These boats, after collecting at a meeting-point on a stretch of canal in the north of the city, 'near the New Bridge', left in convoy for the country, where the garbage was deposited on waste land. Once a year, at New Year, the prefecture undertook a thorough cleansing of the streets and a general clearing-out of the canals.

The houses of the rich had cesspools. But the poor people who lived in the multi-storeyed houses in the poorer districts were obliged to use 'horse buckets' which the scavengers came to collect each day. The nightsoil was doubtless used as manure for the gardens in the environs and for the vegetable plots in the eastern suburbs. The scavengers, commonly called 'the pourers', formed a corporation. Each one had his regular customers, and would be ill-advised to take away theirs from his companions, for should he do so, notes a contemporary with amusement, the affair might grow so acrimonious that it might reach the point of being brought before the tribunal of the prefecture, and the plaintiff would not be satisfied until the case had been decided in his favour.[46]

The establishment of the court at Hangchow seems to have been of great profit to the city; everything was done to improve its appearance and to facilitate the flow of traffic and reduce its dangers. Nevertheless, in spite of the double network of canals and streets, traffic congestion was not unknown on the main thoroughfares. It ocurred chiefly at the gateways to the city, which were too narrow for the seething mass of carriages, horses, donkeys and porters, and also at the approaches to the bridges, which were often narrow and hump-backed, or, as the more poetic Chinese expression has it, 'rainbow' shaped. At Kaifeng, where carts were numerous, it had been customary to harness two mules or two donkeys to the back of the heaviest wagons. They were made to pull against the load on the descent of the slope so as to reduce the speed.[47] Even in Hangchow, where in most districts no carts were to be seen, this type of bridge must have been an impediment to traffic. Some of them had shallow steps which donkeys and mules were trained to go up and down. Finally, on turning off the main streets to penetrate the jumble of alleyways in the poorer districts, an indescribable confusion reigned. According to a contemporary, one only went there at risk of one's life.[48] Pole-porters, animals laden with sacks and pedestrians jostled and bumped into each other in a constant pandemonium.

Thanks to the river, the lake, the paved roadways leading to the city and the canals which ran through it and linked it with the big neighbouring cities, Hangchow was easily supplied with every variety of commodity. A local saying enumerating the products of daily consumption linked them with the four cardinal points: 'Vegetables from the east, water from the west, wood from the south and rice from the north'. And indeed firewood and timber were brought by boats which went up-river towards the interior, the vegetable gardens were numerous in the eastern suburbs where the vegetable market was held, rice came by canal from the plains which extended to the north of Hangchow and on the other side of the Yangtze, and finally, the townspeople's only drinking water was that of the lake to the west.[49]

There were reservoirs known as the Six Wells in the north-west of the city, within the ramparts, which fed into the lake. Made fit for use in the eighth century through the cares of a governor of the city and repaired in the eleventh century, when earthenware conduits had been placed in the channels leading into the lake, they were the sole source of fresh water in the neighbourhood. Water from the river, which, because of the tides, was brackish, contaminated all the wells dug in the sur-roundings of Hangchow. For this reason, jealous care was lavished on maintaining the purity of the lake water. During the years 1265-1274 a censor at the court lodged an accusation against two high officials for having had houses, built on piles, constructed over the waters of the lake, where they washed their hair and did their laundry. 'In this way,' says the accuser, 'the wines offered up in libation to Heaven and Earth and to the Imperial Ancestors cannot have the required purity. Moreover, the townspeople, who drink no other water but this, run the risk of epidemics.'[50] It is not known how the water from the Six Wells was distributed in the town; probably pole-porters carry-ing buckets went about the streets and alleyways of Hangchow.

The two products consumed in largest quantity by the towns-people, and which were their basic foodstuffs, were rice and pork. 'If,' says a contemporary account, 'one excepts the private mansions of princes, the houses of high officials, the residences and dwellings of the rich and of all salaried persons in the administration, the daily consumption of the ordinary people of the town is not lower than 70 to 140 tons of rice.' Another account gives different and more precise figures derived from a source which seems reliable. 'I once had the occasion,' says its author, 'of hearing the head of the officials employed at the pre-fecture say, that if one excludes the families who obtain their supplies directly from outside, there are in the city (within the ramparts) 160,000 to 170,000 people who have to buy their rice in the shops. Now, if one reckons an average of 2½ lb. daily consumption per head, it is clear that a supply of at least 210 to 280 tons of rice is required daily. And neither the suburbs to the north and to the south, nor visiting merchants, nor travellers, are included in this calculation.'[51] Probably the upper classes, who obtained their rice by direct supply, consumed less of this commodity than was the case among the lower classes, because their diet was more varied. But in all, several hundred tons of this cereal must have been brought into Hangchow every day, and the rice-barges coming from the great rice-growing regions of Chekiang and of present-day Kiangsu passed unceasingly along its canals. It was a traffic which went on uninterruptedly night and day, and it was even necessary for Hangchow to import rice from the Huai valley and, by sea, from the region of Canton, nearly a thousand miles away. The barges were unloaded at the Ricemarket Bridge and at the Black Bridge, in the northern suburbs, where their cargo was sold to the innumerable shops and restaurants of the town.[52]

The principal pig-market was right in the centre of the city, off the Imperial Way. In two lanes there several hundred beasts were slaughtered every day. The slaughterhouse opened at the third night-watch, between one and two in the morning, and closed at dawn. Portions of pork and offal were sold there to noodle merchants, tea-houses, taverns and pickled-pork shops, as well as to street-vendors who sold pieces of roast pork. But there also existed, scattered here and there about the city, pork-butchers' shops which did their own slaughtering. In front of their displays, with the various knives and hatchets all shining like new, from five to seven men were occupied in cutting up meat. Every day more than ten sides of pork were sold, and at the festival of the Summer Solstice or at the New Year, which fell at the end of January and the beginning of February, dozens of sides were retailed. Yet, says an inhabitant, if, during the year, the great rich families of the town celebrated marriages or held banquets in several dozen places at the same time, however great the demand might be, everything was delivered promptly.[53]

After rice and pork, salted fish took the first place in the diet of the people of Hangchow. So there were nearly 200 shops selling nothing else but this kind of fish, within and without the ramparts. In addition, there were more than fifteen big markets specializing in the sale of particular products. Most of them were outside the ramparts: the vegetable market outside the New Gate, in the eastern suburbs; the fresh-fish market to the south-east of the city, outside the Gate-where-one-awaits-the-tide; the crab-market on the banks of the river; the cloth-market outside the south ramparts. Also to be noted are the markets for flowers, for olives, for oranges, for pearls and precious stones, for medicinal plants, and for books.[54] Finally, throughout the city and its suburbs, there were shops selling noodles, fruits, thread, incense and candles, oil, soya sauce, fresh and salt fish, pork and rice. 'All these,' says an inhabitant, 'are indispensable products which are everybody's everyday requirements.'

But the districts where the briskest retail trade was done in Hangchow were those adjoining the Imperial Way. It was there that the luxury trade, the best shops, and most of the big taverns and fashionable tea-houses were to be found.

Let us quote Marco Polo once again. Although what he says about the location of the markets within the ramparts does not correspond with the information given by Chinese sources of around 1275, at the end of the Sung period, for the rest his account is exact:

'[There] are ten principal markets, though besides these there are a vast number of others in the different parts of the town. The former are all squares of half a mile to the side, and along their front passes the main street, which is forty paces in width, and runs straight from end to end of the city, crossing many bridges of easy and commodious approach. At every four miles of its length comes one of those great squares of two miles (as we have mentioned) in compass. So also parallel to this great street, but at the back of the market places, there runs a very large canal, on the bank of which towards the squares are built great houses of stone, in which the merchants from India and other foreign parts store their wares, to be handy for the markets. In each of the squares is held a market three days in the week, frequented by 40,000 or 50,000 persons, who bring thither for sale every possible necessary of life, so that there is always an ample supply of every kind of meat and game, as of roebuck, red-deer, fallow-deer, hares, rabbits, partridges, pheasants, francolins, quails, fowls, capons, and of duck and geese an infinite quantity; for so many are bred on the Lake that for a Venice groat of silver you can have a couple of geese and two couple of ducks. Then there are the shambles where the larger animals are slaughtered, such as calves, beeves, kids, and lambs, the flesh of which is eaten by the rich and great dignitaries.

'These markets make a daily display of every kind of vegetables and fruits; and among the latter there are in particular certain pears of enormous size, weighing as much as ten pounds apiece, and the pulp of which is white and fragrant like a confection; besides peaches in their season both yellow and white, of every delicate flavour.

'. . . . From the Ocean Sea also come daily supplies of fish in great quantity, brought twenty-five miles up the river, and there is also a great store of fish from the lake, which is the constant resort of fishermen, who have no other business. Their fish is of sundry kinds, changing with the seasons . . .

'All the ten market places are encompassed by lofty houses, and below these are shops where all sorts of crafts are carried on, and all sorts of wares are on sale, including spices and jewels and pearls. Some of these shops are entirely devoted to the sale of wine made from rice and spices, which is constantly made fresh, and is sold very cheap.'[55]

## AMENITIES OF URBAN LIFE

'Quinsai . . . is the greatest city which may be found in the world,' says Marco Polo, 'where so many pleasures may be found that one fancies himself to be in Paradise.'[56] The wealthy among the people of Hangchow were able to satisfy their refined tastes in furnishings, clothing, good cooking and amusements. There were shops in the centre of the city that specialized in luxury products and that were full of goods from all over China and from the South Seas, India and the Middle East.

Things were to be found in Hangchow which were unobtainable in any other city in China, and according to a contemporary account, featuring among such merchandise were beauty products (ointments and perfumes, eyebrow-black, false hair), pet cats and fish for feeding them with, 'cat-nests', crickets in cages and foodstuff for them, decorative fish, bath wraps, fishing tackle, darts for the game of 'narrow neck', chessmen, oiled paper for windows, fumigating powder against mosquitoes . . .

Moreover, there existed in this city certain trades not known elsewhere: the repairing of ovens, of cooking pots, of articles made of bamboo, knife-sharpening, specialist firms for clearing out wells and canals, etc.[57] Shops known as 'tea and wine kitchens' undertook to supply customers with everything necessary for banquets held on special 'good fortune' occasions (wed-dings, appointments, promotions) or for funerals. These concerns looked after every detail of the feast: food, wine, tea, dishes, tablecloths, decorations, and hiring of rooms, for any number of guests.[58] Marco Polo refers to a similar institution, but as it appears, based on a different principle: 'In the middle of the Lake,' he says, 'there are two Islands, on each of which stands a palatial edifice with an incredibly large number of rooms and separate pavilions. And when anyone desired to hold a marriage feast, or to give a big banquet, it used to be done at one of these palaces. And everything would be found there ready to order, such as dishes, napkins and tablecloths and whatever else was needful. These furnishings were acquired and maintained at common expense by the citizens in these palaces constructed by them for this purpose. Sometimes there would be at these palaces an hundred different parties; some holding a banquet, others celebrating a wedding; and yet all would find good accommodation in the different apartments and pavilions, and that in so well ordered a manner that one party was never in the way of another.'[59]

The intense commercial activity, the extreme density of population, and the constant influx of visitors explain why there were so many places where inhabitants and travellers alike could eat, meet and amuse themselves. The town boasted a multitude of restaurants, hotels, taverns and tea-houses, and houses where there were singing-girls. The rich met at Hangchow's celebrated tea-houses. Wealthy merchants and officials came there to learn to play various musical instruments. The décor was sumptuous, with displays of flowers, dwarf evergreens, and works by celebrated painters and calligraphers to tempt the passers-by. Teas of the highest quality or 'plum-flower' wine were served in cups of fine porcelain placed on lacquer trays, and in summer fritters, medicines against the heat, and beverages for contracting the gall-bladder were also served. Some tea-houses on the Imperial Way had singing-girls on the upper floor. But these were noisy places of ill-fame, and were avoided by the best people.[60]

The fashionable taverns were to be found, as were no doubt the big tea-houses also, in one-storeyed houses which did not give directly on to the street, but on to a courtyard which covered arcades. The garish décor made up in gaiety what it lacked in restraint: red and green balustrades, purple and green blinds, crimson and gilt lanterns, flowers and dwarf trees, elegantly-shaped chairs. In the arcades scores of singing-girls, prostitutes and courtesans, permanently employed there, invited the guests to have drinks. 'From a distance,' says one author, 'their beauty was quite fairylike'.

In these taverns, rice-wine of many kinds was served in little silver cups—a detail which in itself, as a contemporary remarks, shows how well-to-do the proprietors were. Various things to eat were served along with the drinks. A menu was handed to the customers, from which they could choose the dishes they wanted. If they did not intend to drink very much, they did not go upstairs, but sat, as it was said, on 'the horse-track'—the ground floor. It was necessary to be to some extent versed in the ways of the world in these places; the provincial who, by his behaviour, betrayed his inexperience, immediately became the target of jokes at his expense, and the proprietor and the singing-girls took advantage of his ignorance to raise their prices.[61] Some taverns served nothing but pies with the drinks: silkworm pies, shrimp pies, pork pies, or dishes made with mutton. Others, which bore as sign a ladle, a cup or a dried calabash, only catered for clients in a hurry who could not stop for more than one or two cups. These more plebeian taverns were rough shelters made of bamboo trellis and curtains. Others again, where only the lowest class people were to be met (porters, shop-hands, artisans, servants), did not serve anything along with the drinks except beancurd soup, oysters and mussels.[62]

The big restaurants had doors in the form of archways decorated with flowers. From them was suspended half a pig or a side of mutton. The decoration was brightly coloured here too. There were small rooms on each side of the large central banqueting hall. 'As soon as the customers have chosen where they will sit,' says a contemporary account, 'they are asked what they want to have. The people of Hangchow are very difficult to please. Hundreds of orders are given on all sides: this person wants something hot, another something cold, a third something tepid, a fourth something chilled; one wants cooked food, another raw, another chooses roast, another grill. The orders, given in a loud voice, are all different, sometimes three different ones at the same table. Having received the orders, the waiter goes to the kitchen and sings out the whole list of orders, starting with the first one. The man who replies from the kitchen is called the Head Dishwarmer, or the Table-setter. When the waiter has come to the end of his list, he takes his tray to the stove and then goes off to serve each customer with the dish ordered. He never mixes them up, and if by any unlikely chance he should make a mistake, the proprietor will launch into a volley of oaths addressed to the offending waiter, will straight-away make him stop serving, and may even dismiss him altogether.'[63] There were restaurants where all the dishes, includ-ing fish and soups, were served iced. Others specialized in certain kinds of food or in regional cooking of some kind. Others again, of the cheaper variety, only served noodles stuffed with vege-tables or pork and beanshoots with boiled leeks. It is scarcely astonishing that the people of Hangchow were often taxed with being greedy. 'Anyone who should see the supply of fish in the market,' says Marco Polo, 'would suppose it impossible that such a quantity should ever be sold; and yet in a few hours the whole shall be cleared away; so great is the number of inhabitants who are accustomed to delicate living. Indeed they eat fish and flesh at the same meal.'[64]

The multitude and variety of commercial activities was one of the attractions of Hangchow. But not the only one. Outside the ramparts, mainly by the lakeside and in the southern suburbs, were parks and gardens to which the people had free access. On feast days these places were invaded by a holiday crowd who came to admire the rare flowers and exotic trees. Some of them, taking with them something to eat, and carrying musical instru-ments, made a day's excursion on the shores of the lake or on the hills surrounding it. Others hired boats for several cash coins and enjoyed the pleasure of seeing some of the most beautiful and celebrated scenery in China pass before their eyes.

The lake was associated with the memory of two of the greatest poets of T'ang and Sung times: Po Chü-i and Su Tung-p'o, both of whom were prefects of Hangchow, the one at the beginning of the ninth century, the other at the end of the eleventh. The lake had been artificially enlarged during the course of centuries, and was always in danger of getting choked up with mud and with aquatic plants. Between 1041 and 1048 it had been enlarged after the expropriation of estates belonging to great families and to Buddhist monasteries. Between 1086 and 1093, Su Tung-p'o memorialized the Emperor asking for funds for the embellishment of the lake and for the purpose of restoring it to the state it had been in T'ang times. 'The West Lake,' he said in his memorial, 'is like the eyes and eyebrows of a face. It would be a crime to neglect it.' In consequence, the court granted him some certificates of ordination for monkhood (these diplomas constituting at that time a kind of paper money) which he exchanged for cash and for rice. Peasants were recruited for clearing and enlarging the lake.[65]

By 1275 the lake was over nine miles in circumference and nine feet deep. Military patrols, under the command of specially appointed officials, looked after its policing and maintenance; it was forbidden to throw any rubbish into it or to plant in it lotuses or water-chestnuts. The care bestowed over centuries on the maintenance of the lake bears witness to the extraordinary feeling for and delight in beautiful scenery shown by the Chinese of T'ang and Sung times. Its beauty spots were preserved with jealous care, and every new building had to blend in harmoniously with its surroundings. The same was so with the Buddhist pavilions and towers which stood on the hills surrounding the West Lake. Among other edifices of this kind we might single out for mention the pagoda which in the thirteenth century rose up on Thunder Point, a small promontory at the southern end of the lake. This octagonal tower, about 170 feet high, was built in blue brick in 975.[66]

According to a description of Hangchow of 1275, there were always hundreds of boats of all shapes and sizes on the lake: small boats such as those to be seen on the canals of the city, with a large oar fixed to the stern which the boatman worked with his foot;[67] fast boats propelled by wheel or pedals; big flat-bottomed boats 90 to 180 feet long, which could carry thirty, fifty or even 100 passengers; boats 18 to 27 feet long which could hold about twenty people. The finest workmanship had gone into the construction of these boats, and the upper parts were ornamented with fine carvings and painted in bright colours. They moved in such a way that 'one felt the motion no more than if one were on dry land'. Each one had a name: the 'Hundred Flowers', the 'Seven Jewels', the 'Golden Lion', the 'Yellow Boat', etc. Near the gardens of the Little Lake (the part of the lake divided off by a small dyke) were moored the boats belonging to the Emperor, built throughout of cedarwood, with magnificent carvings. Tied up alongside the monastery of the Marvellous Mushroom was a boat which was reputed to cause a storm each time it put to sea, so that it was no longer used and always remained moored at this place.

Some small boats carrying singing-girls, or arranged in such a fashion that the passengers could play various games on them (darts, ball games, etc.), would approach people on the lake-shore without having been summoned. The pleasure boats were never out of work, and on feast days—the 8th of the second moon (in March), the 8th of the fourth moon (towards the month of May) and the Feast of the Dead, around April 5th—it was as well to book passages in advance. On such occasions there was nothing to be had under 200 or 300 cash. The passengers who wanted to dine on board did not have to bring anything with them on these pleasure boats: the boatmen undertook to supply everything— dishes, wine and food. Rich families had their own boats for pleasure trips, and there were high officials who had 'lotus-gathering' boats. These little boats, which only held one or two passengers, were ornamented in the most elegant way and carried deep blue sails. But as well as all these, a swarm of little boats carrying various cargoes crossed the lake from north to south. Vegetables, fruit, chickens, shellfish, flowers, wines, soups, sweetmeats—there was hardly any kind of merchandise that could not be procured from these boats. There were also, near the shore, boats from which fishermen cast their lines, and out in the middle of the lake, boats from which fishing was done by net, when one of the crew would knock against the hull with a long pole to frighten the fish into the nets. There were special boats carrying water-turtles and shellfish which, in accordance with a Buddhist rite, were thrown back alive into the water by their purchasers.[68]

In his description of Hangchow, Marco Polo furnishes information very close to that found in Chinese sources of the Sung period:

'On the Lake of which we have spoken there are numbers of boats and barges of all sizes for parties of pleasure. These will hold ten, fifteen, twenty or more persons, and are from fifteen to twenty paces in length, with flat bottoms and ample breadth of beam, so that they always keep their trim. Anyone who desires to go a-pleasuring with the women or with a party of his own sex, hires one of these barges, which are always to be found completely furnished with tables and chairs and all other apparatus for a feast. The roof forms a level deck, on which the crew stand, and pole the boat along whithersoever may be desired, for the Lake is not more than two paces in depth. The inside of this roof and the rest of the interior is covered with ornamental painting in gay colours, with windows all round that can be shut or opened, so that the party at table can enjoy all the beauty and variety of the prospects on both sides as they pass along. And truly a trip on this Lake is a much more charming recreation than can be enjoyed on land. For on the one side lies the city in its entire length, so that spectators in the barges, from the distance at which they stand, take in the whole prospect in its full beauty and grandeur, with its numberless palaces, temples, monasteries, and gardens, full of lofty trees, sloping to the shore. And the Lake is never without a number of such boats, laden with pleasure parties; for it is a great delight of the citizens here, after they have disposed of the day's business, to pass the afternoon in enjoyment with the ladies of their families, or perhaps with others less reputable, either in these barges or in driving about the city in carriages.'[69]

Outside the east gates the scenery was more austere: sea-going junks with square sails made of matting or of dark-coloured cloth, fishing boats and transport barges, were anchored near the banks, or sailed along the river, which is between one and two miles wide at this point. The great junks that sailed on the high seas rarely came to Hangchow because of the sandbanks which encumber the estuary of the Che river, and the boats usually seen there were of a smaller type with six to eight oars known as 'wind-piercers'. The boats which went net-fishing in the estuary of the Che river as far as Wenchou were called 'sampans' (literally: 'three planks'). It was they which supplied Hangchow with saltwater fish and with crabs. Other boats went up-river for a distance of a hundred miles or more and brought back to Hangchow timber, firewood, oranges and mandarines, salt fish and dried and fresh fruits.[70] But the inhabitants hardly ever made

excursions on this side of the city except at the times of the
great tidal bore. At such times, the tremendous flood of waters
and the wildness of the waves brought along sightseers by the
thousand.

This brief description of the city would not be complete if
mention were omitted of the numerous entertainments which
the townspeople could enjoy in the streets (jugglers, marionettes,
Chinese shadow-plays, story-tellers, acrobats . . . ) and in the
'pleasure grounds' in which huge popular theatres were to be
found where people of all conditions met and jostled together.
There were daily performances there, and exhibitions of dancing,
singing and instrumental music. Hangchow seems to have lived
in an atmosphere of continuous feasting. The incessant activity
in the streets and markets, the pleasures, the luxury, and the
gaiety of the town: all this makes a vivid contrast with the
poverty in the countryside and the hard, monotonous and frugal
life of the peasants.

Without any question, Hangchow in the thirteenth century
was, to quote again the words of Marco Polo, 'the most noble
city and the best that is in the world'. But it should not be forgotten that the order and beauty to be found there were the
result of long years of patient care. The city and its lake were
conquests made over nature dating from the first centuries of the
Christian era. And so the city was a testimony to the genius of
man and his ability to dominate the world he lives in. It was a
concrete example of his ingenuity and perseverance. But there
was also something essentially and peculiarly Chinese about it,
of which this description may have provided a glimpse: the
remarkable administrative organization behind it.

## NOTES AND REFERENCES

References to the *Tung ching meng hua lu*, a description of Kaifeng,
in Chinese, written in 1235, and to similar descriptions of Hangchow: *Tu ch'eng chi sheng* (1253), *Meng liang lu* (1275; referred to
as MLL) and *Wu lin chiu shih* (1280), are to the edition published in
Shanghai by the Ku-tien wen-hsüeh ch'u-pan-she in 1956 under the
title of *Tung ching meng hua lu*.

References to the writings of Marco Polo are either to Volume I of *The Book of Ser Marco Polo concerning the Kingdoms and Marvels of the East*, translated and edited by Sir Henry Yule, 3rd edition revised by Henri Cordier, 2 vols., London, 1926 (referred to as Y); or to Volume I of *Marco Polo, The Description of the World*, edited by A. C. Moule and Paul Pelliot, London, 1938 (referred to as M & P).

References to the *Kuei hsin tsa chih* are to the *Hsüeh chin t'ao yüan* edition, and to *Shuo fu*, to the *Ch'ung chiao shuo fu* edition.

1. *Kuei hsin tsa chih*, Hsü B, § 82.
2. Hsü I-t'ang, article in Chinese on the growth of the city of Hangchow under the dynasty of Southern Sung, *Bulletin of Chinese Studies*, IV, 1, Ch'eng-tu, Sept. 1944.
3. *Tung ching meng hua lu*, I, 1, p. 7. Cf. A. C. Moule, *Quinsai with other notes on Marco Polo*, Cambridge, 1957. It may be noted that city walls in China in the Sung period were usually 24 to 30 feet high.
4. MLL, VII, 1, p. 183. Cf. Moule, *op. cit.*, pp. 13-17 (on the history of the city before Sung times and on the ramparts of the 7th c.).
5. Moule, *op. cit.*, pp. 17-18. On the embankment constructed in 910, see *Feng ch-uang hsiao tu*, *Shuo fu* XXX, f. 14b-15b.
6. *Hou shan t'an ts'ung*, *Shuo fu* XXII.
7. For a reproduction of the plan of 1274, cf. Moule, *op. cit.*, plates.
8. Y, p. 192.
9. MLL, XVIII, 2, pp. 281-2.
10. MLL, XVI, 6, p. 269.
11. Hsü I-t'ang, *op. cit.* Cf. *I chien chih*, *ting* XI, 11th anecdote.
12. *Kuei hsin tsa chih*, Hou § 19.
13. This was also the case in the big commercial port of Chüanchow (Zaytun) in the 14th c. Cf. Ibn Batuta, quoted by Yule, *Cathay and the Way Thither*, IV, pp. 268-9: 'In this, as in every other city of China, every inhabitant has a garden, a field, and his house in the middle of it . . . It is for this reason that the cities of China are so extensive.'
14. MLL, X, 12, p. 215.
15. Quoted by Moule, *op. cit.*, p. 25.
16. M & P, pp. 312-13.
17. Sources quoted in Moule, *op. cit.*, p. 26.
18. Hsü I-t'ang, *op. cit.* Cf. *I chien chih*, *i* 16, 6th anecdote.
19. MLL, XVIII, 7, p. 294.
20. MLL, X, 8, p. 213. E. Balazs, 'Marco Polo dans la Capitale de la Chine', *Oriente Poliano*, pub. by l'Istituto Italiano per il Medio ed Estremo Oriente, Rome, 1957, p. 142.

21. MLL, XVIII, 6, p. 293. Balazs, *op. cit.* An author of the end of the 13th c., Chou Mi, in *Wu lin chiu shih*, VI, 7, p. 444, even goes so far as to assert that in some years, owing to the large number of exemptions, the inhabitants reached the point of being lodged free. But this is no doubt a slight exaggeration.
22. *Tung ching meng hua lu*, III, 11, p. 22.
23. *Feng ch-uang hsiao tu*, chap. II, *Shuo fu* XXX.
24. Hsü I-t'ang, *op. cit.*
25. On fire-fighting organization in Hangchow, see MLL, X, 12, pp. 215-16.
26. Y, p. 188.
27. Hsü I-t'ang, *op. cit.*
28. MLL, XIX, 3, p. 299. *Tu ch'eng chi sheng*, § 12, p. 100.
29. *Kuei hsin tsa chih*, Hsü A, § 75.
30. Hsü I-t'ang, *op. cit.*
31. M & P, p. 327 and Y, p. 200.
32. *Sung shih* [Official history of the Sung dynasty] XCVII, on the canals of Lin-an.
33. *T'ang liang-ching ch'eng-fang k'ao*, by Hsü Sung (19th c.), on the canals of Ch'ang-an.
34. *Ch'ing ming shang ho t'u*, ed. and annotated by Tung Tso-pin, Formosa, Taipei, 1954.
35. MLL, XII, 7, p. 237.
36. *Ibid.*
37. Y, p. 206.
38. MLL, XVI, 6, p. 269.
39. San Tendai Godai-san ki, chap. I.
40. M & P, p. 334.
41. *Tung ching meng hua lu*, II, 1, p. 12.
42. M & P, p. 334.
43. Moule, *op. cit.*, p. 22.
44. *Ibid.*, p. 27.
45. *Hang tu chi shih*, *Shuo fu* XXX.
46. MLL, XIII, 7, p. 245.
47. *Tung ching meng hua lu*, III, 8, p. 21.
48. MLL, X, 12, p. 215.
49. MLL, XVIII, 3, p. 283.
50. MLL, XII, 1, p. 227.
51. The first of these texts is in MLL, XVI, 6, p. 269; the second in *Kuei hsin tsa chih*, Hsü A, § 44.
52. MLL, XVI, 6, p. 269.
53. MLL, XVI, 7, p. 270.
54. MLL, XIII, 1, p. 238. *Wu lin chiu shih*, VI, 1, p. 440.
55. Y, pp. 201-2.

56. M & P, p. 326.
57. *Wu lin chiu shih*, VI, 11, pp. 450-3.
58. *Wu lin chiu shih*, VI, 5, p. 443.
59. Y, pp. 186-7.
60. MLL, XVI, 1, p. 262.
61. MLL, XVI, 2, p. 263.
62. Ibid.
63. MLL, XVI, 4, p. 267. Balazs, op. cit., p. 149.
64. Y, p. 202.
65. MLL, XII, 1, p. 227.
66. Moule, op. cit., p. 33.
67. Ibid., p. 31.
68. MLL, XII, 5, pp. 234-5.
69. Y, p. 205.
70. MLL, XII, 6, pp. 235-6.

# CHAPTER II

# SOCIETY

A WORLD IN PROCESS OF TRANSFORMATION: *The State in China before the Sung dynasty. Vigorous economic expansion between the eleventh and thirteenth centuries.* THE UPPER CLASSES: 1. *Government officials. Administrative organization of China. Recruitment and career of officials. Nepotism and corruption.* 2. *Military officials. Anti-militarism. Armed forces. War.* 3. *The imperial nobility and the Emperor. A civil aristocracy. Political influence of the Emperor's family. Ritual function of the Emperor.* THE MERCHANTS: *Hold of the State on the economy. Forms of currency. Internal and external trade. Urban commercial activity: shops for luxury goods; proliferation of small-scale concerns; the marketing of the main articles of consumption. Guilds. Portrait of a rich merchant.* THE LOWER CLASSES IN URBAN SURROUNDINGS: *Surplus of manpower. Domestics and hangers-on of great families. Shop-hands and artisans. Relations between employers and employees. Forced labour. Pedlars. Entertainers. Prostitutes. Thieves and beggars. Charities and charitable institutions.* THE PEASANTS: *Social differentiation among country people. General poverty and indebtedness. Agricultural work. Administration of country districts.*

## A WORLD IN PROCESS OF TRANSFORMATION

AS WE have seen, the rapid growth of the city of Hangchow between the beginning of the twelfth century and the end of the thirteenth was not solely due to the influx of refugees from the north and the establishment of the court there during the first half of the twelfth century. In fact, it was not during the twelfth century that the most rapid increase in the population of Hangchow occurred, but, on the contrary, during the last years of the Sung dynasty, between 1250 and 1276. Continuous demographic expansion was almost certainly not peculiar to Hangchow, but common to all the big towns in the southeastern provinces. This phenomenon of urban growth in all probability reflects the disequilibrium between town and country which was becoming more and more pronounced, and the found changes which were taking place in the economy, and is indubitably related to the concurrent transformation of the whole fabric of Chinese society.

The political picture China presents in the periods prior to the eleventh century might be outlined as follows: the ruling class formed a very small élite, whose mode of life, ideas, language even, were uniform. They were all steeped in the same culture. But below this thin upper crust was the great inchoate mass of the people with all their different customs, local cults, various dialects and specialized techniques. Certainly they all belonged to the same civilization, but in spite of the frequent efforts on the part of the upper classes to unify customs and usages, the Chinese people—especially the country folk—retained their various pronounced regional characteristics. This multiplicity of varying regions and provinces, still further accentuated by the presence of non-Chinese minorities in some of the outlying provinces, hardly appeared on the surface at all owing to the admirable political organization of the country and to the centralization of government. For all that, it was one of the most important of historical facts. *Mutatis mutandis*, the Chinese world up to the Sung period and even, to a large extent, well into the thirteenth century, is comparable to mediaeval Europe, where 'the Church was the sole depository of the arts and sciences and Latin the sole vehicle for thought; where the common people were conspicuously uncultured save for their folk customs and beliefs.'[1]

But because of new forces at work, the general structure of Chinese society was gradually changing from the eleventh to the thirteenth centuries. Between the ruling élite and the mass of the people a very diversified but very active class appeared and began to occupy a more and more important position: that of the merchants. At the same time, the contrast between the haves and the have-nots, in a society in which a money economy was becoming more and more prevalent, began to acquire a sharpness it had never had in the past, when the élite in the towns and the ordinary people in the country were the only constitutive elements in the social structure. Thus the Chinese world of the thirteenth century was much more complex than it had been in earlier periods. The traditional categories of rulers and ruled tended to relegate the merchants, as before, to the ranks of the

common people, but at the same time the opposition between
capital and labour, which had acquired a new sharpness,
between owners and underprivileged classes, brought the merchants into relation with the élite. Appearances were, indeed,
deceptive. The new forces manifested in the Sung period,
between the eleventh and the thirteenth centuries, slowly sapped
the foundations of Chinese society without ever leading to new
forms of it. In the end they imposed a complicity of interests, in
practice, between the ruling élite and the owners of wealth; they
altered the very nature of the scholar-official. In this sense, the
Sung period, and more particularly the thirteenth century, was
the dawn in China of modern times.

The commercial development of China from the eleventh to
the thirteenth centuries was contemporaneous with a similar
development in Europe. But the vigorous economic expansion
which took place at that time in China is on an altogether
different scale from its Western counterpart. The volume of
commercial growth in China was commensurate with the size of
its population, the amount of its wealth, its vast area, and its
advanced stage of technical development. The exaggerations of
Marco Polo at the end of the thirteenth century merely express
the astonishment of the traveller from the West at finding a
commercial activity far more intense than that of Genoa or
Venice at the same epoch. And yet this sudden increase of
vigour in the economy of both Europe and the Far East had very
different results. In Europe, cut up as it was into a multitude of
separate jurisdictions and powers, the merchant class was able
to assert itself, have its rights recognized, and form an entity of
its own. Towns gained their liberties and urban institutions appeared, the opposition between town and country became permanent, and the rise of a bourgeoisie which was the first step
towards the formation of the Third Estate was to have important
consequences for the future destiny of the West. In China, in
spite of the gigantic scale of development, nothing more happened than that merchants became wealthy. How is such a
difference in the evolution of these two parts of the world to be
explained? In China, an all-powerful central government was
there from the start: any move likely to threaten the supremacy
of the State was unthinkable. Moreover, the State itself canalized
for its own benefit the vigorous economic expansion of the

period; it, too, became a merchant, and drew from its monopolies and from the taxes levied on private transactions the major part of its revenue. Thus it was that a form of social life traditional to China, and one which was later to become the principal cause of its backwardness, was able to be perpetuated. Those typical family and quasi-family relationships that make the whole Chinese world one vast kinship network, in which the only kind of social relations known, the social relations imposed by custom, moral code and laws, were those of recipient to benefactor, client to patron, servant to master, were to make all emancipation of individuals and of social groups radically impossible.

## THE UPPER CLASSES

### 1. Government Officials

The administrative system of China consisted, from the third century B.C. until modern times, of a body of officials for the most part chosen for their merits or as the result of competitive examinations. This was one of China's most original features. But this institution, so greatly admired in Europe when the first accounts of it made it known there in the eighteenth century, did not remain unchanged throughout its history: methods of recruitment, numbers, provinces of origin, and, to a certain extent, social composition of the body of officials varied in the course of the centuries, and, on these various counts, the Sung period (960-1279) marks a turning-point. Moreover, the idealized picture which the Enlightenment formed of the political structure of China was very far from the truth: the government officials all came from a very small number of scholar-families who customarily supplied the State with its executive agents. And if these officials usually showed themselves to be such zealous protectors of the interests of the Empire, it was because the defence of these interests almost always coincided with the preservation of their own prerogatives.

On the other hand, the autocratic character of the supreme power exercized by the Emperor was a cause of instability and of moral corruption: at the highest levels of the administrative hierarchy, the most dire disgrace might follow suddenly and unpredictably upon the enjoyment of the highest favours. The minister or high councillor who had fallen out of favour with the Emperor very often brought down with him in his fall all his protégés, both petty and middle-grade officials. The court was the centre of constant intrigues and plots in which, frequently enough, members of the imperial family, empresses, and eunuchs of the harem were involved. In addition, various other elements, such as individual temperament, family traditions, different interests and connections, all entered in to make the official class in its entirety more diversified than might at first appear. Cliques were formed which sometimes expressed a conflict of political opinions. Under the Sung, desperate battles were waged between the partisans of armed intervention against the Barbarians and the partisans of the policy of paying for peace by offering tribute, or between the innovators and the conservatives; and the violence of the conflicts which occurred within government circles was one of the novelties of the period.

However, in spite of its defects, the administrative organization of the Chinese Empire was admirable. Here is a brief survey of it: supreme power was exercized by the Emperor, aided by a council of no more than three to five ministers. This council, which met daily around dawn, was distinguished from the grand audiences, which all the central ministries attended, by its secret nature and by the absence of protocol. The officials closest to the Emperor after these councillors were the censors, the representatives of the big ministries, and the academicians, whose respective functions were: control of important administrative matters, execution of imperial decisions, and publication of edicts. Below them came the chancellery, the imperial secretariat, and those organs of government which were important because of the number of persons employed: the departments of the various ministers (civil service, finance, rites, war, justice, public works); next, a whole collection of offices dealing either with questions directly concerning the Emperor and the imperial family (cult and sacrifices, banquets, insignia, stables, the Emperor's private treasury), or with technical problems and general directives with regard to agriculture, education, canals, military equipment, foreign relations, or special legal decisions.

To complete the picture, there were two offices, one of which looked after the transmission of memorials and petitions addressed to the Emperor by the provincial officials, and the other the transmission of government decrees to the prefectural governments. Such, in general outline, was the structure of the central administration. Its modernism and its complexity are astonishing when one considers the rudimentary forms of administration in the countries of Europe at this period. Yet it was not new: a similar pattern, which served as model, is to be found from the seventh century or even earlier.[2] A point which is not immediately apparent, and which deserves to be underlined, is the control exercized by the main administrative organs of the central government upon each other. In addition, the tribunal of censors exercized a kind of permanent police supervision upon the whole of the administration, both at the capital and in the prefectures. In the provinces there were Commissioner-Generals who were attached to the tribunal of censors, and whose task it was to keep a check on the chief officials in their districts.

The empire of Southern Sung (1127-1279) was divided into sixteen provinces of varying extent, each of which covered an average area equivalent to a fourth or a fifth of France. Each province consisted of about ten prefectures corresponding in size to approximately two French departments, and each prefecture was in turn divided into three to five sub-prefectures. The sub-prefecture was the smallest administrative unit. In the rural areas where the population was sparse, a sub-prefect administered a population of several tens of thousand inhabitants. On the other hand, if the sub-prefecture was situated partly or entirely within an area of urban concentration, as was the case at Hangchow, its population might amount to several hundred thousand. In such a case, the sub-prefect had assistants beneath him, usually officials at the start of their career, and the sub-prefecture had a much bigger staff than that of a rural area. But in either case, the employees recruited locally (scribes, storekeepers, police, forensic doctors, etc.) as well as the heads of districts and of villages elected by the people for regulating their relations with the public authorities, played no part in the normal carrying out of public affairs. Thus, considering the size of the population administered (over sixty million persons), the number of officials was very small. There were no more than a few thousand in all in the eighth century. It must have been due to the increase in the number of government departments and of monopolies that a figure of 18,700 was reached in 1046, but even so, 6,000 of these were military officials, and over a thousand belonged to the central administration. It is probably a figure of this magnitude that must be estimated for the thirteenth century, at a time when China was cut off from the northern provinces. It is surprising that order should have been maintained at such low cost in an empire so extensive, but the reasons for this will be seen later.[3]

The majority of officials were recruited by means of the examination system. However, success in the final examination was not always or immediately followed by an appointment. All it did was to entitle the candidate to apply for a post in the government. These examinations were a real trial in the fullest and strongest sense of the word: the help of the gods and divine inspiration were required. They consisted of three different stages: the examinations held in the prefectures, those held in the provincial capitals, and finally, those held in the Imperial Palace. They took place every three years, and only a very small number of candidates ever got as far as the capital. To come out first in the examination at the Imperial Palace was a signal honour, which assured the holder the most brilliant and rapid career, particularly when it was a question of doctorate of letters, the most renowned of the various kinds of doctorate (letters, law, history, rites, classical studies). Fraud or favouritism of any kind in these examinations was made impossible owing to the anonymity of the candidates and to a system of triple correcting of papers. A bureau of copyists reproduced the papers of the candidates, two examiners marked each one independently of each other, and a third examiner gave the final decision.

The career of officials was usually fairly secure. It was mainly in the higher spheres of the administration, where factions were rife and calumny all-powerful, that reverses of fortune were to be feared. But the middle-grade officials, at least those who did not owe their career to the patronage of a highly-placed person, ran little risk of being down-graded or unjustly dismissed. Only the central government had the power to appoint, remove or promote an official, and it did so only after going into the matter carefully. A dossier of each official was kept at the capital: records of service, reports from superiors on character, morality, particular merits of the person concerned and the mistakes made by him. In the question of promotion, stress was above all laid on the character of the official: his energy, capacity for hard work, health, courage, sense of discipline. Did he tend to abuse authority? Did he make blunders? Did he give proof of filial piety and of fidelity to his friends? Was his conduct inspired by a fundamental integrity or by ambition? Did he care about the wellbeing of the people he administered? Had he provoked discontent in his district by imposing cruel and unjust punishments or by levying excessive taxes? Had he shown himself to be open to bribes? (In theory, corruption, when discovered, was an act which led to the cancellation of the favour granted by the corrupt official.) The experience of the person under consideration was also taken into account: was he efficient as an administrator and in the various capacities called for? To be a good scholar was a definite advantage, because literary talent was proof of a good education, and more attention was paid to humanistic studies than to technical knowledge. That is why candidates who passed high on the list in doctorate of letters examination always got the most rapid promotion and were sometimes appointed to comparatively important posts right at the beginning of their career. But usually every official started his career in the least important posts in the prefectural administration, or as subprefect in some distant province, or assistant to a sub-prefect. There was no specialization, and most posts could be filled by any official who happened to be appointed. Thus, during the latter part of their careers, most officials had a practical knowledge of the general functioning of the administration both in the provinces and at the capital. A minimum tenure was laid down for each post, for example a sub-prefect usually stayed two or three years in the same town or rural district. But a good administrator was more quickly transferred than a mediocre one.

Retiring age was around sixty-eight or sometimes a little less. Upon retiring, officials received from the Emperor a gratuity in money or in cloth. Sometimes the son or the grandson of a retiring official was granted a grace-and-favour appointment, or the official concerned was himself appointed to an honorific post, in which case he received a pension equal to half the salary attached to the post. In all cases, there was no regular pension on retirement, since it was held, on traditional principles, that children must provide for their parents in their old age.

The examination system reached its perfection during the

Sung period (960-1279), and apart from that, the promotion of
officials was regulated by a whole complex of objective criteria
which ensured that they were protected from injustice and
which favoured the best among them. The very great number of
candidates for the examinations—several thousand per province
—is clear proof of the wide diffusion of education at that period,
particularly in the south-eastern provinces (present-day Chekiang, Kiangsu and Fukien), whence came the best and the
greatest number of the candidates. Although half of those who
passed were the sons and grandsons of officials, recruitment was
from a much wider field than in earlier periods, and it is evident
that new social strata had access to the fabulous career of scholar-
official.[4]

But this picture has another side to it. The examination for
the doctorate was not the only means of access to public appointments, and promotion was not always regular. Indeed
numerous sons, relations and friends of highly-placed persons
were appointed by patronage, and their extremely rapid promotion was not justified by their merits. A system of recommendation which, in theory, was designed to discover hidden talent by
ensuring rapid promotion for obscure but worthy officials had
been diverted from its purpose. It was mainly of profit, all things
considered, to the protégés of the great families, and became an
instrument of nepotism.

Again, the sale of titles and offices was an expedient to which
the central power fairly often had recourse in order to provide a
remedy for the permanent difficulties experienced by the
treasury. The rise of a class of extremely wealthy merchants
dealt a heavy blow to the mandarinate and the imperial nobility.
Traditionally there was, it is true, a whole body of laws laying
down rules for the correct dress, housing, insignia and all the
other details of official life.[5] But the power of the newly-rich
merchants surmounted little by little the hierarchical barriers
that had existed between the holders of political power, the persons ennobled as a reward for exceptional merit, the members of
the imperial family—in a word, all the members of the upper
class—on the one hand, and on the other, the families who had
become rich by means of that vile and despised activity: commerce. Some of the wealthy merchants had a mode of life equal,

or superior, to that of the highest mandarins. But it was essential for the State that it should be able to ensure that its officials enjoyed an unrivalled and brilliant prestige.

There was more. The Mongol menace and their invasion of the northern provinces towards the end of the dynasty made it necessary to maintain a very large army on a war-footing. The sumptuary expenditure of the court, the general impoverishment of China, the deficit in the balance of trade, all brought about an inflation which became more and more acute and led to a dramatic treasury crisis. The officials, of whom there were too many, were poorly paid. Hence corruption got worse from day to day, not only at the level of the petty employees recruited locally, among whom it had always been rife, but even in the highest administrative grades.

One example will suffice: in Hangchow there was a dispensary for supplying pharmaceutical drugs to the common people. This institution, which had been founded at the beginning of the twelfth century, received an annual subsidy of several hundred million cash advanced by the Minister of Finance, who was later reimbursed from the Emperor's private treasury. The clerical staff and also the pharmacists were State officials and employees. This charitable institution gave rise to the most shameless abuses. Misappropriation of ingredients and fraudulent substitution were continual. As soon as a quantity of some drug had been prepared, court officials and 'everyone who had any influence' got hold of it. The court was in ignorance of this, but even had it known of it, it could not have prevented these malpractices, says a contemporary. And so, he adds, although in theory this was supposed to be a charity, never did the minutest quantity of the drugs reach the common people.[6]

The luxurious life led in the towns of south-east China and especially in Hangchow had created new needs. Most members of the upper classes desired to increase their incomes. Many officials from all grades of the hierarchy, besides members of the imperial family and eunuchs of the palace, placed capital in enterprises of a commercial character. But all activity of this kind was theoretically forbidden to officials. However it was always possible to avoid damaging their position by doing business in the name of another person. Thus we learn from a decree of 955 that some officials had been engaged in commercial transactions with foreign countries by means of an agent as intermediary.[7] Pawnshops, of which, in 1275, there were dozens in Hangchow and its suburbs, were extremely profitable.

This institution was of Indian origin and had been introduced into China by Buddhist monks, always desirous of consolidating the economic strength of their Church and sometimes interested in increasing their personal fortunes. But in Hangchow the hold of Buddhism was less in evidence than in the neighbouring region of Fukien, for instance, where education, public works and even the provincial finances were subsidized by the Buddhist communities. So the pawnshops in Hangchow belonged to lay persons, to 'powerful and rich families', according to the expression used by a contemporary, and referring no doubt to persons of high social standing (relations of the Emperor, Palace eunuchs, officials) and to wealthy merchants.[8]

The warehouses protected against fire and thieves that had been constructed in the north of the city were another very rewarding source of income. Let out at very steep rents, since security from thieves and fire was as costly as these two scourges were common, they belonged to the great families, to the Empress, and to wealthy eunuchs.[9] In the same way, many dwelling-houses with rooms let by the month to the poorer people, as well as many shops, must have been the property of members of the upper class, among whom officials were no doubt included. Finally, a few persons in the highest positions in the central government had enormous landed estates to the north of the city, between the Yangtze and the Che river estuary. Their presence at the court had great influence on imperial policy: all attempts at agrarian reform came up against their stubborn opposition. The fact that some officials enjoyed a private fortune which enabled them to live in grand style despite their modest rate of salary made them take a more independent attitude towards the State. In addition, their private interests might come into conflict with the general interests of the empire.

There are, then, clear indications of a deterioration in the mandarinate during the Sung period and particularly during the thirteenth century. Nepotism and patronage, the struggle between rival factions at court, the desire for wealth, the increase in corruption—all these contributed to a progressive lowering of standards. Yet the doctorate examinations attracted an ever-increasing number of candidates. To be a government official was to open the way to honours and esteem for one's family. No other career offered so elevated and so envied a position. An official of high merit ran the chance of receiving a posthumous title after his death or even of having his biography included in the dynastic annals. At the very least, his funeral monument would remain as á lasting tribute to his fame, and this fame would be reflected upon all his descendants.

In spite of the conflicts which arose within their group, the scholar-officials formed a small caste united by common interests. Moreover their cultured literary and artistic tastes, the elegant formality of their manners and their privileges marked them off from the common people, towards whom they adopted a sternly paternalistic attitude. Many of them were acquainted with each other more or less intimately either through having formerly been in the relation of superior and subordinate, or through having been fellow students. Those who had passed the final examination in the same year had particularly close ties with one another. Also, between successful candidates and their examiners there developed relations identical to those that existed between master and pupils or parents and children. An official on his travels would be received by his equals either with warm friendship or with exquisite courtesy. His arrival, his visit, his departure, all served as an occasion for giving banquets at which everyone would give a lively display of literary talent.

2. *Military Officials*
The prestige of military officials was almost entirely eclipsed by that of government officials. The low place held by the army in Chinese society of the thirteenth century is no doubt to be explained both by a climate of opinion which dates back to a remote past, and to historical circumstances which accentuated, in the Sung period, the anti-militarism that was traditional among the scholars. It is clear that the origin of the contempt and suspicion with which the arts of war were regarded lies in one of those choices by which every civilization is characterized, and that this attitude was in sympathy with a concept of human behaviour that put the emphasis on ritual and on the moral code rather than on any form of direct action. As for the historical circumstances, these were of comparatively recent date: from

the middle of the eighth century, political exigencies and the weakening of the central power had led the T'ang dynasty to concede ever-extending powers to the military governors of the provinces.

This derogation of civil powers was to bring in its train a long series of disorders and of wars which continued until the setting-up of the Sung dynasty at the end of the tenth century. Warned by these disastrous events, the Sung emperors and those representing the scholar class remained firmly hostile to any policy tending to encourage the powers of the military. Even in besieged towns, the generals were made subordinate to the local government officials or to imperial commissioners specially delegated by the court. Another factor which must have reinforced the contempt felt by the civil administrators for a social group in which literary culture had been sacrificed to the development of physical prowess, was that most of the military officials came from less illustrious families than was the case with the civil officials. Some of them were even men of the people, of peasant origin. Civil and military officials had little in common. Finally, even among the people, who often produced men of warlike vocation and who furnished the army with its troops, there was an intense hatred for the military. A decent man, it was said, does not become a soldier, and it was indeed the case that the army had been chiefly recruited from the dregs of the population from the time when, at the end of the eighth century, it was no longer composed of conscripts, but of mercenaries. There was a complete lack of discipline, and the soldiers, aware of the contempt and hostility that surrounded them, made abuse of their strength and of their powers.[10] When there was fighting in the vicinity and a scarcity of supplies, the countryside was pillaged. For this reason, troops composed of fellow-countrymen were as much to be feared as enemy troops. In the eyes of the villagers, bandits and soldiers were indistinguishable. 'They hate to see soldiers,' says Marco Polo, 'and not least those of the Great Kaan's garrisons, regarding them as the cause of their having lost their native kings and their lords.'[11]

However, in spite of widely-spread anti-militarism, the importance of the army in China had steadily increased during the Sung period, and its equipment was continually being improved. It had a complement of 378,000 men in 960, which increased to

900,000 towards the year 1000, and reached 1,259,000 after 1041. The dynasty of Southern Sung (1127-1279) established, alongside their land forces, a naval force for the coastal defences and the defence of the Yangtze towns. It amounted to eleven squadrons and 3,000 men in 1130, fifteen squadrons and 21,000 men in 1174, and twenty-two squadrons and 52,000 men in 1237.[12] The land forces consisted of infantry and of cavalry protected by armour made of leather and metal, trained in archery, the use of the crossbow, swordsmanship, wrestling and boxing. Catapults of all sizes and of sixteen different varieties, handled by several tens or several hundreds of men, were used for hurling stones, molten metal, poisoned bullets and bombs. Although cannon had not yet made its appearance, artillery was used more and more during this period. Thus, from 1130, war-junks were armed with catapults that hurled explosive bombs.[13] If the military history of China remains unexplored, it is because the texts are laconic where they are not silent, and because all the information which we possess comes from civilian official sources.

The scant attention paid by the scholar-historians to military affairs can be misleading. Contrary to an opinion which is all too widely held, the military history of China is one of the most eventful and bloodstained chapters in the history of Man. But the historian is often content to summarize a whole series of the most appalling events in one word, as instanced by the use of the single comment: 'floods', which may refer to a cataclysm in which tens of thousands of people perished and which was followed by a terrible famine; or a banal formula such as 'a town was captured', which may imply horrors beyond count and innumerable acts of heroism. All wars, civil or otherwise, were accompanied by massacres and terrible acts of cruelty. All of them followed exactly the same pattern: arson and bloodshed in the countryside and long sieges of walled towns. Ladders and wheeled contraptions and raised causeways enabled the besiegers, holding sticks in their mouths to keep them silent, to hoist themselves up to the level of the ramparts. Usually it was impossible to conclude the siege of a town, many of which were almost impregnable, except by perseverance or by means of a ruse of some kind: promises of immunity or menaces of total destruction in the event of victory, proclamations made at the foot of the ramparts and pamphlets shot by arrow in order to lower the morale of the besieged, disguises worn to make the enemy believe that one of his men had surrendered, spies who attempted to foment dissensions in the enemy ranks.

In spite of the frequent wars that occurred during the Sung dynasty, and in spite of the occupation of Szechwan by the Mongols in the middle of the thirteenth century and the incursions of these barbarians as far as the towns of the middle Yangtze, military affairs always remained peripheral to the main preoccupations of the scholar-officials. In an empire of such wide extent, invading forces only created a limited amount of destruction, and as often as not the horrors of war only affected the common people, both in the country and in the towns. Until the final débacle of the years 1275-1279, the military officials, always regarded as of inferior status, were kept strictly subordinated to the civil powers. Even if they did form a part of the imperial administration, they nevertheless remained, as a group, on the fringe of the upper classes.

3. *The Aristocracy and the Emperor*
The upper classes were mainly composed of the scholar-families who supplied the State with its civil servants. There were many more of them during the Sung period than under preceding dynasties, and by the thirteenth century there must have been several tens of thousands of them. Most of them came from the provinces of the south-east. Many were rich and possessed huge landed fortunes. They were very influential locally, and through those members of the family who had been appointed to government posts they were instrumental in formulating the policy of the imperial government. Such people formed a kind of aristocracy with a hierarchy determined by the Emperor but not immune from alteration.

As well as these, there were officials, civil or military, who were given titles on account of exceptional merit or simply as a result of imperial favour, persons who had no official position but who had been able to get into the good graces of the sovereign, and members of the families of high-ranking concubines, who were integrated into the aristocracy of birth and formed a sort of extension to it. Those nobles who were kinsmen of the Emperor or who had been ennobled by special favour, often received a very high salary, either paid to them by the court or derived from the revenues of land bestowed on them along with the title by order of the Emperor. They also enjoyed, together with officials of high rank, special privileges with regard to the law, which shielded them from the ordinary procedures and guaranteed them immunity for common offences. An anecdote of the eleventh century will illustrate the extent to which this could be of benefit. It has as hero a certain adventurer called Fan Wei, who plumed himself on being the near relation of a defunct celebrity and who, in order to give more weight to his claim, had his grandmother buried in the tomb of the illustrious defunct. For several decades he managed to evade all corvées laid upon the common people, and piled up one misdemeanour upon another. Condemned to forced labour on the frontier, he purchased his acquittal. There was indignation at the capital, but no one made a fuss. However an official of the high court of justice examined his dossier and was on the point of completing his report when he received an order of transfer to another post: Fan Wei had a long arm. It was only the court of censors, better protected no doubt against hidden pressures and against corruption, who were finally able to bring the guilty man to justice.[14]

How much influence did aristocrats of high rank exert at court? Empresses, favourite concubines, princesses, princes, favourites, even if they did not play any direct part in public affairs, were in a position of being able to affect imperial decisions. The fact that their influence was secret did not detract from its efficacy. The atmosphere of the court was eminently suited to the elaboration of intrigues and plots. The ambition and private interests of the members of the imperial family and of the collaterals of the Emperor sometimes came up against the interests of the central administration, and at other times chimed in with the policies of one or other of the official cliques. Apart from certain correctives supplied by ritual codes of behaviour and by the presence of a corps of officials who embodied the wider interests of the empire, it was the atmosphere of an oriental court that reigned in the Imperial Palace in Hangchow.

To this political influence must be added the power procured by wealth, and the near relations of the Emperor disposed of very high incomes. Thus the princes, who in the thirteenth century for the most part had their residences in the northern districts of Hangchow, led a conspicuously sumptuous style of life. In addition, these aristocratic circles, particularly the women and the eunuchs of the palace, evinced a frenzied passion for making money. This was quite in the tradition, as is evidenced by many instances provided during the course of history. We have seen that Empresses and rich eunuchs owned some of the warehouses in the north-east of Hangchow which were let out to visiting merchants and to shopkeepers in the town. Without any doubt these distinguished people also owned, both in Hangchow and outside the city, many other sources of income. Because of the amount of wealth they disposed of and the luxury with which they surrounded themselves, the imperial aristocracy exerted an incontestable influence on the economy of China, and in particular on that of the city of Hangchow.

There remains the empire's highest personage of all. His rôle was of a dual nature: first in rank, he was at the same time head of the administrative hierarchy. He embodied the contradiction between the aspirations of his near relations and those of the scholar-officials. Torn between these two elements forming the upper ranks of society, the Emperor sometimes appeared as the arbiter, but more often as the plaything of the conflicts and rivalries that arose within the very core of the upper class; when all is said and done, it was the fight between the rival cliques which in the end determined the policy of this all-powerful personage.

His dual nature is revealed by the diversity of his functions. Head of the aristocracy, it was he who determined the ranks, titles and emoluments of his near relatives and of those to whom he had given titles. As head of State, he appointed and dismissed officials and issued decrees embodying the general policies of the empire. His ritual acts concerned on the one hand his family, his ancestors, his dynasty, and on the other the empire as a whole; but all exhibited the same fundamental ambiguity: it was often hard to say whether he was acting in his capacity as a private or as a public person. The archaic idea of the religious responsibility of the sovereign which survived in all the imperial ritual implies a similar confusion. Thus, at times of great calamity it was customary for the Emperor to make an act of contrition; for example, after the fire that destroyed more than 50,000 houses in Hangchow in 1201, the Emperor, faithful to the most ancient rites, stayed confined to his apartments,

reduced the luxury of his table, and published an edict in which
he accused himself of having been lacking in virtue.[15]

In fact, everything emanating from the sovereign was more
or less sacred in character; the planes of practical and of religious
acts were never clearly distinguished. In its original essence, the
rôle of the Emperor was to regulate ranks and titles, time and
space. In this sense, the bestowal of a title-deed of office which
confirmed the transfer or the appointment of an official had no
more 'political' significance than the bestowal of an official name
upon some former sage who had become a god, or upon a holy
mountain. In the same way, acts which in all appearance were
religious were not without important political implications: the
promulgation of an amnesty, a change in the name of the reign-
period, the ritual inauguration of the seasons, the institution of
the annual calendar, the various sacrifices performed by the
sovereign, were all as much methods of government as signs of
imperial sovereignty. In a word, the Emperor, who was both the
patron of the scholars and the head of his dynasty, ruled owing
to the power of the rites and of the written word, and in virtue
of the imperial seal.

## THE MERCHANTS

An aptitude for commerce did not assert itself in China until the
eleventh and twelfth centuries; but since then the business
instinct has remained one of the outstanding qualities of the
Chinese. Curiously enough, it was a series of more or less for-
tuitous circumstances which allowed this aptitude for commerce,
so little in harmony with the traditional ethics of China, to
flourish. The most important of these circumstances was the
economic development of South China following upon the
pressure of the barbarians of the North and the invasion of the
northern provinces. The South was much better endowed than
the North for commercial activity. It had the great artery provided by the Yangtze (we must remember that the Yellow River
has too strong a current to be easily navigable), the canals that
had formerly been constructed in the plains of the lower Yangtze
for the provisioning of the capitals and the provinces of the
North, and the south-eastern and southern coasts which, extending for nearly 2,000 miles, lend themselves admirably for coast-

wise traffic and for big-scale maritime trade. There was also, in South China, an already thriving trade which had been begun by Arab and Persian merchants, first at Canton and then at Ch'üan-chou, as well as along the Yangtze and the roads leading to the interior.

But the circumstances were not only of a geographical or historical nature. Towards the middle, or, at any rate, from the end of the eleventh century, the compass, which had for long been used by geomancers, came into use for sea voyages at times when the sky was overcast. Astronomical and marine charts were published, and shipbuilding techniques for constructing vessels to sail the high seas made pronounced advances. Finally, in the sphere of social institutions, the use of negotiable instruments and the spread of promissory notes must have made an important contribution to the extraordinary commercial expansion which China experienced from the eleventh until the thirteenth century. Who knows? The distant repercussions of this sudden efflorescence of commerce in the Far East may have brought about the economic awakening that was to make itself so sharply felt in the countries of Europe at approximately the same period.

But we should first of all take into account one of the most important features of the Chinese economy at this time: the fact that it was almost entirely under the direct control of the State as regards the main products of consumption. Now, since the price of such commodities influences all other commercial activities, it was in fact the total economic development of China that was being regulated by the State. This situation was without question prejudicial to private commerce, but it could also be of profit to it. Apart from the fact that some merchants were able to make a fortune thanks to orders received by them from government authorities (government monopolies and military commissariat), the general control exercized by the State on prices and on the volume of means of payment was bound to ensure a salutory stability for the economy of China.

The fact is that, in spite of competition from the State, private traders flourished during the twelfth and thirteenth centuries. In Hangchow itself, it was the existence of numerous channels of trade that accounted for the intense economic activity of the city. There were four of these channels: State-controlled trade, the large-scale river and maritime trade, the luxury trade, and the trade supplying the city with the main articles of consumption. This diversity in the mercantile life of Hangchow was due to the fact that it was the capital, and also due to its geographical situation, the enormous wealth of part of its population, and the large number of its inhabitants. The term 'merchants' is useful, but it can be misleading, for it cannot be said that merchants existed as a class in Hangchow. Between the wealthiest of the big traders and the little shopkeepers in the poorer districts there was every gradation imaginable. There were many different types and many different categories of merchants, and without any doubt a wealthy shipbuilder would have been scandalized to find himself being put in the same box as some little grocer in the suburbs.

But before analyzing the various categories of merchants and channels of trade, it is essential to say something about means of payment. While, under the T'ang dynasty (618-907), the court, the administration and the army were maintained by means of taxes in kind levied upon the peasants, in the Sung dynasty (960-1279) the State had begun to impose indirect taxes paid in money (commercial taxes, transport dues, State monopolies). Not only were taxes paid in money, but money was being almost exclusively used in transactions between individuals. Taking into account both the amount of coins struck by the official mints and the various types of promissory notes issued, in the first place by rich families and later by the government, the total increase in means of payment is one of the most striking features in the economic history of this period.

Cash coins were the currency mostly used in the markets and shops of Hangchow. These were circular pieces of copper with a square hole in the centre. On one side was an inscription of four characters. At the end of the tenth century and in the eleventh century this inscription simply read: 'Circulating treasure of Sung'. But in the thirteenth century it gave the reign-period when the coin was issued. Thus the cash made during the reign-period *ching-ting* (1260-1264) bore the inscription: 'Principal treasure of *ching-ting*'. The only unit recognized in State accountancy was the string of one thousand cash, in which the coins were tied together by a cord passing through the square holes. In the markets, on the other hand, the unit used was the 'hundred'. In fact, the 'hundred' always consisted of fewer than a hundred cash coins. Already in Kaifeng, the capital of Northern Sung, the official exchange value of the 'hundred' was 77 cash, and it was worth only 75 in cash transactions. Moreover, the rate varied according to the nature of the transactions, and each guild of merchants had its own rate of exchange. Thus, for fish, vegetables and pork, the 'hundred' rate was 72 cash; for gold and silver, 74; for pearls and precious stones as well as for the hiring of domestic servants of the female sex, 68; for copying out written documents of any kind, only 56. In Hangchow, at the beginning of the Southern Sung dynasty (1127-1279), the 'hundred' was worth 77 cash, the same as the officially recognized unit in the markets of Kaifeng. But towards the end of the dynasty it was only worth 50.[16]

Cash of the reign-period Shao-ting (1228-1233). Actual size.
(Musée Cernuschi.)

The cash coin was a currency of very low value, in keeping with the low standard of living of the common people. Under the Northern Sung it was equivalent to approximately one thousandth of an ounce of silver of 37.301 grammes. It was in addition very clumsy to handle, since a string of one thousand cash weighed more than 1½ lb.[17] As well as being inconvenient, a further drawback was provided by the serious shortage of copper, which was accentuated by the exportation of cash coins abroad throughout the course of the Sung dynasty. Thus the State was forced to have recourse to other types of currency. In Hangchow, towards the end of the thirteenth century, discs of tin issued by the Ministry of Finance came into use, each equivalent to a certain number of cash coins. But it was chiefly through the use of paper money that the State solved its currency problems.

It was from the end of the ninth century that the practice which lies at the origin of the use of banknotes in China began to make its appearance among the big wholesalers. Merchants deposited stores of copper currency with wealthy families in exchange for receipts which could be cashed in other towns by certain accredited persons. This was what was called 'flying money'. This practice was extended by the State in its handling of the salt trade at the end of the tenth century: the notes issued by the government permitted the merchants who bought them to exchange them for salt or tea at source, or from the State storehouses. The operation could also be done in reverse: for their deliveries to the military commissariat in the frontier regions, the merchants were paid in notes which were convertible into goods at the capital. Thus, throughout the Sung dynasty, a very large number of notes were issued against which payment was for the most part made in salt. At the beginning of the twelfth century the number of such notes issued in a single year amounted to the value of 26 million strings of cash. However, these notes were not valid beyond a certain number of years, after which they could no longer be cashed. In addition, they were only valid in the designated zones (vast enough, it is true) for which they had been issued.[18] It was not until the years between 1265 and 1274 that the government put notes into circulation which were backed by gold or silver and were valid throughout the empire. From this time on, says an inhabitant of Hangchow, commodities went up in price enormously, and cash coins lost much of their value: banknotes had made their appearance.[19]

The notes in circulation at Hangchow in the thirteenth century were of varying values, probably ranging from one string of cash to one hundred at the most. They must have been similar in appearance to the banknotes of the Mongol period or to that of the notes issued by the barbarian State of Chin which was still in occupation of North China at the beginning of the thirteenth century. A plate for the printing of a Chin note has been discovered at an archaeological site in Jehol. It dates from the year 1214. The notes for which it was used measured 10 by 19 cm., and had a value of a hundred strings of 80 cash coins. They bore a serial number, the number of the series, and, among other inscriptions, two which are reminiscent of the first promissory notes in France: 'Counterfeiters will be decapitated', and 'The denouncer will be rewarded with three hundred strings of cash'.[20]

The issue of currency was a privilege reserved for the State. This privilege, together with the monopoly on certain main articles of consumption, enabled the State to do just as it liked with the economy of the empire. State monopolies had been established for salt, alcoholic liquors, tea and incense. The government did not allow private enterprise to touch these trades except in areas where it could not itself supervise transport and distribution. In Hangchow the army owned thirteen large, and six small stores of alcoholic liquor, and, dependent upon these stores, there existed taverns in which were housed State prostitutes. The city possessed several large public granaries in which rice was stored which had been either bought, requisitioned or paid in tax. One of them got its supplies from the government estates which were established towards the end of the dynasty to increase the supply required by the army, and received more than six million hundredweight per annum.[21] In addition, there were numerous dwelling-houses in Hangchow which, as we have seen, were let out by the State.

These facts suffice to demonstrate the competition offered by the State, in all the various economic spheres, to private enterprise. A large area of commercial activity escaped its clutches, but the State also benefited substantially from this trade in the form of direct and indirect taxes on commodities, and on the sale and transport of them. But this hold that the government had on trade did not have merely negative effects. The traders who, at the State's expense, undertook the transport and sale of products under State monopoly, and the merchants who supplied cereals, fodder and building materials to the armies stationed on the frontiers, were believed to have accumulated vast fortunes. They were regular potentates. They lent their capital at a high rate of interest to government commercial concerns or to the peasants, and they often had the local government in their pay.

Without doubt there must have been many of this type of *nouveau-riche* among those described by an inhabitant of Hangchow as merchants who had made their money in the big-scale trade carried on along the river. According to his account, the biggest fortunes in the city had been made in the trade on the Yangtze and its tributaries and in foreign maritime trade. Most of these big shipowners were not natives of Hangchow, but had established themselves there, attracted, no doubt, by the luxurious life lived there, by the convenience of the city's situation midway between the Yangtze and the ports of Fukien, and by the presence there of the central government. Almost all of them lived on Phoenix Hill, to the west of the Imperial Palace, which was why the townspeople had got into the habit of calling this district 'the hill of the foreigners'.[22] The Yangtze, which was easily reached from Hangchow by means of the Grand Canal which terminated at Chen-chiang, downstream from Nanking, was navigable for nearly two thousand miles, as far as the south of Szechwan province. Big markets had grown up along its banks where the roads leading from north to south crossed the river. One of them was situated to the north of Lake Tung-t'ing, another near present-day Wu-han, yet another south of Nanking. The products of the entire empire, from Canton to the Han valley, from Szechwan to the region of the lower Yangtze, could be found there.[23]

Thus there existed in China during this period the embryo of a 'national market', and owing to the ease of transport afforded by the waterways, a certain regional specialization of products developed.

At the same time, foreign trade became of greater importance than it had ever been since the time when the Arab and Persian ships had begun to ply between the Persian Gulf and Canton. This great port, which must have had a population that was half Muslim at the beginning of the ninth century, had ceased to be the most important one for foreign trade. Its place had been taken by Ch'üan-chou and Fuchow, on the Fukien coast. At the same time, Chinese shipowners had replaced the merchants from the Middle East, although at Hangchow there was still a small number of foreign merchants in the maritime and in the inland trade: Kaifeng Jews who had followed the court in its exodus to the south in 1126,[24] Muslims from Central Asia or from India, Syrians, Persians, Arabs, etc. They were less numerous than a few decades later, under the Mongols. Indeed these barbarians, full of distrust for the Chinese, but themselves incapable of governing a country as densely populated and as civilized as

China was, were to call upon foreigners from all the countries of
the West to fill administrative posts[25] — Marco Polo is one
example of those Western merchants to whom the Mongols
entrusted high administrative posts—and, as a result, a great deal
of trade went out of the hands of the Chinese merchants. But,
although the Chinese sources of the Sung period make hardly
any reference to them, the small colonies of foreigners that must
have existed in Hangchow on the eve of the Mongol conquest
should not be forgotten.

Chinese junks went to Japan, the Hindu kingdom of Champa
on the coast of Annam, Malaya, the coasts of South India and of
Bengal, and the coast of Africa. These large junks, almost square
in shape, with a raised prow and poop which were also square,
had eight to ten pairs of oars (each oar worked by four men in
calm weather), two stone anchors, and sails of matting or of
canvas. Watertight compartments gave greater safety in the
event of shipwreck. In the bows there were several dozen
individual cabins. The junks towed behind them a boat carrying
supplies of wood and water which were laid in at ports of
call.

Navigation was by the stars and the position of the sun, aided
by astronomical and marine charts, when the sky was clear.
When it was overcast, the Chinese compass, in use for sea
voyages since the end or perhaps even the middle of the eleventh
century,[26] pointed to the south and enabled ships to continue on
their course.

The biggest junks could carry five to six hundred people and
several dozen tons of goods. They very seldom came up as far as
Hangchow owing to the sandbanks in the Che river, and dropped
anchor further east. The goods were transported by boats which
sailed up-river coastwise to Shao-hsing, to the south-east of
Hangchow;[27] or else the junks made Kan-p'u their port of call, a
small port on the north coast of the estuary. The crews, composed not only of sailors but also of archers and crossbow-men,
whose arms were put into store at every Chinese port of call, had
officers in charge of them. Black men, probably coming from
Malaya, did the heavy work on board. Each junk had to have a
paper issued to it by the Commissariat for merchant ships, which
had been transferred to Hangchow since about the year 1000.
This document, sealed with a red seal, bore the names of the

ābers of the crew, the dimensions of the junk, and informa-
ı about the cargo.[28]

The freight brought to Chinese ports was composed of very
valuable articles: rhinoceros horns from Bengal, ivory from
India and Africa, coral, agate, pearls, crystal, rare woods (chiefly
sandalwood and aloe), incense, camphor, cloves, cardamom . . .
Outgoing cargoes consisted of silks and brocades, porcelain and
earthenware. Also raw products were often exported: gold,
silver, lead and tin, and, in spite of all government prohibitions,
copper cash. Archaeological excavations have discovered cash
dating from the Sung dynasty in several countries in the Far
East,[29] and Chinese ceramics in the Philippines, Indo China,
Malaya, the Indian coast, and even as far afield as Egypt, in the
vicinity of Cairo.

The workshops for ceramics, each with its own style and pro-
cesses of manufacture, were in the south-eastern provinces
(Kiangsi, Chekiang and Fukien). In Hangchow itself there were
two great factories. One was situated within the precincts of the
Imperial Palace, at the foot of Phoenix Hill, and supplied the
court with the finest celadons that have ever been made, some of
which were exported. The other was near the altar for the sacrifices to Heaven, about a mile outside the southern ramparts.
There were also workshops in Fuchow, the big port on the
Fukien coast, which was not so wealthy as Hangchow, but better
situated for the maritime trade.

Yet, in spite of the growth of the export trade in porcelains
and silks, China experienced a steady impoverishment from the
beginning of the twelfth century. There was a deficit in the
balance of trade, as is proved by the export of precious metals
and cash coins to foreign countries. China was living above her
means, and the unbridled luxury of a tiny segment of Chinese
society was one of the principal causes of this disequilibrium.

The passion for luxury and pleasure was particularly strong
in Hangchow. It was there that the court, the very high officials
and the richest merchants had their residence. No other town
had such a concentration of wealth. The riches and elegance of
the upper classes and of the prosperous merchants account for
the importance of the luxury trade. Celebrated products which
were the specialities of various towns were on sale in the shops

in the centre of the city, either on or just off the Imperial Way. Silks from Suchow could be found there, lacquers made at Wenchou on the south coast of Chekiang, jasmine in pots which came by sea from the provinces of Fukien and Kuangtung, fans made at Nan-chang, a town situated to the south-west of Lake P'u-yang, between four and five miles from Hangchow, renowned rice-wines produced in the provinces of Chekiang and Kiangsu.

Hangchow itself was celebrated for its makers of jewellery, of hair ornaments in gold and in silver, of artificial flowers, of combs, of necklaces and pendants of pearls. Children's toys, gold brocades and printed books were also among Hangchow's specialities. An inhabitant obligingly describes for us every one of the renowned products which could be obtained in the city, but we shall not follow him into every detail. It will suffice for us to know that the best rhinoceros skins were to be found 'at Ch'ien's, as you go down from the canal to the little Ch'ing-hu lake', the finest turbans 'at K'ang-number-eight's, in the street of the Worn Cash-coin' or 'at Yang-number-three's, going down the canal after the Three Bridges'. The best place for buying works of literature was at the bookstalls under the big trees near the summer-house of the Orange Tree Garden. Finally, one could get wicker cages in Ironwire Lane, ivory combs at Fei's, folding fans and painted fans at the Coal Bridge.[30]

The shops and workshops that specialized in well-known products made every effort to keep up their reputation. Some of them had been established for over a century.

We must also remember the very great number of small shopkeepers who sold articles of everyday use to the common people: cloth, dried fish, noodles, candles, soya sauce, etc. In contrast to the well-known specialist shops and workshops, these little grocery shops did not usually employ any staff, but were looked after by the family of the managers or owners.

That there was an artificial overdevelopment of commercial activity in Hangchow is clear. What we know of the prices fetched for the sale of shop premises points to an extreme scarcity of capital. In the twelfth century, twenty-five strings of cash sufficed for the purchase of a small grocery business.[31] This is a very modest sum when one realizes that the cash was the smallest monetary unit used in the markets. On the other hand, profits were high: a profit of one per cent on capital per day was considered normal. This economic situation was obviously very hard on the common people and had besides resulted in an excessive proliferation of shops, to which neither the government nor the guilds seemed able to put a stop. Well-to-do families in the upper circles of society did not hesitate to buy a business for a son who had failed in the final examination, if the family influence was not powerful enough to get him a small government post. These shopkeepers-by-accident were known in the town by the name of 'mandarins' (*kuan-jen*), and they were apparently occupied in the more exclusive trades. One did not let a young man of good family end up as a butcher or a noodle-merchant, but as a pharmacist, a bookseller, a 'brusher of teeth' (which probably meant a dentist) or a vendor of the special caps with long 'ears' worn by scholars.[32]

Yet however great the amount of this small-scale trade might be, the main part of Hangchow's commerce consisted in the provisioning of its inhabitants, so vast in number for that period. We have seen that there were about fifteen big markets outside the ramparts for the main articles of consumption. The rice-trade alone, which, we may recall, dealt each day in several hundred tons of this cereal, provided occupation for a whole crowd of big dealers, agents, shopkeepers, porters, makers of sacks. It was a most complex organization, and yet, according to one inhabitant of the town, everything went without a hitch and without disputes, despite the scale of operations. The varieties of rice were countless, and it was quite an art to be conversant with all of them. Let us mention, among other kinds, the early and late varieties, new-milled rice, husked winter rice, first quality white rice, rice with lotus-pink grains, yellow-eared rice, rice on the stalk, ordinary rice, glutinous rice, ordinary yellow rice, short-stalked rice, pink rice, yellow rice and old rice. The wholesale and retail trades were separate, and the same was probably the case for other articles of main consumption such as pork and fish. 'Let us now speak,' says the author of the description of Hangchow in 1275, 'about the shops of the rice-merchants in the city and in the suburbs. Each shop-owner consults the heads of his guild about market prices. It is they who are the direct suppliers of the rice (which has been ordered from them), and it goes on sale immediately. The shopkeepers (receive their deliveries before paying for them and) come to an arrangement with the heads of the guild about the date of payment. But there are also small agents who attend the markets and operate a personal delivery service to their clients, the shopkeepers. There is also, outside one of the gates of the city, a rice-market (nearer to the centre of the city than the big rice-market) where a cluster of thirty to forty agents do business with their clients and take their orders.'[33]

Merchants, artisans and members of all professions were grouped into guilds similar to that which existed for the rice-trade. There was an amazing variety of these guilds: jewellers, cutlers, gilders, gluemakers, dealers in antiques and *objets d'art*, dealers in crabs, olives, honey, ginger . . . Even the doctors, soothsayers and scavengers had their guilds. Some of the trades bore fanciful names. The bootmakers, for instance, were called 'the companions of the double thread', the keepers of bathing establishments 'the companions of fragrant water', and the jewellers 'the companions of the abrasive powder'.[34]

Local guilds of this kind often corresponded to the actual grouping together of certain trades in particular districts of the city, and the term for guilds was originally applied to the streets in a market where all the merchants or artisans belonging to the same trade were to be found. In Hangchow some trades were still localized in one particular part of the city. Thus, the stretch of the Imperial Way which lay between the Sweet Harmony district and the district known as South-of-the-markets was called the 'pearl-market' because of the large number of jewellers' shops in this neighbourhood. Further north, between the Five-span Pavilion and Officials' Lane was the money-changers' quarter. Their shops occupied both sides of the street. There they dealt in precious metals, salt-exchange bills and other kinds of promissory notes. They displayed, piled up on their stalls, articles in gold and silver and also copper coins.[35]

Those trades which were not grouped together in the same street had their guilds nevertheless, for there were numerous advantages in forming an association of this kind. Each one was presided over by a 'head' or a 'dean', and they exercised a general control over their members, came to the aid of those in need or who had no family, and insisted upon each member's absolute integrity. Arab merchants who visited China in the ninth century or later were unanimous in extolling the honesty of the Chinese merchants. 'The Chinese,' says one of them, 'are scrupulously honest in the matter of money transactions and of debts'.[36] And Marco Polo for his part is of the opinion that 'both in their commercial dealings and in their manufactures they are thoroughly honest and truthful'.[37] No one ever went back on his word, and in so far as manufacture of goods was concerned, the State saw to it that certain standards were complied with.[38] Since the guilds were religious associations of a kind, or at least associations modelled on the same pattern, they had their annual feast-days in honour of their patron saints, who might be legendary beings or deified heroes. On such occasions, the members met together for a banquet, towards which each member contributed his quota, and they exhibited their *chefs-d'oeuvre*.[39]

One of the principal advantages of forming trade guilds was that they provided merchants and artisans with a means of regulating their relations with the State. It was to the heads of guilds that government authorities applied when making requisitions of any kind, whether of goods from the shops or of artisans from the workshops. In this way, official intermediaries ensured that fair prices and fair wages were paid.[40]

The *nouveau-riche* merchants possessed everything they could want — wealth, luxury, influence — except the social standing that was denied to them by those whom the traditional hierarchy had placed above them. It is therefore understandable that their one desire was to raise themselves to the level of the upper classes. The *bourgeois gentilhomme* is universal, or is at least a human type inevitably to be found in certain forms of society.

Certainly the shipowners, the salt traders and the proprietors of the luxury shops in the city made the greatest efforts to give their children a good education; they hired tutors for them, and hoped that they might attain to the career of a scholar-official. To this there were two obstacles. The first was of an official nature: sons of merchants were in theory not allowed to enter for the civil service examinations. But it is by no means certain whether, in practice, there were not ways of getting round this. The other obstacle was of a psychological nature: the most immediate desire entertained by the sons of rich merchants is to

squander the paternal fortune. 'A père avare, fils prodigue', as
the French proverb has it ('Miserly father, wastrel son'). This,
while often true of the bourgeoisie in the West, was all the more
so among the families of wealthy merchants in China, for there
were no economic principles that make a virtue of thrift, and
work, far from being extolled as a good-in-itself, as in Christian
countries, was despised. People in high positions did not work;
they directed. Thus each generation laid itself open to the dangers of dissipation and exhibited a ruthless desire to make money.
The gilded youth of Hangchow certainly number among its
ranks a good many sons of nouveau riche merchants, and the
feeling that their offspring belonged to the fashionable world of
the town must no doubt have flattered the vanity of parents who
in any case seem to have usually been inclined towards indulgence.

There were other ways of satisfying their vanity. At the end
of the Southern Sung dynasty, a few years before the Mongol
invasion, the State decided to open up vast agricultural estates
run by managers, in order to increase supplies for provisioning
the army. To raise funds for the purchase of land for this enterprise, the court put up for sale petty titles of nobility for both
men and women. A number of merchants must have used this
method of gaining a title for themselves or for their sons or
wives. Others must have invested their fortune in landed estate,
a secure investment and one which brought a title into the bar-
gain, unless they had already bought a title direct, such titles
being by no means merely nominal.

The vanity of the nouveau-riche found a further source of
satisfaction, as did that of Monsieur Jourdain, in imitating the
usages and customs of the higher circles of society and in affect-
ing the 'grave and decorous behaviour', to use Marco Polo's
expression, of the well-to-do. The few lines in which the
Venetian traveller describes the rich merchants of Hangchow
provide an illustration of this:

'The leading and wealthy owners of these shops do no work
with their own hands and affect, on the contrary, a grave and
decorous behaviour. The same is true of their ladies who are very
handsome, as we have just said; they are brought up to acquire
habits of great timidity and delicacy, and their dress displays
such magnificence of silks and jewels that it would be impossible

to estimate the cost. And, although it is prescribed by the laws of their former kings that each man must exercise the profession of his father, yet it is permitted to them, when they have made their fortune, to dispense with the necessity of doing manual work, on the understanding that they keep up the ancestral establishment and employ workmen to carry on the hereditary trade.'[41]

Wealthy merchants had pretensions to the aristocratic tastes of the scholars. At the entrances and inside the rooms of the big taverns and tea-houses on the Imperial Way were hung paintings and specimens of calligraphy commissioned from well-known painters. And on the occasion of the wedding of a son or daughter, no expense was spared on the decoration of the banquet hall. According to Marco Polo, the merchants devoted fabulous sums to such outward signs of culture. Their houses, he says, 'are well built and elaborately finished; and the delight they take in decoration, in painting and in architecture, leads them to spend in this way sums of money that would astonish you'.[42] But this was a debased kind of art, vitiated in its very nature by its venality, and without any real aesthetic value, since its sole purpose was to flatter the bad taste of parvenus.

Another psychological trait deserves mention. The people in Hangchow who made the biggest fortunes, the merchants who had made money in the maritime and river trade, had a great propensity for works of charity. Charity for them was one way of making up for being excessively wealthy, a kind of tax paid to the gods. It is worth quoting what a contemporary tells us about this, if only because at the same time it reveals the extreme poverty of a large part of the population.

'Among these people,' he says, 'there are some who like to acquire merit by being extremely charitable to the poor, the orphaned and the aged. Every time they see some unfortunate sitting sadly in front of his unsold merchandise, they take notice of him and give him a few coins. When a poor person dies and the family has nothing with which to pay the funeral expenses, they supply the coffin or contribute to the cost of cremation. When, after heavy falls of snow have blocked the streets, adults and children go about groaning, half naked, frozen and starving, these rich men go round from door to door to find out which families are worst off, take note of their distress, and, when night

falls, push through the cracks in their doors some scrap gold or
silver, or else cash coins or notes. So that when the people open
their doors in the morning, they find these presents which seem
to them to have dropped from heaven. Or again, our rich men
may distribute quilts or clothing lined with floss silk. By all these
acts of charity they gain the eternal gratitude of poor families.
'Those who do good,' says a popular saying, 'bring upon themselves happiness a hundredfold and the blessing of the gods.
Those who do evil receive retribution a thousandfold and the
devils are bent on their destruction. Rapid in reply as the shadow
and the echo are the recompenses and the punishments of
Heaven.'[43]

## THE COMMON PEOPLE IN URBAN SURROUNDINGS

The concentration of wealth in the towns and the poverty in the
countryside combined to promote a constant influx of peasants
into the great urban centres. They quickly adapted to urban life,
and it was they who formed the greater part of the population of
Hangchow. Their numbers increased year by year until the
phenomenon began to take on the aspect of a catastrophe. The
existence of large towns in thirteenth-century China is in itself
concrete proof of the malady from which the economy was
suffering. Their overpopulation reflects the artificial overdevelopment of commercial activity and the immoderate growth of the
luxury trades at the expense of the production of basic necessities.

All the ordinary people of Hangchow—whether poor devils
who slaved all day long to satisfy the demands of their masters
or employers, or porters, prostitutes, petty tradesmen with stalls
set up at street corners, entertainers, pickpockets, thieves and
beggars — had one thing in common: they had nothing to
depend on for their living but the strength of their muscles or
the sharpness of their wits. They had endless stores of patience
and of courage, of guile and cunning. The struggle was hard,
because while capital was scarce and brought in a big return to
its possessors, labour, on the contrary, was superabundant and
wages always low.

The effect of the abundance and cheapness of labour was to
produce an extraordinary degree of specialization. This was

almost a kind of luxury not at all in keeping with the level of wealth and of techniques reached in China at that time. The labour market was remarkably well organized thanks to the guilds, who acted as employment exchanges. It was to them that both employers and employees applied, since no transaction was ever carried through without recourse to an intermediary (and it is probable that the guilds did not permit independent practice of any trade). It was through the heads of the guilds that merchants and members of the upper classes in Hangchow were able to procure managers for pawnshops and shops for selling rice-wine, for restaurants and pharmacies, or stewards for private mansions, gardeners, secretaries, accountants, cooks, specialists for heating and lighting. Some of these employment agencies even offered, on a short-term basis no doubt, concubines, dancers, young boy-singers (pederasty, let us note, was common and accepted), embroiderers, chair-porters, and escorts for people of rank proposing to travel, either in order to return to their native province or to make a tour for their education, or for officials travelling to take up their posts.[44]

The wealth of the great families and of the *nouveau riche* merchants acted like a magnet to all the masses of poor people; most of the lower classes were either servants in the houses of, or suppliers to the demands of the rich. Imperial princes, high and middle-grade officials, wealthy shipowners, owners of huge landed fortunes, all maintained a crowd of dependents in their vast town houses or luxurious country estates. It was a sign of social success to keep a large establishment, and even newly enriched courtesans were accompanied by a retinue of servants, according to Marco Polo. The wealthiest families, particularly the princes, had their own artisans: jewellers, sculptors in ivory, embroiderers . . . They also had their own private militia, and the staff of a great family was divided among various service departments. They were known in Hangchow as 'the four services and the six offices'. The four services consisted of the servants in charge of furnishings (chairs, tables, curtains, blinds, mats, hangings, screens, paintings and scrolls of calligraphy); those in charge of alcoholic liquors and teas; those in charge of the table-furnishings for banquets and the masters of ceremony who led in the guests and attended to the sending out of invitations and to the ceremonies at marriages and funerals; and those in charge of the kitchen and the kitchen staff. The six offices had tasks that were more precise and more limited: the decoration of dishes ready for serving, the purchase of fruits, the purchase of snacks for accompanying drinks, lighting, the purchase of incense and perfumes and of medicines, the heating, cleaning and decorating of the rooms.[45]

This large staff of domestic servants did not, however, by any means complete the number of persons employed in the great houses. There was, at a higher level, a whole bevy of people, not strictly servants, who were maintained on a permanent or a temporary basis by the great families in virtue of their social talents or special gifts: tutors, tellers of tales ancient and modern, chanters of poetry, zither players, chess players, horsemen, painters of orchids, literary men, copyists, bibliophiles. There were others who gave exhibitions of cock-fighting or pigeon-fighting, who could imitate animal noises, train performing insects, pose amusing riddles, or who were experts in hanging paintings or arranging flowers for interior decoration, or who served as go-between with fashionable courtesans and undertook to deliver notes to them.[46]

The people who depended on the wealthy families for their living certainly formed one of the largest groups among the lower classes because dozens of people were employed by the great houses in various capacities. On the other hand, the number of people employed in the workshops, pork-butchers' shops, restaurants, tea-houses and luxury-trade shops was confined to as few hands as possible. But the relationship between all these people and their masters or employers was everywhere the same: a paternalistic attitude on the part of the master, and one of respect and submission on the part of the servants or employees. The latter formed part of the family, and sometimes served from father to son in the same houses. Their complete economic dependence together with the persistence of the old family system provides an explanation for the strength of this bond. There were no big factories nor yards in Hangchow, and almost the only revolts of any kind were those which broke out in the provinces, either among the peasants or in the big industrial concerns, both public and private, such as the salt-wells in Szechwan, where a large number of poverty-stricken people were employed.

As for the guilds, they were too numerous and too varied to allow their influence to be felt. There was no consciousness among the lower classes of their unity vis-à-vis the rich. Not only an indefatigable zeal, but complete devotion as well was expected of servants and employees. Their slightest faults were severely punished, and the State gave every assistance towards maintaining the requisite sense of duty and obligation. The law provided sanctions for any deviation from the traditional relationship between master and servant.[47] Moreover, heads of families and owners of shops and workshops were usually careful to ensure that their dependants had no cause for revolt. They refrained from any crying injustice, saw to it that they amassed some savings, and did their best to arrange marriages for them. These dependants, although they were early to rise and late to bed and constantly at the beck and call of their masters or of the chief steward or shop-manager, had one great advantage over the peasant: a relative security of livelihood. A particular advantage attendant upon being a servant in a rich family was the certainty of finding a wife among the domestic staff of his master, and this was one of the main incitements to acceptance of this particular form of servitude.

All those who did not belong to the comparatively fortunate class of servants and employees and who had therefore not succeeded in linking their fortunes with those of a master or employer, lived for the most part from hand to mouth. They occupied a lower level in the stratification of the lower classes. Among them were the heavy labourers: navvies, water-carriers, scavengers, etc., they, too, with their guilds—for what trade was without one? One tends to imagine these thirteenth-century coolies as having the same characteristics as their modern counterparts: faces marked by a life of toil, thin as an ascetic, yet full of humour. Also to be included are the numberless pedlars of various types who went about the streets shouldering their poles, or set themselves up at street corners or in the markets: vendors of tea who could be seen going their rounds at night on the Imperial Way or from door to door in the poorer districts, and who were favourites with the gossips because they knew all the tit-bits of the neighbourhood; sellers of toys, of cooked food, hot-water pedlars squatting at the doorways of bathing establishments, horoscope pedlars, physiognomists, soothsayers, sellers of sugarcane from which one sucked the juice, of honeycomb, of jujubes, or of sweets for children: little figures, animals, birds, flowers and fruits fashioned out of sugar made from soya beans, sugarcane, barley or sesame.[48] Each had his special street cry, if he did not simply attract the attention of customers by beating on a piece of wood or metal.

Some of them worked in the pay of shopkeepers, and there were even some concerns which used only pedlars for selling their goods, pedlars 'poor and honest', in the words of an inhabitant, who went at dawn to collect their merchandise from shops known as 'factory workshops'. At the end of the day they brought back the money they had earned, and were given a commission of ten per cent. The products sold by these poor wretches were ready-cooked dishes carried in a series of small boxes which could be packed away inside each other, sweets, and a fumigating product for getting rid of mosquitoes.[49] All such people, whether working on their own account or in the pay of some shopkeeper or artisan, only just managed to scrape a living from the few cash they earned on their unwearying rounds. No doubt many of them were recent arrivals from the country.

People engaged in popular entertainment were innumerable: actors of little comic or historical scenes, storytellers, puppeteers or producers of Chinese shadow-plays, jugglers, acrobats, tight-rope walkers, exhibitors of wild animals, etc. They gave their shows in the 'pleasure grounds', covered bazaars of a kind situated in the markets and at the approaches to bridges and frequented by all classes of society.

Some of them came in from the country on feast-days and could be seen 'on the bridges and in the streets, trailing their children along with them'; others drew crowds by displaying stupendous muscular strength, and to the roll of a drum lifted iron weights, wooden beams or blocks of stone. Sometimes these were old soldiers, such as the Strong Man at one time celebrated in Ch'ang-an (Si-an) under the T'ang, who had this proud device tattooed on his arms: 'Alive, I fear not the governor of the capital; dead, I fear not the king of the infernal regions'.[50] It is quite remarkable how large a number of the lower classes in Hang-chow were occupied in the popular entertainment industry. However, the show people only put on their best turns during the times of the great annual festivals when business in the town had a sudden burst of feverish activity that went on day and night without stopping.

Prostitution was very widespread in Hangchow. In Cambaluc, the Mongol capital, the walls of which were slightly further to the north than those of present-day Peking (vestiges of them are still to be seen today), Marco Polo had been struck by the large number of prostitutes in this cosmopolitan city. 'And again I tell you another thing,' he says, 'that inside the town dare live no sinful woman . . . but . . . they all live outside in the suburbs. And you may know that there is so great a multitude of them for the foreigners that no man could believe it, for I dare tell you in truth that they are quite twenty thousand who all serve men for money, and they all find a living . . . Then you can see if there is great abundance of people in Cambaluc since the worldly women there are as many as I have told.'[51]

The Mongols, stricter in morals than the Southern Chinese, had relegated the prostitutes to the districts outside the walls of their capital. In Hangchow, however, prostitution had infiltrated everywhere. There was hardly a single public place, tavern, restaurant, hotel, market, 'pleasure ground', square or bridge where one did not encounter dozens of ladies of the town. A contemporary gives a list of the districts and addresses where low-class prostitutes were to be found in large numbers together. There were also brothels: 'singing-girl houses' and taverns, which had for sign a bamboo shade over the light at the entrance.[52]

It is difficult to assess the social status of the prostitutes in Hangchow. They must, actually, have formed a cross-section of urban society. The humble origins and poverty of many of them points to their inclusion among the lower classes. But all degrees of poverty and wealth were to be found among them. Some, like the geishas of ancient Japan, were celebrated as courtesans, and having got rich quick, lived in luxury of the most exotic kind and only consorted with people of the upper classes. Their names have been preserved by contemporaries.[53] Talented singers and musicians, they were invited to the banquets held by high officials or noble families. A fashionable marriage was not complete unless 'singing-girls' were included in the celebrations. The most celebrated ones were even invited to the court to play before the Emperor on the evening of the 15th of the first moon, the feast of lanterns. They played, seated, on the zither or on the p'i-p'a, a kind of guitar of Central Asian origin, or sang standing up, accompanying their song with sinuous movements of the body. A description of a singing-girl runs: 'Her face is the colour of peaches, her lips are like cherries, her fingers delicate as jade, her eyes brilliant and bewitching, and her body sways as she sings'.[54]

Some courtesans were frequented by the gilded youth of Hangchow and by the students from the big colleges. The State taverns, which were run in connection with the big storehouses of alcoholic liquor, had their own singing-girls whose names were kept on special lists. Each of these taverns also kept several dozen official courtesans of whom a list was supplied to the regular customers. But the most celebrated of them usually stayed confined to their apartments and were only on view to important visitors. The entrée to these taverns was theoretically reserved for the students of the big colleges in Hangchow (the National University, the Imperial Academy and the Military Academy) but wealthy young men had access as well.[55]

Here is what Marco Polo has to say about prostitution in Hangchow:

'Certain of the streets are occupied by the women of the town, who are in such number that I dare not say what it is. They are found not only in the vicinity of the market places, where usually a quarter is assigned to them, but all over the city. They exhibit themselves splendidly attired and abundantly perfumed, in finely garnished houses, with trains of waiting women. These women are extremely accomplished in all the arts of allurement, and readily adapt their conversation to all sorts of persons, insomuch that strangers who have once tasted their attractions seem to get so bewitched, and are so taken with their blandishments and their fascinating ways that they never can get these out of their heads. Hence it comes to pass that when they return home they say they have been to Kinsay or the City of Heaven, and their only desire is to get back thither as soon as possible.'[56]

This description obviously only applies to those wealthy singing-girls who had been able to emancipate themselves from all forms of protection. A Chinese author of the end of the thirteenth century tells us how one of them succeeded in attaining wealth and fame. She was a native of Suchow, a town to the north of Hangchow celebrated for its beautiful women. A petty official who came of a very rich family had heard of her charms and went by boat to Suchow to make her conquest. The gift of a sumptuous wardrobe of clothes, and handsome presents to her domestics, brought no results: the young lady was well aware of the wealth of her admirer. She did not yield until he had presented her with five hundred pounds of silver and a hundred rolls of silk. In six months the unfortunate young man had squandered several million cash, but the fame and fortune of the lady were assured. The gilded youth of Kiangsu besieged her doors. Her house, although small, was extremely luxurious. It lacked nothing: pavilions, summer-houses, belvederes, flower-gardens and artificial lakes. The floors were carpeted with brocade, the walls covered with hangings woven with gold thread, the beds decked with priceless covers. The domestic staff ran to more than ten servants and musicians. As for the ornaments and vases in gold, silver and jade, the paintings and the calligraphy scrolls, all were chosen with the most exquisite taste. At her death, the Lady Hsü Lan was buried on Tiger Hill, the burial place for people of high rank, and a student at the College composed her epitaph.[57]

Successes of this kind were exceptional. The majority of the singing-girls, even those who lived in comparatively easy circumstances, did not succeed in emancipating themselves entirely from some kind of protection. Even if they did not actually live in one of the 'singing-girl houses', they remained attached to certain taverns or restaurants whose proprietors no doubt found it advantageous to round out their income by allowing singing-girls to entertain customers in their courtyards. In the best tea-houses in the city there were no singing-girls. But they were to be found, upstairs, in five tea-houses on the Imperial Way. However, according to a contemporary, these were noisy places with a bad name where decent people did not venture to go.[58]

As for the singing-girls of the lowest category, they were to be found by the dozen in the markets and near the bridges in the poorer districts. Their musical training seems to have been scanty. They were not usually called 'singing-girls' or 'artistes', but simply 'flowers'.[59]

A word should be said here about male prostitution, which

appears to have been a phenomenon peculiar to the big cities in the Sung period. Already in Kaifeng at the beginning of the twelfth century the existence of certain inverts who prostituted their charms is noted. They simpered, used cosmetics, decked themselves up, sang and danced just as their feminine counterparts did. During the years 1111-1117 an imperial decree authorized their arrest and imposed a punishment of a hundred strokes of the rod. A reward of fifty strings of cash was promised to anyone catching one of them or making a deposition or denunciation. But finding out such prostitutes, while difficult enough in Kaifeng, was still more difficult in Hangchow, where the population was both numerous and more fluid. Doubtless also there was far greater tolerance after the court had moved south. So a considerable number of inverts were to be found in Hangchow, probably several hundred, who had no other means of support but prostitution. Better organized than the singing-girls, being a more homogenous group, they had their special haunt outside the ramparts, near the New Gate.[60]

The dregs of the population consisted of thieves, ruffians, swindlers and beggars, all grouped into guilds. There were criminal gangs. A small troop of them would block the streets and rob the citizens in full daylight, in spite of being pitilessly hunted down by the city police. Others, experts in housebreaking, slipped into wealthy houses through holes made in brick walls or in bamboo partitions and took boxes of valuables. There were 'daylight robbers', selling bogus wares: imitation silk clothing made of paper, lumps of lead or copper that looked like ingots of silver or gold, drugs which were nothing but earth and sawdust. A contemporary is unable to restrain his admiration: 'The cunning of these people is extraordinary'. Sneak-thieves threaded among the crowds in the markets and the lanes snatching purses and necklaces. Swindlers hid their reprehensible activities behind attractive offers that seemed socially advantageous. There were 'services' which, owing to supposed influence in high places, undertook to procure for their clients appointments, promotions, court favours, success in legal proceedings or in commercial transactions. Others, bearing the name of 'Beautiful Ladies Service', dealt in the sale of gay ladies as concubines, while yet others specialized in lotteries and gambling.[61] Theft and fraud could not be entirely suppressed in a town containing such a large conglomeration of people. Marco Polo may be correct when he declares that 'the city was so safe that the doors of the houses and shops and stores full of all very dear merchandise often stayed open at night as by day',[62] but his account is only valid for the period of the Mongol occupation, when the police in the city must have been reinforced.

The number of paupers, beggars, thieves, country girls turned prostitutes, and poor devils living from hand to mouth by peddling worthless wares—sleeping anywhere they could find, nearly dying of cold and hunger—probably varied sharply from year to year and from month to month. The least rise in the price of rice was enough to double or triple the number of those who had to live by their wits in Hangchow. The great mass of humanity that filled the city of Hangchow to overflowing was sometimes subjected to violent shocks, and the resulting sudden increase in poverty and starvation became a matter of concern to the State. The frequency of such crises made it necessary to take precautionary measures. The court and the prefecture decided to make distributions of rice and cash at times when there was heavy snow or extreme cold, or following upon big fires, summer floods and autumn droughts. Thus, after the excessive rains in the Hangchow region in 1223, there was a famine in the town in the 3rd moon of the following year (about April), and the government had to distribute aid.[63]

The great official ceremonies and the great annual festivals were also made the occasion for distributions to the poor: 'At times when prayers for fine weather or for rain are offered by the Emperor and his ministers, when snow falls or when there are lucky omens, on the occasion of the birth of a prince or on the Emperor's birthday, when there is an eclipse of the sun, or excessive rains, or intense cold, when the townspeople are in want or when the grand rites of the Sacred Palace are celebrated or ceremonies of congratulations offered to the Emperor are performed — at all these times, an imperial notice is published announcing the gift of 200,000 strings in paper money for the army and the same for the common people.'[64]

Those in want could also look to private charity. To enhance their prestige, officials on being newly appointed or promoted would distribute cash to the poor.[65] And we have seen how the rich shipowners who lived on Phoenix Hill in the south side of the town devoted a part of their immense fortunes to works of charity. But that was not all. Buddhism had, from the fifth century, introduced and developed in China various charitable institutions (hospitals, alms-houses, dispensaries, .centres for the distribution of aid to the poor) which were supported by the income derived from the land with which they had been endowed. Following upon the widespread confiscation of property belonging to Buddhist communities in 845, the alms-houses and hospitals had been taken over by the public authorities. On moving to Hangchow, the court had established there a big dispensary which distributed drugs through seventy branch dispensaries scattered all about the urban area, and we have seen how the medicaments, which were supposed to be sold at a third of their price to the people of the town, were actually misappropriated by the employees and officials serving in these dispensaries. But other charitable institutions were run with greater honesty: hospitals for the aged and the penniless, orphanages for foundlings, free funerals and public cemeteries for the poor, homes for the infirm. This last institution still existed at the beginning of the Mongol occupation, if Marco Polo is to be believed: ' . . . if in the daytime', he says, 'they find any poor cripple unable to work for his livelihood, they take him to one of the hospitals, of which there are many, founded by the ancient kings, and endowed with great revenues. Or if he be capable of work they oblige him to take up some trade.'[66]

## THE PEASANTS

We know very little about the people of the countryside. No one took the trouble to give a detailed account of village life and of its social structure. Such information as we possess is fragmentary and sparse, and it is only on the hypothesis that country life changes little and slowly that one ventures to draw a picture composed of data as diverse chronologically as they are geographically. Let us first of all underline an economic fact of general application: the growth of the towns in the southeastern provinces could not have taken place except to the detriment of the countryside. The town consumed more than it produced, and many of its richest citizens owed their entire fortune to the income from their vast domains to the north of Hang-chow. The rents from private estates and State domains, commercial taxes that bore upon products of daily consumption, obligatory purchases of salt imposed by the State in certain areas —every form, in short, of direct and indirect taxation, brought about a progressive impoverishment of the countryside. Depopulation in the villages was doubtless accounted for by the flow of people into the towns.

However, there was considerable diversity in the social life of country districts, and there must have been an appreciable difference in the standard of living enjoyed by middle and small peasant proprietors, managers of private estates, superintendents of State domains, tenant farmers and agricultural labourers. For another thing, even if rice-cultivation predominated in the plains of the lower Yangtze, there was a greater variation in types of cultivation and in economic pursuits in the areas surrounding this great rice-growing zone.

In the mountainous regions in the southern part of Chekiang province, the main occupations were fishing, hunting, forestry and tea-growing; in the marshy regions along the coast, bamboo plantations, salt-extraction, and fishing along the coasts of the Che river estuary. It goes without saying that rural districts varied according to the main occupation of the inhabitants: villages in the rice-growing plains presented quite a different appearance from fishing villages. Finally, there was one part of the country population that was controlled by, and directly dependent upon, the State: those who worked in State enterprises, whether mines or salt marshes.

These people led the most poverty-stricken existence imaginable, their wages touching starvation level. In the ninth century the State paid 6½ lb. of corn per day and 40,000 cash per annum to the families working on the salt-lakes in the south of Shansi province.[67] Later, in the salt-marshes of the Huai valley, the ministry responsible for the salt-tax bought the salt produced by the workers employed by the State at a low price, and at the same time fixed the production figure that had to be met for the year. In the Huai marshes, nearly 280,000 families—that is, about a million persons—lived in a condition of semi-slavery.[68] In debt through loans they had contracted with the officials of the salt administration, reduced to penury by excessive requisitions and by delays in payment, the workers in the salt industry could find no means of escape save by flight or enrolment in the army. Their situation cannot have been very different in the thirteenth century in the State enterprises in Chekiang and Kiangsu.

The small peasant proprietors, tenant-farmers and agricultural labourers in the great rice-growing regions did not enjoy a much more enviable fate. Even a good harvest scarcely brought in enough to supply their basic needs. Bad years brought debts and very often famine. The renting-out or the sale of their land, the sale of children for domestic service, departure from the village, brigandage, suicide — such were the desperate measures they were reduced to take by the extremes of poverty. The rate of interest on loans was very high: 20% per month for the loan of cash, 50% for cereals at harvest time. Contracts for loan or hire must have been similar to those which have been found in Central Asia, near Tun-huang, dating from the ninth and tenth centuries. Here is an example of one concerning a loan of cloth (cloth serving at that time as a means of exchange in this region):

'On the first day of the third moon of the year [marked by the cyclical signs] *chia-tzu*, Fan Huai-t'ung and his brothers, whose family is in need of a little cloth, have borrowed from the monk Li a piece of white silk 38 feet long and two feet and half an inch wide. In the autumn, they will pay as interest 40 bushels of corn and millet. As regards the capital, they will repay it [in the form of a piece of silk of the same quality and size] before the end of the second moon of the following year. If they do not repay it, interest equivalent to that paid at the time of the loan [that is, 40 bushels of cereals] shall be paid monthly. The two parties having agreed to this loan in presence of each other shall not act in any way contrary to their agreement. The borrowers: Wen-ta, Huai-ta, Huai-chu and their elder brother Huai-t'ung.'[69]

Another document from the same period shows how the sale of agricultural labourers was concluded:

'Contract agreed on the third day of the 11th moon of the year *yi-wei*. The monumental-stonemason Chao Seng-tzu, because . . . he is short of commodities and cannot procure them by any other means, sells today, with the option of repurchase, his own son Chiu-tzu to his relation [by agreement] the lord Li Ch'ien-ting. The sale price has been fixed at 200 bushels of corn and 200 bushels of millet. Once the sale has been concluded, there will neither be anything paid for the hire of the man, nor interest paid on the commodities. If it should happen that the man sold, Chiu-tzu, should fall ill and die, his elder brother will be held responsible for repaying the part of the goods [corresponding to the period of hire which had not been completed]. If Chiu-tzu should steal anything of small or great value from a third person, either in the country or in town, it is Chiu-tzu himself [and not his employer] from whom reparation will be demanded . . . The earliest time-limit for the repurchase of Chiu-tzu has been fixed at the sixth year. It is only when this amount of time has elapsed that his relations are authorized to repurchase him. Lest a higher price should then be asked for him, this contract has been drawn up to establish proof of the agreement.'

The signatories to this contract were Chiu-tzu himself, his elder brother, 'vendor and guarantor', the monumental-stone-mason 'who has agreed on the amount of the commodities and has received them', and four witnesses, one of whom was a villager whose fields adjoined the vendor's.'[70]

Contracts for the hire of agricultural labourers are more precise. The man is hired for the season, generally from the first moon (February) until the ninth (October). His wage is one 'load' (about eight bushels) of cereals, corn and millet, per month. His employer undertakes to furnish him with free clothing: a 'spring outfit', a shirt and trousers for the summer and a pair of leather shoes. In exchange, he must work without stopping from morning until evening. For each day's work missed, 3⅓ bushels would be deducted from his wages during the months when the work was heaviest, only 1½ during the other months. If he falls ill, payment for the days when he is not at work is deducted from his wages. If he loses or damages the agricultural goods entrusted to him (wicker baskets, sacks, harvesting knives, hoes and spades) he has to see that they are replaced. Finally, as was the custom, his employer will not be held responsible if he is guilty of theft with respect to a third party, whether it is a case of corn or millet, melons, vegetables, fruit, a sheep or an ox.[71]

The indebtedness and poverty of the countryside accounts for the existence of vagabonds and brigands. Varying in numbers according to region and period, this type of person never completely disappeared. Even the most important roads were not secure from them, and merchants did not venture to travel singly. Bands of brigands had their haunts in the mountains and in the swamps where the vegetation was thick enough to allow them to escape pursuit. Thus there was a region covered with reeds and marshes, 'the desert of a hundred *li*', to the north-east of Lake Tung-t'ing, which was infested with brigands. A high official who went by boat from Szechwan to Suchow in 1177, and who has left us a diary of his journey, notes in it when passing through this deserted region traversed by a stream running parallel with the Yangtze: 'The moon was so bright that everything was as clear as daylight. The escorting soldiers, full of courage, called out to each other from one boat to another all through the night. Bows and crossbows were kept at the stretch, and as we made our way, they kept up a continuous beating of drums and small bells.'[72]

The low-lying, humid plains stretching to the north of Hangchow as far as the Yangtze and beyond, are covered with ricefields. These are small squares or rectangles often no more than ten yards long. They are surrounded by narrow raised paths. Flooded or dry depending on the season, they are cultivated by a two-pronged hoe with a very long handle which the peasants hold with both hands, lifting it above their heads and bringing it down again with a sudden movement. Only lightweight tools are required to turn over the light soil of the ricefields. The plough, which is light, is drawn by men or by one buffalo. But beasts are scarce, and the buffalo is often on loan, or owned in common by several families. When work is at its peak, between the months of June and September, the peasants are in the fields from dawn to dusk. The midday meal is brought to them by the wives and children. In Szechwan, the communal labour in the ricefields was regulated by a waterclock. A drum was beaten to call the workers together, provide work-rhythms, spur them on in their tasks, and prevent them from chattering. The sound of the drum could be heard in the fields from morning to night.[73]

Winter was the only slack season. The men busied themselves with winnowing, the women with weaving. They stayed up late and sometimes joined company to save oil for the lamps. The rearing of silkworms and weaving were delicate and absorbing tasks. As for the children, they were employed throughout the year in looking after the buffaloes, feeding the animals in the yard (pigs, chickens, and sometimes edible dogs), collecting firewood, which was always scarce, and fetching water from the well. But in some villages there were schools for them in the winter where they learnt the rudiments of writing and doing sums.

Peasant life, usually laborious and monotonous, did also have its moments of relaxation and jollity. Such were the annual festivals, chief of which were the New Year festival, about the end of January or beginning of February, and that for the sacrifices to the god of the soil. The great festival of the god of the soil fell at the end of August or early in September. Its official date was the fifth day marked by the cyclical sign wu following the 'establishment of autumn', a date in the solar calendar corresponding approximately to August 7th. The villagers gathered together near a local sanctuary to watch games, theatrical entertainments, clowning and juggling, sometimes performed by wandering players specially hired for such great occasions. Pigs and chickens were killed, rice of superior quality was eaten, and everyone got drunk. The poorest among them borrowed in order to be able to celebrate in a fitting manner these special days of the year which influenced the fortune and happiness of everyone.

There was very little contact between the government and the rural population. The sub-prefect lived in town, within a fortified citadel containing his residence, the administrative offices, the audience-hall and the prison. He was a distant being who was hardly ever seen and who was surrounded by an aura of dazzling prestige. The State for its part did not interfere in the life of the peasant communities, or rather only did so for essential purposes: collecting taxes, collecting men for the forced labour that was demanded for public works, when sometimes as many as several hundred thousand men were required, and for taking defensive measures against subversive movements. For these, villages and families were held collectively responsible — and sometimes organized into groups of families with collective responsibility—so that whenever a rebellion broke out anywhere, the repression was terrible.

The principle underlying the whole administrative system in China was that above all, peace must reign. There was to be no stirring up of trouble: a sub-prefect who allowed disturbances to arise in his area of jurisdiction was a bad administrator, and it was he who was blamed, whatever the origin of the disturbances might have been. His immediate superiors ran a considerable risk of having their promotion retarded. From another point of view, the people administered were hesitant about referring to the public authorities for settling their differences, and it was only when all other solutions (compromise or arbitration) had failed that they presented themselves before the court of justice held by the sub-prefect. An accused person was immediately thrown into prison: even an innocent person wrongfully accused was guilty of having disturbed the peace of the locality and the tranquillity of the judge. Besides, since the idea of accusing him had arisen, his innocence was not complete. As for the accuser, he too was regarded with the greatest suspicion. Furthermore, it was expensive to have recourse to public justice, since an accusation could not be laid without making the usual offerings to the judge: it was a matter of decorum.

Chinese justice insisted on certain kinds of objective proof (a thief could not be condemned if the object stolen had not been found, nor a supposed murderer if there was no trace of violence on the corpse), but at the same time it was one of the most cruel systems of justice that have ever existed. All the penalties consisted of extremely severe corporal punishments. The accused were kept in prison for lengthy periods in wretched conditions. They received no nourishment except from their relations, who, however, were needed for work in the fields. Torture (whipping, beating, the iron collar and manacles) was normally employed to induce recalcitrant prisoners to confess. Also miscarriage of justice was comparatively frequent. In short, it was a system of justice apparently designed to discourage people from acquiring a taste for legal proceedings, and it is easy to understand why the peasants preferred to settle their quarrels among themselves, either by coming to an agreement, or by arbitration. Only the most serious cases came before the official courts of justice.[74]

Collective responsibility, the cruelty of repressive measures, the authority of the elders of the village and the local district, the authority of heads of families, village solidarity and the horror of legal proceedings—these are the factors which explain why peace reigned in the countryside. Only a great famine or the most crying and widespread injustice stirred up troops of rebels. It was troops of this kind, inflamed with messianic hopes and grown to the size of veritable armies, that usually put an end to dynasties and sometimes swept one of their leaders to the throne of the Son of Heaven.


## NOTES AND REFERENCES

1. M. Mauss, *La Nation, Année sociologique* 1953-1954, p. 28.
2. On the general organization of Chinese administration, see R. des Rotours, *Traité des Examens*, Paris 1932, introduction; and E. A. Kracke, *Civil Service in Early Sung China* (960-1067) Cambridge (Mass.), 1953.
3. See below, *The Peasants*.
4. Most of the information given in this passage is taken from the work by E. A. Kracke already cited.
5. These rules and regulations, the functions of which were at one and the same time economic, social and psychological, have long treatises devoted to them in the official histories. Infringements were punished by law. Cf. *T'ang lü shu i* (the T'ang Code), chap. XXVI, art. 15: 'All those who contravene the regulations when having houses or carriages built, clothes, vases and other utensils made, or animals carved in stone for funerary purposes, are punished by a hundred strokes of the rod'. For instance, mandarins whose grade was below the third degree did not have the right to have animals carved in stone placed among the approaches to their tombs.
6. *Kuei hsin tsa chih, pieh chi* A, § 14.
7. This decree is mentioned by L. C. Goodrich in *A Short History of the Chinese People*, London, Allen & Unwin, 1958.
8. MLL, XIII, 3, p. 240.
9. *Ibid.*, XIX, 3, p. 299.
10. In times of peace, the soldiers, who were very badly paid, took to trading. This was traditional. Cf. *T'ang liang-ching ch'eng-fang k'ao* (Researches on the walls and districts of the two T'ang capitals) by Hsü Sung (1718-1848), the paragraph on the West

Market in Ch'ang-an: The soldiers of the Imperial Guard made a comfortable living selling silks. The strongest of them became popular entertainers; they wrestled, competed in tugs-of-war (two teams contesting a rope), or were weight-lifters of blocks of wood or pieces of iron. In Hangchow, in the 13th c., soldiers were sellers of rice-wine.

11. Y, p. 205.

12. Goodrich, op. cit.

13. On the Chinese navy in the 12th and 13th centuries, see Lo Jungpang, 'China as a sea-power', Far Eastern Quarterly, XIV, 4, 1955. On the first use of gunpowder for military purposes in China, see L. C. Goodrich and Feng Chia-sheng, The early development of fire-arms in China, Isis, XXXVI (1946), pp. 114-23, 250-1, and XXXIX (1948), pp. 63-4.

14. R. H. van Gulik, T'ang yin pi shih, 'Parallel cases from under the Pear-tree', Leiden, 1956, p. 149.

15. Sung shih [Official history of the Sung dynasty], XXXVIII, first year chia-t'ai, 3rd moon.

16. On the units in use at Kaifeng at the beginning of the 12th c., cf. Tung ching meng hua lu, III, 9, p. 22; on those of Hangchow, cf. MLL, XIII, 2, p. 238.

17. According to the Yen pei tsa chih by Lu Yu-jen of Sung (end of 13th c.), Shuo fu XXII, f. 7a, ten cash of the reign-period Hsien-p'ing (993-1003) weighed one ounce, that is to say 37·3 grammes. Cf. also Wen hsien t'ung k'ao, II, 2, f. 19b, which says that in Szechwan—where iron cash were in circulation—the weight of a string of cash was about 16 lb.

18. See Lien-sheng Yang, Money and Credit in China, Harvard University, 1952.

19. MLL, loc. cit.

20. J. Mullie, Une Planche à Assignats de 1214, avec une Figure dans le Texte, T'oung Pao, XXXIII, 1937, pp. 150-7. We might recall here what Marco Polo recounted about the Mongol banknotes of the end of the 13th c. (M & P, p. 238): 'And all these sheets or moneys . . . are made with as much authority and formality as if they were of pure gold or silver, for many officials who are deputed for this write their names on every coin [i.e. note], placing there each one his mark [these were official, not private, seals], and when it is all done as it ought to be, the head of them deputed by the lord stains the seal entrusted to him with cinnabar and impresses it upon the coin so that the pattern of the seal dipped in the cinnabar remains printed there, and then that money is authorized. And if anyone were to counterfeit it he

would be punished with the last penalty . . . ' On the history of money in China, consult Lien-sheng Yang, op. cit., and more specifically for the Mongol period, H. Franke, Geld und Wirtschaft in China unter der Mongolen-Herrschaft, Liepzig, 1946.

21. MLL, IX, 13, p. 208.
22. MLL, XVIII, 7, p. 294.
23. On the market of Wu-ch'ang (on the right bank of the Yangtze opposite present-day Hankow) cf. Wu-ch'uan lu (of 1177), chap. II, f. 16a, which describes this market as being a town of several tens of thousand houses extending along the banks of the river. The Meng liang lu, XIX, 3, p. 298, also mentions, as being important markets, Sha-shih (near Chiang-ling, to the north of Lake Tung-t'ing) and T'ai-p'ing-chou (between Nanking and Wuhu).
24. L. Wieger, Textes historiques, III, pp. 1880-90.
25. Cf. M & P, p. 215: 'And you must know that all the Cataians hated the rule of the great Kaan because he set over them the Tartar, and for the more part Saracen, rulers, and they were not able to bear it, seeming to them to be like slaves. And then the great Kaan had not the rule of the province [of] Catai by right, but rather had obtained it by force; and not trusting them he gave to rule the lands to Tartars, Saracens and Christians who were of his own household faithful to him, and were not of the province of Catai.'
26. One of the first texts mentioning the use of the compass for sea voyages is the P'ing-chou k'o-t'an, chap. II, f. 2b in the edition of the Shou-shan-ko ts'ung-shu. On the marine compass, see Li Shu-hua, an article in Oriens Extremus I, July 1954.
27. T. Fujita, Hang-tschau als Seehafen in der Zeit der Sung und Yüandynastie (in Japanese), Shigakuzasshi XXVII, 9, Sept. 1916.
28. On the build, crews and armaments of merchant ships in the Sung period, see Kuwabara J., On P'u Shou-keng, Memoirs of the Research Department of the Toyo Bunko, No. 2, 1928, pp. 66-72.
29. The places where Chinese cash dating from the Sung period have been found are: Japan, Java, Singapore, southern India, the island of Zanzibar, and the Somaliland coast. Cf. Kuwabara, op. cit., pp. 25-7.
30. MLL, XIII, 4, pp. 240-1, gives a long list of the shops in Hangchow celebrated for the quality of their products before and after the reign-period Ch'un-yu (1241-1252).
31. This information is supplied by a story of the Sung period which has been translated into English under the title of 'Fifteen strings

of cash' in *The Courtesan's Jewel Box*, Foreign Languages Press, Peking, 1957.

32. Cf. MLL, XIII, 4, pp. 240-1, where several *kuan-jen* [mandarins] appear in a list of celebrated traders of Hangchow.
33. MLL, XVI, 6, p. 269. Cf. Balazs, op. cit., p. 144.
34. MLL, XIX, 3, p. 239.
35. MLL, XIII, 4, pp. 239-40.
36. J. Sauvaget, *Relation de la Chine et de l'Inde rédigée en 851*, Paris, 'Les Belles Lettres', 1948, p. 19.
37. Y, p. 204.
38. The T'ang Code, of which most of the articles were still in force during the Sung period, allotted a punishment of sixty strokes of the rod for all fraudulent imitation in the manufacture of goods (flimsiness, use of unsuitable materials, measurements not according to the regulations—particularly in the case of cloth). Cf. *T'ang lü shu i*, chap. XXVI, art. 30.
39. MLL, XIX, 4, p. 300.
40. MLL, XIII, 3, pp. 238-9. For the history of the Chinese guilds in T'ang and Sung times, see the article by Sh. Kato in *Memoirs of the Toyo Bunko*, VIII, 1936.
41. Translation from the French of the *Livre de Marco Polo*, ed. by A. J. H. Charignon, pub. by Albert Nachbaur, Peking, 1928, p. 87.
42. Y, p. 204.
43. MLL, XVIII, 7, p. 294.
44. MLL, XIX, 6, pp. 301-2.
45. MLL, XIX, 7, pp. 302-3. Cf. *Tu ch'eng chi sheng*, § 6, p. 95.
46. MLL, XIX, 5, pp. 300-1. Cf. *Tu ch'eng chi sheng*, § 13, pp. 100-1.
47. Cf. the Sung story translated in *The Courtesan's Jewel Box* under the title 'Fifteen strings of cash', and the numerous articles in the T'ang Code dealing with relations between master and servant.
48. MLL, XIII, 7, p. 245.
49. *Wu lin chiu shih*, VI, 6, p. 444.
50. *T'ang liang-ching ch'eng-fang k'ao*.
51. M & P, p. 236.
52. *Tu ch'eng chi sheng*, 3, p. 92.
53. MLL, XX, 1, p. 310.
54. MLL, XX, 3, pp. 309-10.
55. MLL, X, 9, p. 214.
56. Y, pp. 202-3.
57. *Kuei hsin tsa chih*, Hsü B, § 7.
58. MLL, XVI, 1, p. 262.

59. *Wu lin chiu shih*, VI, 4, p. 443.
60. *Kuei hsin tsa chih, Hou*, § 71.
61. *Wu lin chiu shih*, VI, 8, p. 444.
62. M & P, p. 313.
63. *Ch'ien-t'ang hsien chih* (local gazeteer of one of the two sub-prefectures of Hangchow compiled at the end of the 16th c.), § *chi shih*, 'things worth recording'.
64. MLL, XVIII, 6, pp. 292-3.
65. *Wu lin chiu shih*, VI, 7, p. 444.
66. Y, p. 188.
67. *Sung hui yao*, chap. CXXXII, 23-4.
68. Ibid., 18b-23.
69. Cf. Pelliot collection of Chinese Mss. from Tun-huang in the Bibliothèque nationale, Paris, No. 3565. Contract on paper of the 9th or 10th c.
70. Ibid. No. 3964.
71. Cf. Pelliot collection No. 3150 and No. 3649 verso (dated 957). The Stein collection of Mss. from Tun-huang in the British Museum No. 1897 (dated 924), published in *Tun-huang to-so*, p. 440, and Tun-huang Mss. in the National Library of Peking, published in *Tun-huang hsieh-ching t'i-chi yü Tun-huang tsa-lu*, II, p. 127.
72. *Wu ch'uan lu* by Fan Ch'eng-ta, chap. II, f. 15b-16a, in the edition of the *Chih-pu-tsu chai ts'ung-shu*.
73. Lien-sheng Yang, 'Schedules of Work and Rest in Imperial China', *Harvard Journal of Asiatic Studies*, XVIII, 3-4, Dec. 1955.
74. An excellent summary of the administration of Chinese justice, based on contemporary accounts of Sung and Ming times, is to be found in the introduction to R. H. van Gulik's translation of the *T'ang yin pi shih*, Leiden, 1956.

# CHAPTER III

## HOUSING, CLOTHING, COOKING

HOUSING: *Techniques of construction. Different types of buildings. Gardens. Luxury of the Imperial Palace. Interior decoration of rich people's houses.* PERSONAL TOILET: *Baths. Bathing establishments in Hangchow. Wallowers in filth and ablution maniacs. Cosmetics and perfumes.* CLOTHING: *Official regulations. Hair styles and headgear; girdles. Footwear. Stylishness of Hangchow people.* COOKING: *Various kinds of regional cooking. Provisioning facilities in Hangchow. Differences in diet of the poor and of the rich. Banquets. Alcoholic drinks and varieties of tea.*

### HOUSING

NOT ALL the inhabitants of Hangchow were fortunate enough to have a roof over their heads. Beggars and penniless wretches slept in the open, and, since overcrowding was often exacerbated by the frequent fires which ravaged the city, others were always having to be provided with temporary accommodation. The cells and courtyards of monasteries, boats on the lake, military barracks and hastily erected shelters made of waterproof matting were put at the disposal of homeless families and of victims of disasters. One section of the population lived permanently on the boats on the canals—the boatmen and their families.

As for those people of the lower classes who did have somewhere to live, they had to crowd six or seven together, possibly more, in one tiny room. In spite of the multi-storeyed houses in the poorer districts, there were too many people for the available accommodation in a town squeezed between the river and the lake. Streets, markets and houses overflowed with people. But buildings were constructed quickly, well, and economically. From time to time, when the great ceremonies of the official cult took place, vast constructions made of bamboo stakes, wooden poles, knotted cords, matting, screens and curtains, were erected in a few hours in various parts of the city or near the altar for the sacrifices to Heaven in the southern suburb. One of them might serve as the hall for exhibiting the ceremonial chariot of the Emperor, another as a hall for lustrations.[1] The rapidity with which these temporary buildings were erected is typical of Chinese building as a whole. Even edifices intended to last were built of light materials and constructed with incredible dexterity and skill.

The basic materials were wood and bamboo brought by boat from the region south of Hangchow, and bricks and tiles. The timber requirements of the city, enormous for that time, had altered the nature of the economy over a distance of one or two hundred miles to the south. The peasants of the prefecture of Yen had given up the cultivation of rice, which brought small returns, for forestry work, and they sold quantities of cryptomeria-wood to merchants in the city. Stone was reserved for bridges, balustrades, paving for streets and roads, for the ramparts, the dykes, and for Buddhist towers. It was a noble material fit for ornamentation and carvings, but not to be employed in the construction of dwelling houses or even for government buildings.

Houses for the rich and houses for the poor, edifices and temples, whether public or private, were all built by the same methods. The main structure did not consist of foundations and bearer-walls, but of wooden pillars spaced about three yards apart, resting on stone supports sunk ten to twenty inches in the ground. The size of a house, or of a covered arcade or a gateway, was reckoned in the number of spaces between pillars, or, as one might say, in spans. The lightness and rigidity of the whole structure meant that it could be raised from the base, so that the entire building could be moved elsewhere if necessary.

All buildings, without exception, were rectangular in shape; they were sometimes subdivided across their width by one or two partitions. As many constructions of its kind as might be required were scattered about the parks and gardens of the rich, either set at right angles to each other to form a U enclosing a courtyard, or else separate. They had a ground floor only, or one storey at the most. In the poorer districts, on the other hand, the houses formed an uninterrupted façade along the lanes. Joined one to another and extending in depth, they no doubt gave on to small courtyards at the back. Many of them consisted of several storeys, if the accounts of Marco Polo and of Arab and

European travellers of the fourteenth century are to be believed.[2] Was the method of construction for these multi-storeyed houses any different from that used in low buildings, and, in particular, did they have foundations? Probably not. In these crowded districts of Hangchow, adjacent buildings would provide some support, and extra support was probably found to be unnecessary in view of the lightweight materials used both for structure and furnishings. Indeed, when compared with houses built in Europe at the same period, these buildings were more like scaffoldings.

The roof, the most important and the most expensive item in house-building, was put on as soon as the pillars for supporting it were in place. It always had two slopes, and rested on a combination of mainbeams and crossbeams, and sometimes on exterior brackets as well, which, in the finest buildings, gave an effect of a roof detached from the rest of the building and floating in the air. The parts of the roof-timbers exposed to view were adorned with carvings and painted in bright colours. The finest roofs, with tiles glazed yellow, pale green or jade-green, and with slightly upturned edges, harmonized to perfection with near-by trees and with the varied curves of the hills surrounding the lake.

The custom of making roofs with upturned edges was probably fairly recent in the thirteenth century. It cannot have become widespread until the T'ang dynasty (seventh to tenth century), and the method of obtaining the required curves was still rather clumsy at that time. An architect of the eleventh century who wrote an important treatise on the rules of his art, and who invites us to share his admiration for the builders of the T'ang period, adds that they were not very skilled in curving the edges of their roofs upwards.[3] It is worth noting, incidentally, that curved roofs were reserved, by imperial decree, for the houses of people of high rank and for government buildings. As for constructing roofs for shops and ordinary houses, no one would have thought of spending money on such a costly method.

Similarly, ornaments in the form of aigrettes and small terracotta animals, dragons and phoenixes, which were to be seen on the ridge and eaves of roofs on the houses of nobles and officials, as well as on government buildings, were forbidden to the common people.[4] At the beginning of the twelfth century, the roofs of Kaifeng, the capital of Northern Sung, as far as can be seen from contemporary paintings, were covered with two different kinds of tiles, and this was probably also the case in Hangchow, where every effort was made to copy the customs of Kaifeng. One kind, known as 'panel-tiles', were long flat slabs which were laid horizontally, and were only used to roof shops and lower class houses; the other kind were rounded, similar to those used in the south of France, and were reserved for public buildings and the houses of people of rank.[5] It was only this kind of tile that was considered worth the trouble of glazing.

The use of pillars to bear the weight of roof and flooring meant that the outside walls were independent of the main structure. Apart from the filled-in parts which were lightly built of brick, offering little resistance to rats and thieves, they consisted of blinds, screens and bamboo trellises. The filled-in parts, except for the gable-end walls which were windowless, only rose to a height of about twenty inches above ground-level. This enabled the occupants to enjoy the cool of the evening and, if the house had a good situation, the beauty of the view. Windows were made of square trellis-work with the spaces covered by oiled paper which could be procured in the markets of Hangchow.[6] These square-paned windows were extremely decorative.

The houses in the poorer districts gave directly on to the street, unless there was a courtyard in between. In either case, shops, restaurants and small workrooms were always on the ground floor. These houses with fronts open on to the street were no doubt typical of all the towns of South China, and gave Hangchow a friendly air which the capitals of T'ang times, with their houses closed in on themselves and their districts shut off with walls of dry earth, had never known, except perhaps in a few of the busiest streets. The blind walls along the lanes in present-day Peking probably give a fairly good idea of the appearance presented by the residential quarters of the great cities of the North in T'ang times. But walls of this kind, with no openings other than doors, were also to be found in some parts of Hangchow in the thirteenth century. They hid from view official buildings, temples, palaces, monasteries, and the residences of important people, high officials and rich merchants.

Behind them were tall single-storeyed buildings with roofs extending into porches, dwelling-houses with courtyards surrounded by covered arcades, and detached two-storeyed buildings and small summer-houses scattered among trees and flower-gardens. The main residential quarters of wealthy establishments consisted of a group of buildings set at right angles or placed parallel to each other, separated by a series of courtyards varying in number. The ground-level of the buildings was slightly higher than that of the courtyards, and the main hall was reached by several steps placed in the centre of the building. The front gate leading into the first courtyard was a square structure, also above ground-level, which was roofed. It served as shelter for the gate-keepers. Sumptuary regulations did not allow private persons to have gates more than one span wide.[7] Only important dignitaries of the empire might have gates with several passageways, such as were to be seen at the Imperial Palace. Gates had a screen in front of them consisting of a wall six feet high which hid the entrance and was supposed to keep out baleful influences. We might mention here another form of protection against bad luck and demons: the gate gods. Painted images of them were placed one on each side of the gateway to prevent evil spirits from entering the house. These gods were historical persons who had been deified—two captains of the guard who, according to the legend, kept armed guard at the door of the apartments of the first T'ang emperor and thus put an end to his nightmares.

The group of buildings composing the residential quarters of the finest houses, with their upturned roofs and porches one behind the other and their long covered arcades, presented a total effect that was most harmonious. But each single one of the detached buildings was designed to produce some special picturesque effect. Each pavilion was built for a particular purpose: perhaps one from which the moonlight could be admired, another for music-making, another for banquets, yet another, set in the shade of bamboos and pines and hung with paintings of snow scenes inside, for keeping cool in hot weather. Sometimes summer-houses were built on piles over an artificial pool which could be reached by boat or by a little wooden bridge. It was said that many wealthy people had spent a fortune on constructing and making improvements to their residences. Sometimes rare woods, aloe and sandalwood, imported from tropical countries, were used for the pillars and framework. The floor was often paved with glazed bricks, and there is even one case cited of a rich man who had his floor inlaid with a floral design in silver.[8]

Just as much thought was given to gardens and artificial pools as to the actual buildings. It was the harmonious lines of the total effect that was considered important. A poet of T'ang times recommended that, for a well-planned residence, a sixth of the total area should be assigned to the house, half to lakes and ponds, and a third to plantations of bamboos.[9] The natural scenery of these gardens was all man-made: little artificial hills, winding streams with waterfalls, ponds in which swam those gold and silver fishes that were sold in the town under the name of 'long-life fishes' and were reared in large quantities outside one of the north-west gates.[10]

No fine house was without its rare flowers or without pine-trees with gnarled trunks and twisted branches; no good garden without the curious stones it was then the fashion to collect. These rocks worn by wind or water were like miniature mountains. Sometimes they were placed so as to represent one of the famous sites where Taoist immortals were supposed to dwell. Planted perhaps with dwarf trees (probably already used at that time), pierced with little grottoes where perfumes could be burnt to make smoke that looked like clouds, and with little lakes here and there, these curious rocks invited ecstatic excursions. Those who delighted in them, shrunk, as sometimes happens to immortals, to dimensions in accord with the little paths and tracks that wound about these mountains in miniature, could wander freely there in imagination.[11] This is a particular form of expression of the Chinese aesthetic sense which comes from an ancient magical conception of the art of representation, and which is also to be found in the landscape painting and in the art of landscape gardening. Gardens were sometimes laid out to represent some famous mountain site. Wandering there, one derived strength from contact with its strange stones, ancient trees and rare plants, and, as one contemplated the fish darting capriciously hither and thither, a sense of renewal from the feeling of natural spontaneity which the scene conveyed.

Marco Polo's description of the Imperial Palace deserves to be quoted in its entirety, because it is full of interesting details about the imperial residence, which formed a small walled city of its own. Marco Polo's account is all the more valuable because the Chinese sources are not very illuminating on this subject. He got his information from an old Chinese merchant. 'All this story,' he says, 'was told me by a very rich merchant of Quinsai, when I found myself in that city, who was very old, and had been an intimate friend of the King Fanfur [that is to say, one of the last emperors of Southern Sung] and knew all his life, and had seen the said palace in being, into which he was pleased to lead me. And because the king deputed by the Great Kaan stays there, the first pavilions are still as they used to be, but the rooms of the girls are all gone to ruin and nothing else is seen but traces. In the same way the wall which enclosed the woods and gardens is fallen to the ground and there are no longer either animals or trees.' But let us turn to the beginning of the description:

'Now we will speak of a most beautiful palace where the King Fanfur lived, whose predecessors had had a space of country enclosed which they surrounded for ten miles with very high walls and divided it into three parts. In the middle part one entered through a very large gate, where were found on one side and on the other very large and broad pavilions on the level ground, with the roof supported by columns which were painted and worked with gold and the finest azures. Then at the head was seen the principal one and larger than all the others, painted in the like way with the pillars gilt, and the ceiling with the most beautiful ornaments of gold; and round about on the walls the stories of the past kings were painted with the greatest skill. There every year on certain days dedicated to his idols the King Fanfur used to hold court and give a banquet to the chief lords, great masters, and rich artificers of the city of Quinsai, and ten thousand persons at one time sat at table there conveniently under all the said pavilions. And this court lasted ten or twelve days, and it was a stupendous thing and past all belief to see the magnificence of the guests dressed in silk and in gold with so many precious stones upon them, because each one did his utmost to go with the greatest display and wealth in his power. Behind this pavilion of which we have spoken, which was entered through the middle of the great gate, there was a wall with a door which divided off the other part of the palace, where on entering one found another great place made in the manner of a cloister with its pillars which held up the portico which went round the said cloister, and there were various rooms for the king and queen which were likewise worked with various

works, and so were all the walls. Then from this cloister one
entered into a walk six paces wide, all covered; but it was so long
that it reached down to the lake. On this walk ten courts on one
side and ten on the other stood facing one another, fashioned like
long cloisters with their porticoes all round, and each cloister or
court had fifty rooms with their gardens, and in all these rooms
were stationed a thousand girls whom the king kept for his service. And sometimes he went with the queen and with some of
the said [girls] for recreation about the lake on barges all
covered with silk, and also to visit the temples of the idols. The
other two parts of the said enclosure were laid out with woods,
lakes, and most beautiful gardens planted with fruit trees, where
were enclosed all sorts of animals, that is roe-deer, fallow-deer,
red-deer, hares, rabbits; and there the king went to enjoy himself
with his damsels, some in carriages and some on horseback, and
no man went in there. And he made the said [damsels] run with
dogs and give chase to these kinds of animals; and after they were
tired they went into these woods which faced one another above
the said lakes, and leaving the clothes there they came out of
them naked and entered into the water and set themselves to
swim some on one side and some on the other, and the king
stayed to watch them with the greatest delight; and then they
went back home. Sometimes he had food carried into these
woods, which were thick and dense with very lofty trees, waited
on by the said damsels.'¹²

The Chinese sources tell us nothing of these gambols. But it is
possible that they were not a mere figment of the imagination,
for we do learn that in front of the Palace of the Refreshing
Spring, within the walls of the imperial enclosure, was an artificial hill covered with old pine-trees and tall bamboos which
gave complete protection from the heat of the sun. Even in the
hot-weather months (July and August) it was agreeably cool
there. There was also a Palace of Coolness, made of Japanese
pinewood, ivory white. In front of it were several ancient pine-
trees. An artificial waterfall cascaded into a lake covered with
pink and white water-lilies. In the vast courtyard surrounding
the palace were hundreds of urns containing jasmine, orchids,
pink-flowering banana, flowering cinnamon and other rare and
exotic flowering shrubs. They were fanned by a windmill so that

their fragrance should penetrate within the great hall of the palace. Along each side of this hall were receptacles in bronze filled with snow, and vases containing rare perfumes, choice fruits, sugarcane juice and other refreshments for the emperor's delectation.[13]

Interior decoration was always simple, elegant, and unobtrusive. The furniture consisted of small, low, rectangular tables with thin, straight legs, of little pedestal tables, of armchairs and low chairs with tall backs, of circular stools with feet rounded on the outside which were decorated with openwork carving, and of light chairs with legs crossed in an X, known as 'barbarian seats'. Chairs had only come into use in China two or three centuries before this. Brought in from India via Central Asia, they did not find favour in T'ang times, when only wide armchairs with heavy backs were used, upon which one sat cross-legged, since the practice of being seated on a chair was unknown. Beds were made of wood of various kinds, and consisted of planks joined together and supported on a carved frame. Sometimes they were closed in on three sides by partitions hung with paintings. Furniture in rich people's houses was very often of black lacquer, especially the beds. By an imperial decree of 1029, red lacquer beds were reserved for the use of the emperor. For bedding, everyone used rush matting, covers lined with floss silk, and a pillow in the form of a parallelipiped with a depression in the centre. The ordinary kind of pillow was of plaited rush, but the best ones were made of lacquered wood or painted pottery. The beds, which were screened by curtains,[14] provided a hard, flat surface for sleeping on, but the pillow and mattress had the advantage of being cool during the hottest weeks in the summer.

Black and red were the dominating colours in interior decoration. Scrolls, usually landscapes, sometimes covered an entire wall. Fine specimens of calligraphy were also the fashion, and antique vases such as were sometimes discovered during excavations, or else copies of genuine antiques—there was a thriving antique trade in Hangchow—as well as small terracotta animals. These last were probably in imitation of the pottery figurines and animals found in ancient tombs, and provide another indication of the taste for antiques of all kinds that was so prevalent at that time,

Flowers were one of the most important elements in the décor of a well-appointed house, and the art of flower arrangement, which Japan inherited and which is still very much alive in that country, was one of great skill. Rare flowers demanding special attention were much sought after. That is why jasmine became so much the fashion in Hangchow. A very fragile plant, it was brought in pots by sea from the provinces of Fukien and Kuangtung. Special skilled and complicated treatment was required to produce very large flowers and make the plant last over the summer. Among other prescriptions, one recommends watering the plants with the liquid obtained from fermented fish on the 10th of the 6th moon. The region around Hangchow itself, though, also produced some beautiful flowers: nearly ten kinds of winter and autumn peonies, over seventy varieties of chrysanthemums, and numerous varieties of daphne, magnolia and orchids, not to mention the blossom of a wide range of fruit trees, such as plum, pear, peach, pomegranate and cherry.[15]

The people of Hangchow paid much more attention to the decoration than to the comfort of their houses. In the hot season, the common people sallied forth from their stifling living-quarters and, in summer attire, strolled about the streets or in the gardens near the ramparts. The wealthy took refuge in the coolest of their pavilions or in those best protected from the sun. But in winter there were no adequate heating arrangements, and the thin partition walls offered very poor protection against the cold. The little portable charcoal-burning braziers that were placed in the centre of the room cannot have been very efficacious. As for the poor people, they probably had no form of heating and depended only on warm clothing and quilts to protect them in the really cold weather. The k'ang, the bed made of bricks which is hollow to allow heat from the cooking stove to warm it, was probably only to be found in country districts.

In the wealthy houses, perfumes and incense were often burnt, especially when guests were being entertained, to freshen the atmosphere.[16] Another product, used more widely on account of its modest price, was sold in the streets of Hangchow under the name of 'mosquito smoke'. This was doubtless a fumigating powder which would be much required in all houses, particularly at sundown, when the mosquitoes are at their worst.

In the houses of rich families and high officials, yellow-and-white cats were kept, called 'lion-cats', which their owners valued highly. They were useless for catching rats and were only kept as pets. As we have seen, pet-cat fanciers could find in the Hangchow markets all the necessary requirements: 'cat nests' and 'fish for cats'. But long-haired cats for rat-catching could also be bought in the town, and watch-dogs whose tails were usually docked.[17]

## PERSONAL TOILET

Nothing in China had so much regional variation as bathing habits. As a general rule, people washed more frequently in the South and in the East than in the North and in the West. The people of Szechwan, near neighbours of the Tibetans, whose horror of water is notorious, contented themselves with wiping their faces with a cloth during hot weather, and, according to a popular saying, only got washed 'twice in their lives: at birth and at death',[18] these being times of ritual washing laid down by custom. But the Hangchow region was, on the contrary, one where a taste for bathing was highly developed. Both the town itself and its inhabitants were clean. Parasites were rare, in distinction to North China and the interior regions, where everybody was permanently infested with fleas and lice. An author who recounts the various methods of getting rid of lice, describes having seen at Yen-chou (a small town situated about a hundred miles up the Che river from Hangchow) an elegant and well-dressed young woman who owned a fine tea-house with doors lacquered in gold—a clear sign of wealth—engaged in a delousing operation. Her clothes were laid out on a small table, and she popped all the lice she found into her mouth. And this operation was carried on with such skill and rapidity that the movement of hand to mouth was almost continuous. And, adds the author, the people present found it amusing, and were not the least disgusted. They found it the most natural thing in the world.[19]

In ancient times it had been the custom among the upper classes to take a bath in their own house every ten days, and this bath-day was made the pretext for a day's leave given to officials. Not only the body, but also the hair was washed on such occasions. For this reason, official salaries were known as 'emoluments of the bath and hair-washing', and the word for bath came to mean a period of ten days, first, middle and last 'baths' indicating the three ten-day periods of each month. Bathing and washing the hair were regarded as an important operation, and it was not considered as contrary to the rules of etiquette to allow the attendance of visitors. It was, in fact, a kind of rite which might be classed in the same category as ablutions of a more clearly defined ritual character, such as baths taken before imperial audiences by officials authorized to approach the emperor, baths given to new-born infants, baths taken before the marriage ceremony, and the ritual washing of the corpse before dressing it.

In Hangchow and in southern parts of China the habit of taking frequent baths may derive from ancient peasant customs which survived longer in the South than in the North. During the marriage festivals held by non-Chinese peoples in the southern provinces, there was still a bathing ceremony in which both boys and girls entered the fecundating waters of a river or lake, a rite which was shown to have existed in Ancient China by Marcel Granet in his *Festivals and Songs*. But the ruling class, whose outlook was governed by northern prudishness, disapproved of these bathing ceremonies in which men and women took part together. A well-brought-up Chinese did not bathe in the presence of a woman or of a near relation belonging to a different generation. This modesty, which was carried to extremes among the scholar-officials, did not, incidentally, exclude a very pronounced taste for erotic refinements, and for various forms of erotic titillation to accompany bathing. It is this attitude of false modesty, which was very widespread, that accounts for a remark made by a thirteenth-century author about customs in Cambodia. Cambodian women, he says, enjoy plunging naked into pools in order to wash themselves, and the Chinese merchants living in the country come in a group to watch them.[20]

While the original religious significance of bathing may have survived in certain customs, in Hangchow baths were usually taken for pleasure. There were a great many bathing establishments in the town which had as sign a pot hung up over the door. During his stay in Hangchow in 1072, the Japanese pilgrim Jôjun visited one of them, and noted in his travel diary that the price for entrance was ten cash.[21] According to Marco Polo, there were as many as three thousand of these commercial enterprises, and each establishment could accommodate a hundred bathers at a time. No doubt it was possible to get massaged there, and be served with tea or alcoholic drinks, and presumably prostitution was not absent from these places. The people of Hangchow frequented them almost daily. They were supplied with cold water brought from the lake, but Marco Polo assures us that there were also hot baths for foreigners, probably provided for Muslims accustomed to the stifling heat of the Turkish bath. 'There are many streets which open on to the aforesaid squares [along the Imperial Way],' says the Venetian traveller, 'and in some of these there are many baths of cold water, supplied with many men-servants and maids who are in waiting to bathe both men and women who go there; because from childhood they are used to be bathed in cold water at all times, which thing they say is much to be recommended for health. They also keep in the said baths some rooms with hot water for foreigners who could not bear the cold, not being used to it. They are accustomed to wash themselves every day, and would not eat if they were not washed.'[22] Pedlars hung around the doors of these establishments selling hot water for washing the face, and various medicines.[23]

It was probably the ordinary people who frequented these establishments, since rich people had their own bathrooms. The baths were made of wood, metal or earthenware. They had a small bench placed inside them for the bathers to lean on. The bottom had a mat laid on it, and towels or scarves were used for drying oneself. Ladies had a screen put round when they were taking a bath. A metal jug and bowl were used for washing the face and hands, which was done every morning. As for soap, it was made of a mixture of peas and herbs, and was in liquid form. In order to heat the water in tubs and baths, a piece of hot metal or stone was immersed in it.

As well as this general enjoyment of bathing which characterized both the upper and the lower classes in Hangchow, mention should also be made of certain eccentrics noted for their extreme attitudes: some poets, philosophers and aesthetes who were celebrated either for their mania for ablutions or, conversely, for their incorrigibly filthy habits. The great eleventh-century reformer Wang An-shih, for instance, was well known for the dirtiness of his person and for his repulsively unkempt head of hair. Two of his colleagues forced him to bathe once a month, and left out clean clothes for him to put on when he came out of the bath. On the other hand, there were maniacs who had an almost religious phobia for dirt of any kind, and who washed their hands every few minutes, such as the great eleventh-century calligrapher and painter, Mi Fu; or, to give another instance, an aesthete of the same kind who lived during the Mongol period, and who carried his love of cleanliness to such a degree that he changed the water he washed his face in several dozen times, and ten times over shook the dust off his cap and clothes before putting them on. He even had the trees and stones outside his studio washed and polished. There were also bathing voluptuaries, such as a certain P'u Tseng-meng, who every day performed a major and a minor face-washing, a major and a minor foot-washing, as well as taking a major and a minor bath proper. He had a dozen servants to aid him in his ablutions and used five tubs of hot water for each bath. Final mention should be made of those superstitious persons who would not for all the world have washed themselves on the day of the Rat or of the Hare, these days being considered unlucky for bathing.[24]

The Chinese of the thirteenth century were unacquainted with the use of the toothbrush, and after eating, they wiped their gums with a handkerchief. Another of their customs scandalized the Arab merchants of the ninth century: 'They are not clean,' says one of them. 'They never wash themselves with water when they have defecated, but wipe themselves with Chinese paper.'[25]

It seems to have been only the ladies who used cosmetics and perfumes. In the region of Peking girls of well-to-do families covered their faces in wintertime with a kind of ointment with a vegetable base, to protect their complexion against the cold and the wind. They kept on this paste, known as 'Buddha adornment', until the spring, and when their complexion was then exposed to view after being preserved from contact with sun and wind for so long, it was said to have the beauty of jade.[26] However in Hangchow, with its more temperate climate, the make-up worn by the ladies consisted of a white foundation, with powder of a deep rose shade placed on the cheeks. Hangchow women also took great care of their nails. They tinted them with a product made up from pink balsam leaves crushed in alum. The colour, pale at first, deepened with several applications, and then remained indelible for several weeks. 'Actually,' says one author, 'the older ladies tint their nails in this way every sixty or seventy days. But Muslim women adore this dye, and some of them even use it all over their hands. There are people who find it amusing to tint cats and dogs with it.'[27] The ladies were fond of putting oil on their hair to make it smooth and shining. One case is cited of a very smart young lady who applied an oil which was not suited for that purpose and found her hair coagulating into such a compact and solid mass that there was nothing to be done but cut it off.[28] Another fashion, known in China since before the Christian era, recalls one which came into vogue in Europe before the last war: the fashion of plucking the eyebrows and pencilling them in with a black line, which often gives the face a rather impersonal expression, but which is thought to make it more attractive.

Foot-binding for girls was another way of improving upon nature: the atrophied small feet give greater grace of movement when walking. Foot-binding does not seem to have appeared in China until the tenth century.[29] Perhaps it was not yet widely in use in Hangchow three centuries later. Perhaps it was mainly reserved for little girls destined for the gay life.

At all events, ladies of rank, wives of merchants and courtesans all lavished the greatest care on their appearance. They kept their cosmetics, their jewellery and their polished-metal mirrors in boxes made of lacquered wood, jade, gold or silver, and wore perfume-sachets hung from their girdles.

## CLOTHING

It was commonly held in China that the essential function of clothing was protection from the cold. Certainly, methods of heating were rudimentary even in the houses of wealthy people, and were practically non-existent among the poor in south-east China. Coal was scarce and expensive. Hence the main protection against intense cold was clothing lined with floss silk and fur-lined coats. But clothing was also one of the obvious signs of social standing. Among the ruling class, clothing was just as much an indication of rank as were insignia of various kinds or the number and style of one's retinue. The colour and ornamentation of the dress to be worn, the shape and type of headgear, the particular style of girdle—all such details were laid down, for every occasion and for each grade of the hierachy, by imperial decree, in fulfilment of ritual requirements.

The official histories contain monographs entirely devoted to describing in the minutest detail the costumes, headgear, girdles, carriages and seals of the Emperor, of his close kin, and of high dignitaries of the court and other officials. A large number of decrees were concerned with questions of this kind which to us moderns seem of minor importance. Not so to the Chinese of those times, for the regulation of ceremonial details had the double purpose of keeping a check on expenditure and of producing a desired psychological effect. The regulations perpetuated the age-old attachment to the outward signs of prestige, and, through the very importance attributed to them, they in turn aroused appropriate emotions. According to the Chinese expression, their purpose was to bring the outward and the inward into harmony with each other. In order to believe, there is nothing better than to begin by wholeheartedly complying with the ritual gestures performed by believers: faith will then come of itself and without the asking. In our day, only the army, with its ranks, its uniforms and its rituals, can help us to understand the traditional Chinese world, the purest manifestation of which was to be found in T'ang times.

At the beginning of the Sung dynasty, towards the end of the tenth century, there was still a series of colours prescribed for each grade in the hierarchy of the mandarinate: above the third degree, robes must be purple; above the sixth, vermilion; above the seventh, green; above the ninth, turquoise.[30] Black and white were only worn by ordinary individuals. However these regulations soon fell into disuse, because the court granted the right to wear purple indiscriminately to officials of all grades.

The same thing happened with the round parasols of blue-green silk which in the first instance had been reserved for princes of the imperial family. From the end of the tenth century permission was granted to certain officials to carry these parasols; then it was granted to women of the palace when they paid visits to town. In 1012 a faint effort was made to stem the tide: only members of the imperial family were to have rights to the parasol. A little later, there was not a single official who did not strut about with his parasol. In the whole sphere of clothing regulations there was hardly one privilege that did not succumb to a similar fate, whether it might be a matter of girdles, or headgear or anything else. The prosperous merchants, whose arrogance increased from one day to the next, contributed largely, either directly or indirectly, to the disintegration of the rules for ceremonial details.[31]

It was by their costume that, at first glance, people of rank and *nouveau-riche* merchants could be distinguished from the common people in the streets of Hangchow. The former wore a long robe that reached down to the ground, the latter a blouse that came down below the waist and trousers made of light-coloured material. The women wore either long dresses, or blouses which came down nearly as far as the knee, jackets with long or short sleeves, and skirts. When they went walking in the streets, women and young girls sometimes threw over their shoulders a square scarf, purple in colour, which was called a 'head-cover'.[32] As distinguished from men, their clothes were fastened on the left side and not on the right. Men of rank had self-coloured robes for everyday wear, and robes with symbolic designs embroidered on them for ceremonial occasions: phoenixes, dragons, or birds with lucky plants held in their beaks. The fastenings were the same as those used in present-day Chinese dress: little oblong buttons fastened by loops of cloth. Robes were often edged with cloth of a deeper colour round the neck and sleeves. The sleeves, which had very wide openings, could be used for carrying small articles in them. An illustration of this is afforded by a story about an old man who was sunk in vice and was an incorrigible skirt-chaser — a sort of Chinese counterpart to Baron Hulot in *La Cousine Bette*. At the end of a life of debauch this individual, formerly an honoured government official, procured for himself a young concubine whom he spoiled like a child. Every time that he was invited out by relations or friends he made sure of taking some tit-bit home to her. One day, on meeting an acquaintance in the street, he was obliged, in compliance with the demands of politeness, to cross his hands in that silent salute that was still in use among the Chinese not so very long ago. As he did so, a little parcel wrapped in a lotus-leaf fell from his sleeve, unwrapped itself, and, to the general hilarity of the passers-by, lay open to view: it was a portion of duck.[33]

Trousers, a cultural borrowing from mounted barbarians which had first come into use in North China during the fourth century B.C., were worn not only by the common people, but also by soldiers, who wore them with the lower part of the legs tucked into boots that came up to cover the calf.

Fine clothes were made of silk, and sometimes, for special occasions, of gold brocade.[34] Ordinary people usually wore clothes made of hempen cloth. Cotton, which was first cultivated by non-Chinese peoples in the southern provinces, had begun to spread to Kiangsu in the region south of present-day Shanghai, but it was still a luxury. For protection against the cold, quilted clothes and fur-lined coats were worn, and people readily put on several layers of clothing if the cold was specially intense.

Footwear of many kinds was to be found in Hangchow: leather shoes sold under the name of 'oiled footwear', wooden or hempen sandals, satin slippers. Grand people went about perched on buskins of a sort, to make them taller. No one ever went about barefoot, just as no one ever went bareheaded. Even the very poorest were shod and wore some kind of headgear, and it was only Buddhist monks who went about the streets with their shaved heads unprotected by any kind of covering.

But it was never a cap or a hat that the women wore. Their headwear was confined to hairpins and combs stuck into their hair, which was always most artistically arranged. Ladies of rank, princesses and imperial concubines, officials' ladies and the wives of rich merchants, also wore head ornaments in gold and silver wrought in the form of phoenixes and flowers. Archaeological excavations have unearthed several specimens of pieces of jewellery of this kind and revealed their exquisite workmanship. The phoenix ornaments, placed one on each side of the head, rose up like two wings and hid the hair almost completely. Ladies also wore chignon rings and ear-rings. This love of head ornaments which was so much in vogue in Hangchow had already existed and been remarked upon by Arab travellers in the ninth century. 'The women,' says one Arab account, 'go about with head uncovered and put combs in their hair. Sometimes a woman will wear as many as twenty combs made of ivory and other materials.'[35] But instead of having the hair piled up high on the forehead as had been the fashion in T'ang times, women now wore it combed back and gathered into a chignon.

Servant girls could be recognized by the peculiar style in which their hair was worn: it was brought forward to the front of the head and tied into two tufts by ribbons of many colours, and a fringe was worn on the forehead.

Most men were cleanshaven, but a few wore long side-whiskers and a goatee beard, particularly military men: it was a sign of virility to have a vigorous growth of hair. Hence the soldiers who were boxing champions wore side-whiskers and beards and long hair hanging down to their shoulders.[36] As for children, their heads were shaved, leaving only a small tuft on top at the front.

The men of the ruling class wore a great variety of headgear, each with a different name. But it was the Emperor whose wardrobe was particularly rich in headwear of all kinds designed for special ceremonial occasions. One of them consisted of a cap surmounted by a horizontal board from which hung twelve pendants. Most headgear was made of black silk. The kind of cap usually worn by the scholars covered the hair completely and was tied behind by two ends which stuck out like two long, rather stiff ears. Some people defied ridicule and wore caps in antique style, and there were shops that specialized in old-fashioned headgear of this kind.[37] As for the common people, they usually wore turbans of a sort. It was still possible in Hangchow, as it had been in Kaifeng at the beginning of the twelfth century, to recognize a man's trade from the shape and colour of his turban.[38] But there were other types of headgear as well: round straw hats for wearing in the rain, and hats made of leather.

Another essential article of clothing, as well as headgear of some sort, was the girdle: these were the two things which distinguished the Chinese from the barbarian. The girdle, which very often was an article of value, was always worn, both with a robe and with a blouse. The finest girdles had plaques or buckles in jade, in gold, or in rhinoceros horn. The horn was imported from India, and in particular from Bengal, which was supposed to have the best horn. This was an old luxury trade, and had for long been in the hands of Persian and Arab merchants. 'The Chinese,' says an Arab account of the ninth century, 'make from this horn girdles which fetch a price of two or three thousand dinars or more . . . ' The astonishing prices

fetched by these horns and the intense delight taken by the
Chinese in ornaments made from them can hardly be explained
by their rarity-value alone: superstition as well as artistic taste
must lie at the root of this passion. And indeed we find that
'sometimes the horn is in the image of a man, or a peacock, or a
fish, or some other thing.'[39] The more unusual and handsome
the image, the higher the price of the horn. For it was also a kind
of talisman. Other girdles were ornamented with plaques of jade,
gold, bronze or iron. This article of apparel also had its official
regulations, which, at the end of the tenth century, laid down
what type of girdle was to be worn by each grade in the
hierarchy.[40] But we have seen how, under the Sung, such ceremonial regulations got quickly undermined.

From the girdle there usually hung a purse, very tempting for
thieves, which contained money and small articles such as handkerchief, keys, knife, sharpening-stone, abacus.[41] Fans were
another article of dress used both by men and women. They
were of two kinds. One, the typical Chinese fan, was round and
stiff and made of white silk. The other was the folding fan which
was brought in from Korea in the middle of the eleventh century. Some fans were decorated with painting or calligraphy.

Wealth, luxury and refinements of all kinds were characteristic of thirteenth-century Hangchow. It was the centre of
elegance of the time. Its people, says Marco Polo, 'the men as
well as the women are fair and handsome and always dress for
the most part in silk, because of the great abundance which they
have of that material which is produced in the whole territory
of Quinsai, besides the great quantity which is continually
brought in from other provinces by merchants . . . [The]
ladies and wives [of the rich shop-owners] . . . dress with so
many ornaments of silk and jewels that the value of them could
not be estimated.'[42] There were also a number of dandies extremely occupied with their personal appearance. One of them,
while dressing, would 'give a quick glance to left and then to
right to see if his clothes were hanging properly, and if there was
anything the least wrong with the cut, he would call his tailor
immediately to put it right. His shoes and stockings were made
of fine satin and Suchow silk. At the slightest sign of their being
soiled he would discard them and would only wear those which
had been newly washed.'[43]

## COOKING

Descriptions of Hangchow in the thirteenth century contain hundreds of names of dishes served in its innumerable restaurants and taverns or at court banquets. Truth to say, the names remain for the most part incomprehensible to us, because we do not know what the recipes for these dishes were. But since there is nothing more tenacious than culinary traditions, some of these recipes must still be in use at the present day, and to judge from the ingredients most often mentioned, from the seasonings used (pepper, ginger, pimento, soya sauce, oil, salt and vinegar) and from the principal methods of preparation, Hangchow cuisine in the thirteenth century does not seem to have been very different from the Chinese cuisine of today. The only difference, if any, is that it seems to have been even more varied then than now.

Various factors account for the excellence and the extraordinary variety of this cuisine. Owing to its vast size, China has a great deal of regional diversity, and this, together with the fact that Hangchow had a large number of refugees and temporary visitors from all parts of China, accounted for the town's having several varieties of regional cooking, while the predominant cuisine found there was itself a combination of that of Honan (the cuisine of the former Sung capital, between 960 and 1126) and that of Chekiang.

Accounts say that in the Northern Sung period there were restaurants in Kaifeng which specialized in Southern cooking— that is to say, the cooking of the south-eastern provinces, Kiangsu and Chekiang. They had been opened for the benefit of officials and of members of grand families who had come from the south-east to the capital, and who probably found that Northern cooking was not highly seasoned enough for their taste.

Rice, imported from the Huai valley and from regions further south, had, however, already become one of the principal foodstuffs of Kaifeng people, and had entered into competition with corn in Honan cooking. Conversely, when the barbarian invasion of North China had swept people of the upper classes belonging to the Kaifeng region towards the lower Yangtze, it was the south-east that had had thrust upon it the culinary traditions of North China. At that time, it was said, most of the restaurants in Hangchow were kept by people from Kaifeng. Dishes were served there imitated from the cuisine of the former capital and of the court.⁴⁴ Thus it was that a century later a kind of synthesis had been arrived at of the two main traditional cuisines of China.

But in Hangchow there were also restaurants which specialized in various regional cuisines: Szechwanese restaurants serving dishes which were probably largely flavoured with pimento; taverns where, along with the drinks, dishes characteristic of Shantung or Hopei were served; or the so-called Ch'ü-chou restaurants (a town situated about 250 miles south of Hangchow) with cooking of a popular variety: minced meat and noodles with fish and shrimps.⁴⁵ Finally, there must have been restaurants, although there is no actual proof of it, where the religious taboos of Muslim merchants were respected, and which did not serve the foods, such as pork, dog or snails, which, although abhorred by them, were eaten without any scruples by the Chinese, but only the flesh of animals slaughtered in accordance with the strictest Koranic laws.⁴⁶

Eating habits of foreigners do not seem to have had the slightest influence on Chinese cooking during the Sung period. However, a few exotic and expensive products were normally imported in Hangchow, these being mainly wine made from grapes, and raisins and dates. In the eleventh century, the date was still a curiosity in China. The proof of this is given by notes made by a Chinese official posted in Canton at that time. Having been invited by a rich Arab merchant of the town to taste some 'jujubes from Persia', he afterwards took the trouble to write this description of them. 'This fruit,' he says, 'is the colour of sugar, its skin and its pulp are sweet, and it gives the impression, when you eat it, of having first been cooked in the oven and then allowed to dry.'⁴⁷ As for wine made from grapes, it had been known in China since the Han conquests in Central Asia, but was still, in the T'ang period (seventh to tenth centuries), a luxury reserved for the Emperor's table, and was made from vines grown in the imperial park. In the twelfth century this luxury was available in Hangchow for such wealthy families as could afford it. 'Neither grapes nor wine are produced there,' says Marco Polo, 'but very good raisins are brought from abroad, and wine likewise. The natives, however, do not much care about wine, being used to that kind of their own made from rice and spices.'[48]

There is another reason for the excellence and variety of Chinese cooking: it is based on ancient peasant traditions which arose in rural surroundings where undernourishment, drought and famines were frequent, and so it makes judicious use of every possible kind of edible vegetable and insect, as well as of offal. There is no doubt that in this sphere China has shown a greater inventiveness than any other civilization.[49] It is also to be noted that there were no religious taboos about food. Only fervent Buddhists and ascetic Taoists abstained, the former from eating vegetables with a strong smell (onions or garlic), meat and eggs, the latter from cereals. Milk and cheese were absent from the diet, but this was because there had never been any dairy-farming in China. For the same reason, Hangchow people did not eat beef: the ox was the farmer's faithful companion. More-over, it was an animal that was scarce and dear to buy, even in the North, and it did not acclimatize so well in the warm, humid climate of the lower Yangtze as the water-buffalo. As for human flesh, it was perhaps not the object of such a violent repulsion as is the case in the West. One author relates—deploring the thing it is true — that people from North China, where habits of cannibalism had spread after the wars and famines at the begin-ning of the twelfth century, had opened restaurants in Hang-chow where human flesh was served. Dishes made from the flesh of women, old men, young girls and children each had a special name, and were served in the same way as mutton, human flesh in general being euphemistically called 'two-legged mutton'.[50]

Because of its climate, China had a much more extensive area and a greater range of plants for cultivation than Europe, and hence a greater variety of crops. Moreover, agronomic skill had, over the centuries, selected a greater number of varieties of edible vegetables. In the region of Hangchow itself, eighteen different kinds of haricot and soya beans were cultivated, nine kinds of rice, eleven kinds of apricots, eight of pears, and there was hardly any vegetable or fruit that did not have a large number of different varieties.[51]

Hangchow's exceptionally favourable situation and its supply facilities account for the diversity of products on sale in its mar-kets: freshwater fish from the lake and from the river, fish from

the sea caught mainly off the south coast of the Che river
estuary, game from the hills and mountains which rise to the
south of the city, vegetables from the gardens to the east of its
ramparts, rice from the plains to the north, geese and duck from
the lake, pigs and edible dogs from farms in the vicinity. With
regard to the dogs, it is to be noted that this was a food probably
eaten only by the lower classes, since it does not figure on the
bill-of-fare of the big restaurants in Hangchow. Probably dog-
meat was eaten no more frequently than snails are in France.

There were such extremes of wealth and poverty in the classes
forming the population of Hangchow that a distinction must be
made between the food eaten by the rich and the food eaten by
the poor. Rice, pork and fish formed the main diet of the lower
classes. According to contemporary estimates, the daily consumption of rice per person was just over 2 lb., and, as we have seen,
the rice-trade and the transport of rice by canal boats and even
by sea from the Canton region occupied an important place in
the economic activities of the city. Night and day strings of rice-
barges arrived without interruption in the northern suburbs
where the principal rice-markets were situated. The cereal was
sold in the husk, and had to be dehusked in mortars. There had
long existed in China mortars with machinery driven by water-
power, but the surplus of labour in Hangchow no doubt explains
the absence of such machines in the town, and a local saying
refers to the prodigious sale of wooden pestles among the people
of Hangchow.[52]

As we have also seen, several hundred pigs were slaughtered
daily in the abattoirs situated right in the centre of the city, and
in addition there were the numerous pork-butchers who killed
their own pigs. As for salt fish, another item of daily consumption, it was brought in by the boatload from the towns and
villages of the Che river valley. Offal was also a common article
of diet among the lower classes—liver, lights, kidneys and tripes.
' . . . the rest who are of low position,' says Marco Polo, 'do
not abstain from all the other kinds of unclean flesh without any
respect.'[53]

There were a number of restaurants which served food at
popular prices, among them the so-called Ch'ü-chou restaurants
which we have already mentioned. Others served ravioli stuffed
with pork and leeks served with bamboo shoots. But apart from

restaurants and taverns, ordinary people could at any time of the day find something to eat on the streets, and even at night as well. There were always pedlars selling cooked food for a few cash.

The food served at large banquets and the food eaten by the well-to-do was naturally richer and less monotonous than the diet of the people. The court, the princes of the imperial family, high officials and rich merchants took a keen delight, as much from inclination as from vanity, in exotic dishes. Rice, pork and salt fish, the diet of the poor, played a very subordinate rôle in the cuisine of the rich. Fowl, geese, mutton, shell-fish and fresh fish of all kinds were the foods which figured most often among the dishes served in the most celebrated restaurants. The upper classes also ate game, which strikes one as unusual, since, as a result of the deforestation of China, this is an item which has almost entirely disappeared from the Chinese diet of today. Let us recall the list given by Marco Polo: 'Roebuck, red-deer, fallow-deer, hares, rabbits, partridges, pheasants, francolins, quails . . .'. The information supplied by the Venetian traveller is confirmed by the Chinese sources: an inhabitant of Hangchow tells us that the fallow-deer sold on the markets is often really nothing but donkey or horse-flesh, and he counsels buyers to be distrustful so as to avoid getting poisoned.[54]

Many restaurants in Hangchow specialized in certain kinds of dishes. There was one, for instance, where only iced food was served, and others which were noted for one particular dish. Formerly, writes an inhabitant in 1275, the best-known specialities were the sweet soya soup at the Mixed-Wares Market, pig cooked in ashes in front of the Longevity-and-Compassion Palace, the fish-soup of Mother Sung outside the Cash-reserve Gate, and rice served with mutton. Later, around the years 1241-1252, there were, among other things, the boiled pork from Wei-the-Big-Knife at the Cat Bridge, and the honey fritters from Chou-number-five in front of the Five-span Pavilion.[55] Among the more exotic dishes, let us mention scented shell-fish cooked in rice-wine, goose with apricots, lotus-seed soup, pimento-soup with mussels, fish cooked with plums; and among the most common, fritters and thinly-sliced soufflés, ravioli and pies. There was a special kind of cake, made of cornflour, which contained peas, sugar-beans and candied fruits.

One work cites more than two hundred dishes that could be served at a grand banquet, and even mentions the correct order for serving them. It lists in succession 41 dishes of fish, shrimps, snails, pork, goose, duck, mutton, pigeon, fried, sautéed, grilled, roast on the spit, roast in the oven, or boiled; 42 dishes based on fruits and sweetmeats; 20 dishes of vegetables; 9 of boiled rice served with different ingredients (sugar, sweet soya, cakes cut in thin slices, beans . . . ); 29 dishes of dried fish; 17 refreshments (li-chee juice, honey or ginger drinks, paw-paw juice, pear-juice . . . ); 19 kinds of pie and 57 desserts (cakes and dishes of vegetables and meat which could be served as dessert).[56]

Hangchow people ate three meals a day: at dawn, about midday, and at sunset. But there were no fixed hours for them. From dawn onwards fried tripe, pieces of mutton and goose, pies, boiled rice and blood and offal soup were sold on the Imperial Way.[57] At night, the fashionable restaurants along this grand avenue remained open until a late hour.

In the houses of wealthy people, food was served on low tables in little porcelain dishes. The variety and number of dishes was more important than the quantity of each. They were brought in on lacquer trays. The table was laid with chopsticks and spoons, as is the custom today; there were no knives on the table, because everything was cut up small enough to allow it to be picked up by chopsticks. Because of the abundance of domestic servants and the low wages they were paid, no one would dream of allowing guests at a banquet or even clients of a cheap restaurant to cut up their meat themselves.

It was usual at a banquet to serve a small cup of rice-wine with each different dish. Custom had changed since T'ang times, when one drank after the meal, and when each guest only raised his cup when it came to his turn to drink. Alcohol was always drunk tepid, at body-warmth. Before serving, it was warmed in bowls of hot water.

Rice-wine was also drunk between meals, either at receptions or in the taverns of the town. Along with it were served vegetables, probably seasoned with salt and vinegar, salted seeds and nuts, and various things of this kind designed to increase thirst. When the customers had given their orders, the dishes laid out in front of them were removed and more interesting ones brought.[58] Singing-girls and musicians beguiled the customers of taverns, and these establishments stayed open until midnight and after at all seasons of the year. Alcoholic drinks sold in Hangchow were all made from rice, but the variety of tastes and flavours was astonishing: there were supposed to be no less than 54 different kinds of these rice-wines, most of which were made in Hangchow itself or in the neighbouring towns.[59] The delicious flavour of these drinks explains the lack of interest evinced by the inhabitants for the wine made from grapes that was imported by sea. 'Instead of wine,' says Marco Polo, 'they make a drink of rice, and they make the rice boil with very many other good spices mixed together, and they make it in such a way and so well and with such a flavour that it is better worth drinking than any other wine of grapes and men could not wish better.'[60] Drunkenness was certainy a vice that was very prevalent in Hangchow. Festivals were often the occasion for bouts of drinking when everyone made it a point of honour to get drunk, and the large number of taverns is evidence of a widespread addiction to alcohol.

Apart from alcoholic drinks, the only other drink for daily consumption was tea.[61] There were a great many varieties of tea, and everyone was a connoisseur of the different types and flavours. Hangchow people drank prodigious quantities of it. The Hangchow region only produced three varieties: Jewel tea, Forest of Fragrance tea, and White Clouds tea. But tea was imported from central China and from Szechwan. Prices varied considerably. The tea sold by pedlars which one could drink on the street or on the markets only cost one cash at the end of the twelfth century. On the other hand, the tea served in the fashionable tea-houses could cost as much as some alcoholic drinks. If it is taken in sufficient quantity, tea can produce a certain intoxication. Hence the scholars used to write short compositions in praise of this beverage in which they even went so far as to compare the respective merits of tea and wine. It would be difficult to explain the extraordinary vogue that tea enjoyed in China and later in the Muslim world if it was not a drink that produces some kind of euphoria and artificial stimulus. For another thing, to make tea it was necessary to boil water which was not always as clean as it might be (we must remember that Hangchow's water supply consisted of well water brought by canals from the lake to within the ramparts), so that the general and constant use of tea afforded an effective protection against epidemics: no one would have dreamt of drinking plain water.

## NOTES AND REFERENCES

1. *Wu lin chiu shih*, I, 3, p. 341.
2. Cf. above, chap. I, *Overpopulation and Scarcity of Accommodation*.
3. For a detailed analysis of this work on architecture which dates from the end of the 11th c., see P. Demiéville, *Le Ying-tsao-fa-che*, *Bulletin de l'Ecole française d'Extrême Orient*, 1925, pp. 213-64.
4. On the use of these roof ornaments, which had regional variations, see *P'ing-chou k'o-t'an*, chap. II, f. 8b.
5. Tung Tso-pin, *Ch'ing ming shang ho t'u*, Formosa, Taipei, 1954, pp. 2-3 of the notes at the end.
6. *Wu lin chiu shih*, VI, 11, p. 452.
7. On the regulations about building in the Sung period, cf. *Sung shih*, end of chap. CLIV.
8. *Kuei hsin tsa chih*, Hsü B, § 68.
9. This recommendation is attributed to Po Chü-i (cf. *T'ang liang-ching ch'eng-fang k'ao*, on the Lu-tao district of Lo-yang), and also to Hsieh Yeh-ho (cf. *Kuei hsin tsa chih*, Hsü A, § 3).
10. MLL, XVIII, 3, p. 291.
11. R. A. Stein, 'Les Jardins en Miniature d'Extrême-Orient', *Bulletin de l'Ecole française d'Extrême-Orient*, XLII, 1, Hanoi, 1943.
12. M & P, pp. 338-9, n.
13. *Wu lin chiu shih*, III, 8, pp. 379-80.
14. Cf. *I chien chih*, chia 5, f. 8a in the edition of the *Shih-wan-chüan-liu ts'ung-shu*.
15. MLL, XVIII, 3, pp. 285-9.
16. *Kuei hsin tsa chih*, Hsü B, § 68.
17. MLL, XVIII, 3, p. 290. The *Kuei hsin tsa chih*, Hsü A, § 22, explains the advantages of docking dogs' tails: 'The dog is an animal that is very sensitive to cold. Every time it goes to sleep, it protects its nose by covering it with its tail. It can then keep warm while asleep. If one wants to have dogs that are good watchdogs at night, their tails should be docked. Not having anything to protect their noses from the cold, they stay awake and bark all night.'
18. *Kuei hsin tsa chih*, Hsü A, § 28.
19. *Chi le pien*, *Shuo fu* XXVII, f. 4b.

20. Chou Ta-kuan, *Account of the Customs of Cambodia* (end of 13th c.), quoted by E. H. Schafer in 'The Development of Bathing Customs in Ancient and Mediaeval China and the History of the Floriate Clear Palace', *Journal of the American Oriental Society*, LXXVI, 2, 1956.

21. *San-Tendai-Godai-san ki*, chap. 1. (Account in 8 chapters of the journey of the Japanese monk Jôjun (1011-1081) across China, from the south of Chekiang to the north of Shansi.) Ed. Dainihon bukkyôzensho.

22. M & P, pp. 328-9 n.

23. MLL, XIII, 5, p. 242.

24. On baths in China, see E. H. Schafer, *op. cit.*

25. J. Sauvaget, *Relation de la Chine et de l'Inde*, p. 11.

26. *Chi le pien, Shuo fu* XXVII, f. 8a.

27. *Kuei hsin tsa chih*, Hou A, § 43.

28. *Chi le pien*, f. 12a (paragraph on the various kinds of oil).

29. Tung Tso-pin, *Ch'ing ming shang ho t'u*, initial notes, p. 5 (*ting*), which quotes the *Cho keng lu* by T'ao Tsung-i (end of 14th c.): 'The custom of binding the feet first appeared under the Five Dynasties (10th c.) and was not widely adopted before the reign-periods *Hsi-ning* and *Yüan-fu* (1068-1085). But recently this fashion has become so common that it is considered shameful not to adopt it.'

30. *Sung shih*, chap. CLII, f. 13a in the Ch'ien-lung edition.

31. On the decline of the sumptuary regulations, cf. *Sung shih*, chap. CLIII, f. 13a *et seq.*, where a high official, in a report to the throne, expressly mentions 'the rich merchants who ride on horseback on lacquer saddles'.

32. *Ch'ing po tsa chih*, by Chou Hui, *Shuo fu* XXII.

33. *Kuei hsin tsa chih, pieh* A, § 56, f. 31b.

34. 'In the T'ang period, the adoption, under Iranian influence, of Western weaving methods had revived the textile arts, which were further perfected under the Sung. It was then that there appeared brocades woven with gold thread.' (*L'Art de la Chine des Song*, catalogue pub. by the Musée Cernuschi, Paris, 1956, p. 32). The *Chi le pien, Shuo fu* XXVII, f. 12b-13b, contains quite a long passage on the most important weaving techniques. Cf. also *P'ing-chou k'o-t'an*, chap. II, f. 14b in the edition of the *Shou-shan-ko ts'ung-shu* on gauze manufactured by the nuns of the Lien-hua convent at Fuchow, south of Lake P'o-yang.

35. J. Sauvaget, *Relation de la Chine et de l'Inde*, p. 11.

36. MLL, XV, 5, p. 312.

37. On the history of headwear in China and Tibet, see the long note on the pigtail in P. Demiéville, *Le Concile de Lhasa*, pp. 207-12.

38. MLL, XVIII, 1, p. 281. Cf. *Tung ching meng hua lu*, V, 1, p. 29.
39. J. Sauvaget, *op. cit.*, pp. 13-14.
40. *Sung shih*, chap. CLIII, f. 4a *et seq.*
41. Lien-sheng Yang, *Harvard Journal of Asiatic Studies*, XIX, p. 48.
42. M & P, pp. 332, 330.
43. *I chien chih*, ting 6, quoted by Hsü I-t'ang, *op. cit.*
44. *Tu ch'eng chi sheng*, 4, p. 93, and MLL, XVI, 4, p. 267.
45. *Tu ch'eng chi sheng*, 3, p. 92, and 4, p. 94.
46. On Muslim cooking in China, cf. J. Kuwabara in *Memoirs of the Toyo Bunko*, II, 1928, pp. 48-50, where the *P'ing-chou k'o-t'an* by Chou Yü (1119), chap. II, is quoted: 'The foreigners (Muslims in Canton) never eat pork . . . They never eat the flesh of an animal that has not been killed in accordance with their own customs.'
47. J. Kuwabara, *ibid.*, p. 40.
48. Y, p. 202.
49. On the special foods in various regions of China, cf. *P'ing-chou k'o-t'an*, chap. II, f. 8b in the *Shou-shan-ko ts'ung-shu* edition: Little frogs in Fukien and Chekiang, large frogs in central China, snake soup in Canton. The islanders of Hainan eat various insects (flies, gnats, earthworms) cooked in pieces of bamboo. The foreigners in Canton, Muslims for the most part, flavour their food with sugar, honey and musk. In Manchuria they eat dairy products flavoured with sour butter. In general, remarks the author of this work, food is salty in the South and acid (seasoned with vinegar) in the North. Non-Chinese people in China and villagers like sweetened food, while those in the plains of the Yellow River and town-dwellers prefer unseasoned food. Referring to Cantonese cooking, the *Chüan yu tsa lu*, *Shuo fu* XXXIII, f. 3a, notes that people in the extreme south eat snakes, but change the name to 'brushwood eels'. Similarly, they eat grasshoppers under the name of 'brushwood shrimps', and rats under the name of 'household deer'.
50. *Chi le pien*, *Shuo fu* XXVII, f. 14a-b.
51. Cf. MLL, XVIII, 3, pp. 283-4.
52. *Wu lin chiu shih*, VI, 11, p. 452: 'The inhabitants of Hangchow purchase daily 90 yards of rice-pestles'.
53. M & P, p. 328.
54. *Kuei hsin tsa chih*, Hsü B, § 66.
55. MLL, XIII, 4, p. 240.
56. *Wu lin chiu shih*, VI, 9, pp. 445-9.
57. MLL, XIII, 5, pp. 242-3.
58. MLL, XVI, 2, p. 263.
59. *Wu lin chiu shih*, VI, 10, pp. 449-50.

60. M & P, p. 249.
61. It appears that tea had been known in China since before the 3rd century A.D., but tea-drinking only came into fashion in the 7th or 8th c.

# CHAPTER IV

# THE LIFE CYCLE

THE FAMILY CIRCLE: *Traditional moral outlook. Family relationships and social relationships. Break-up of families and the spirit of independence.* BIRTH: *Different attitudes towards birth. Infanticide and abandonment and sale of children among the common people. Birth ceremonies among the rich.* UPBRINGING AND EDUCATION: *Gentleness and kindness. Spread of education. State schools. Preparation for the examinations. Views on education.* MARRIAGE AND THE POSITION OF WOMEN: *A family affair. Marriage ceremonies. The married woman. Feminine virtue and the severity of morals. The rôle of women.* ILLNESS: *Medical theories. Diagnostics. Therapeutics. Official and private medicine. Pharmacies.* DEATH: *Cremation and burial. Funeral ceremonies.*

## THE FAMILY CIRCLE

THERE WAS, in China, an ideal conception of the family: that of the extended family with several generations living together — grandparents, parents, married sons, grandchildren and servants. This was a conception which left out of account the development of smaller units consisting of parents and children, which stifled individuality, and which demanded from its members an absolute respect for the hierarchies based on age and generation. It was based on the type of rich and influential family found among the upper classes, the scholar-family, several members of which had served or were serving the State in the capacity of officials. It imposed itself easily as a model wherever the family structure approached the ideal type—for example, in certain rural areas—but with more difficulty elsewhere; so that one may take it that whenever the existence of the extended family was threatened, the traditional moral outlook belonging to it was threatened also.

What was the nature of this moral outlook based on respect for the family hierarchy? The youngest members were expected to be obedient and respectful to those senior to them and still more so to members belonging to older generations. The servants, who were part of the family, were obliged to show the same respect and humility towards their masters. But everything was a question of degree: the degree of difference in age, generation and proximity of relationship. Nothing was considered more blameworthy than that a husband should show more affection for his wife than was considered proper. In the matter of family relationships, too much was as much to be condemned as too little, and it was an art requiring skill and subtlety to know how to adjust one's behaviour according to the complex gradation of duties. Only a few Sages of antiquity arrived at perfect mastery in this domain.

Nevertheless, the family relationships supposed to exist in the ideal family were the foundation of the entire moral outlook, and even the law, in its total structure and its scale of penalties, was nothing but a codified expression of them. According to the T'ang Code, which in its general lines was still in force in the thirteenth century, those who lifted a hand against parents or grandparents deserved to be beheaded. Those who struck an older brother or an older sister were condemned to two years and a half of forced labour, but those who struck an older cousin only received a hundred strokes of the rod. A father who broke the bones of his son in administering an overdose of punishment was liable to a less severe penalty than if he had done the same to a stranger. A master who beat his servant to death got no more than one year's forced labour, but a servant who killed his master accidentally was condemned to death by strangling.[1]

As well as being the foundation of morals, these ideal family relationships were also the basis for social relationships. They expressed to perfection the only type of relationship to be found in all forms of social contact: that of inferior to superior, of recipient to benefactor. Even if they did not entirely exclude affection, it cannot be said that affection was essential to them. Family feeling was at the same time stronger and more diffuse than we are inclined to imagine. The respect owed to parents was not given to them as individuals: it was part of a kind of cult that made them into abstract figures and foreshadowed, in their lifetime, the cult of the ancestors. It was an anonymous feeling, impersonal and eminently transferable.

The extended family with its various age-groups all living together also taught the art of give-and-take. If, in spite of frequent opportunities for friction — especially between the women, among whom quarrels often broke out on account of jealousy or disagreements—peace nevertheless reigned in a large family, the local officials would send a report to the court so as to make known the exceptional virtue of the head of the family. Petty events of a miraculous or symbolic nature (piglets and puppies fed by the same mother, crows and pigeons sharing the same nest) would sometimes occur to confirm the greatness of his virtue, and the house would be deemed worthy of having a notice put up for the information of passers-by.

In short, the extended family was the ideal school for life in society, since society as a whole owed its cohesion entirely to personal relationships, there being no abstract principle governing it. For this reason, everyone felt the urge to devote himself to someone more powerful than himself in the hope of gaining his protection, and to bind himself to his equals by exchange of presents and of services. The individual could not stand alone. The more relations he had, and the wider the circle of relations his family had, the more dignified he appeared in his own eyes and in the eyes of others, and the greater was his sense of security. Not only did all those who bore the same family name —and there were scarcely thirty of the commoner of these names—feel bound by mutual obligations, but it was also possible to create artificial bonds of kinship with a stranger, include him as a member of the family, or become his blood-brother. Society as a whole was nothing but a vast network of family-to-family and person-to-person relationships. Particularly when it was powerful, the Chinese family was an organism with many tentacles.

Such were the general ideas most commonly accepted. Everyone tried to imitate the way of life, the moral outlook and the behaviour of the upper classes. But the extended family typical of the upper classes was not by a long way the only type of family found in China. The family unit varied in size and in cohesion depending upon regional differences and social stratification. Natural calamities and poverty, wars and invasions, might reduce its membership to two or three, and multiply the number of isolated individuals. Thus, the extended family does not seem to have been usual either in the countryside around Hangchow or in the poorer districts of the city itself. Even among the upper classes it was far from being the rule. The exodus to the South caused by the wars and famines which ravaged North China from 1126 onwards must have resulted in a dispersion of families and in a weakening of kinship ties. The emigrants, who for the most part belonged to the upper classes in the Northern provinces, were decimated by malaria in the extreme south, and by starvation during an exceptionally hard winter in the region of Lake Tung-t'ing.[2] They were more fortunate in the Hangchow region. But, cut off from their homes and often separated for good from their closest kin, many exiles must have begun to show a more independent spirit. The moral freedom that reigned in the great city of Hangchow is perhaps partly to be explained by the presence there of a large number of refugees.

## BIRTH

Stress has often been laid, and quite rightly, on the need felt by Chinese families in traditional China to perpetuate themselves— to ensure, by giving birth to children, the continuity of the ancestral cult and also, when all is said and done, the survival of the individual family. This need was certainly felt all the more strongly in virtue of the fact that the individual had no real existence apart from the group. But it goes without saying that it was in the powerful families, with the widest circle of relationships, and with numerous members who had had illustrious careers in the mandarinate, that the ancestral cult acquired its full significance. It was in such families, small enough in number, that the traditional principles held full sway. But if these principles demanded a large number of descendants, it was not merely in order to ensure that the ancestral cult should continue without break, but also so that the children should reinforce the power of the family. Here, religion and social prestige are indistinguishable.

'The whole power structure of the old Chinese society requires children, as power is exercised by families and groups of families, tied together by intermarriage. Children are thus necessary in order to protect the status and the power of the family by occupying key posts in the administration.'[3] The richer and more influential a family, the more it endeavoured to add to its power and the number of its members by births, advantageous matrimonial alliances, and the extension of its area of patronage. But there is a corollary to this: the poorer and more lacking in support a family, and the more it was forced by the necessity of survival to break up into smaller units, the weaker were its motives for having numerous descendants. The ancestral cult could only be perpetuated by male children, since daughters became completely integrated into the family of their husbands. This was why the birth of a boy was in general the more favourably viewed, and wives and concubines sought by all possible means—medical, magical and religious—to give birth to sons. But it would be wrong to suppose that the birth of a boy was always welcomed and that of a girl in every case viewed with disfavour by the parents. Economic circumstances could alter this completely, and did in fact do so among the most underprivileged classes in Hangchow. With them, while it was indeed always difficult for a man to find a way of earning his living, girls, on the contrary, could be placed in rich families as concubines, companions, embroiderers, actresses, zither-players, chess-players, cooks . . . and their parents did their best to give them some training in whatever direction their talents lay.[4]

During the twelfth and thirteenth centuries the splitting-up of families and reduction in numbers of their members was particularly pronounced among the common people because economic conditions were not in their favour. Although it was something frowned upon as being contrary to custom (and in these matters it was the upper class families that set the tone), it was nevertheless common, in the countryside in Chekiang, to find sons setting up on their own while their parents were still alive. It is also easy to see why, contrary to what happens in our capitalistic society, it was poor families who had the fewest children: infant mortality must have been greater among them, and also these families could not, as in the upper classes, afford numbers of concubines. Above all, poverty obliged them to have their children separated from them as soon as possible, and sometimes even drove them to infanticide.

The birth of an unwanted child in a lower class family which was in need was indeed felt to be a catastrophe. It was one mouth more to feed, and, in the country, where land was scarce, it meant a further subdivision of the inheritance. Thus an author of the end of the 12th century tells us that in Fukien 'if a man should have numerous sons he brings up no more than four and keeps no more than three daughters. He claims that he has not the means for bringing up more'. At the moment of birth, a bucket of water was kept ready for drowning the infant immediately. This was called 'bathing the infant'. This practice was commonest at that time in the central regions north-west of Fuchow.[5] Elsewhere, the custom was known as 'harrowing the progeny': all children born after the inheritance had been divided among the sons were drowned.[6] But drowning seems to have been mostly confined to country districts. In Hangchow the preference was for abandoning newly-born infants in the streets. As for abortive drugs, which were in common use in Chinese towns towards the end of the Manchu dynasty,[7] they were only used rarely and when there was no other way out, because they were considered dangerous. The mother of Prince Shao-ling, who was of low birth, had been obliged to attempt to induce abortion by these means. The infant was born nevertheless, but remained weak and sickly all his life.[8]

The abandonment of infants, on the other hand, was of such frequent occurrence that the court had to prohibit the practice in 1138, and accompanied the prohibition with the foundation of foundling hospitals.[9] 'In those provinces [of South China],' says Marco Polo, 'they are wont to expose their new-born babes;. I speak of the poor, who have not the means of bringing them up. But the King used to have all those foundlings taken charge of, and had note made of the signs and planets under which each was born, and then put them out to nurse about the country. And when any rich man was childless he would go to the King and obtain from him as many of these children as he desired. Or, when the children grew up, the King would make marriages among them, and provide for the couples from his own purse. In this manner he used to provide for some 20,000 boys and girls every year.'[10] This account of Marco Polo's is confirmed by a Chinese author of the Mongol period. 'In the Sung period,' he says, 'there were offices for the protection of children in all prefectures. If a poor family had a child which it could not afford to bring up, the parents were allowed to hand it over to this administrative body. Note was taken of the exact date of birth, and the child given into the charge of a nurse. Families who, on the other hand, wanted to adopt children could come and get them from the foundling hospitals. In bad years, crowds of babies were brought there. Thus there were no new-born infants abandoned in the streets.'[11]

Poor families had yet another means of getting rid of children whom they could not provide for: they placed them with better-off families who brought them up or employed them as domestic servants. It is this very widespread form of adoption, which sometimes included purchase, that is noted after its own fashion by an Arab account of the fourteenth century: 'I may observe here by the way that young slave girls are very cheap in China; and, indeed, all the Chinese will sell their sons as slaves equally with their daughters, nor is it considered any disgrace to do so. Only, those who are so purchased cannot be forced against their will to go abroad with the purchaser; neither, however, are they hindered if they choose to do so.'[12]

Presumably the ceremonies accompanying and following upon a birth were rather simple among the common people in Hangchow. But this was by no means the case with the upper classes. The month preceding the confinement, the maternal grandparents sent the mother 'presents for hastening the birth'. These were silver plates filled with rice-straw and covered over with brocade or paper. On them were placed flowers and choice foods, jujubes, chestnuts, and clothes embroidered in bright colours for the baby. On the day of the confinement, as well as on the seventh, the fourteenth and the twenty-first day after the birth, relations and friends presented the mother with fine rice, coal and vinegar.

At the end of the first month, the ceremony of the bath took place: the infant was plunged into a silver bowl filled with scented warm water. The family elders stirred the water with gold or silver hairpins. Jujubes were thrown into the bowl and the young women present fought for them and ate them. This rite, which perhaps retained a memory of ancient customs (wading through rivers and gathering fecundating plants) was supposed to encourage the birth of male children. The baby-hair of the infant was put into a little gold or silver box. The mother, with her baby in her arms, then went round the assembled company and thanked each of them separately. Then she handed over her child to her sisters-in-law, and this was called 'changing the nest'. There was another celebration on the hundredth day after the birth, and yet another on the first anniversary of the birth. This was the time when various objects were placed round the child: classical or Buddhistic books, a bushel measure, scales, a knife, silk cloth, flowers, needle and thread, toys. According to the object which the child grasped, prognostications were made as to its future vocation.[13]

In all circles, extreme importance was attached to the date of the birth and care was taken to note the exact hour if possible. This date was held to influence every moment of a person's destiny, and knowledge of it was required for all the important actions and events of his life: for every time, that is to say, that it was thought advisable to consult a soothsayer. Births on the 5th day of the 5th moon, the day belonging to the maleficent animals (scorpion, wasp, centipede, snake and toad), were regarded with horror. Infants born on this day were thought to be predestined either to suicide (Ch'ü Yüan, the great poet of the 4th century B.C. committed suicide on the 5th of the 5th moon) or to murder at the hands of their father and mother.[14]

'. . . the people of this city of Quinsai,' says Marco Polo, 'have a custom . . . that as soon as the infant is born . . . the father or the mother have the day and the minute and the hour that he was born written down immediately, and they make the astrologers say in what signs and what planets he is born, and they write it all . . . And when anyone is grown up [if he is about to do business, or go on a journey, or get married] he goes off to the astrologer with the aforesaid note, [who] when he has seen this and considered it all, he sometimes says things, and if they are found to be true the people put the greatest faith in him . . . And of such astrologers as these, or magicians [rather], there is a vast number on every square. No betrothal would be celebrated unless the astrologer told them his opinion.'[15]

## UPBRINGING AND EDUCATION

Children were brought up to be affable, gentle and obedient. They were taught to prize self-restraint above everything else, and had to learn to be content with their lot and to live on good terms with relations, friends and strangers. The rules of politeness, widespread even among the lower classes, had no other aims but these. They reflected a certain understanding of life that had its own touching and genuine charm, for politeness was no mere outward form, but went with, and aroused, the feelings it expressed, all the more so since it was the only permissible way of expressing feelings. Thus the rules for the art of living taught to children awakened in them a feeling of respect for elders and betters. They were taught not to answer back when their parents spoke to them, not to sit down if a superior—father, mother, a friend of the parents or someone senior to themselves—remained standing, not to refuse a drink when invited by a superior. There are edifying texts among the late T'ang documents discovered in Central Asia which contain precepts of this kind. The devoted son or friend, or the faithful wife, who carry their filial piety or faithfulness to the extremes of heroism, were the ideals set up before the young.

This kind of upbringing stifled individuality and tended to produce an admirable stereotype of the socially-adapted person. It was scarcely the kind of training to foster rebelliousness or ambition. Nor did it encourage belligerent characters or the fighting spirit. It is to be noted that sports were not much cultivated in the thirteenth century, and the practice of them had actually declined since T'ang times, when upper class people displayed an extraordinary passion for a game which came from Iran: polo. In the thirteenth century, however, boxing, wrestling, fencing, polo, archery and football were only practised by army officers and soldiers. There was a sharp contrast, in the Sung period, between the games of physical prowess and of skill which were enjoyed by the common people, and the aristocratic games of the scholar class: chess, calligraphy and literary composition. Skill in the use of arms was rare and not encouraged. This was why it was chiefly from among the uneducated and the peasants that men with a military vocation arose, and that swashbuckling types were recruited.

'The natives of this city [of Hangchow],' says Marco Polo, whose astonishment may be imagined when one considers the habits of Europeans at that time, 'are men of peaceful character . . . They know nothing of handling arms, and keep none in their houses. [This was in fact forbidden by law.[16]] You hear of no [family] feuds or noisy quarrels and dissensions of any kind among them . . . and there is such a degree of good will and neighbourly attachment among both men and women that you would take the people who live in the same street to be all one family.'[17]

Early childhood was one of the happiest times of life. Children were allowed to roam about the streets in groups. They were never beaten, and to silence the really naughty ones nothing more stern was done than to threaten them with some sort of a bogeyman. One of these was Liu-the-Barbarian, with a dark skin like an Indian or a Malay. In the Huai valley and in Hupei, children were frightened into being good by warning them that Big-eyes Yang with the terrible voice would come. In southern Kiangsu, on the other hand, appeal was made to a kind of demon who had the power of curing malaria.[18] To judge by the number of sweetsellers and toysellers who went about the streets of the town, children must have been more often spoilt than punished. It was not until a fairly advanced age, about seven years, that they were either sent to school, or, in wealthy families, given a tutor. For the children of the imperial aristocracy and the high mandarinate there were special schools in Hangchow where they remained from the age of seven until the age of thirteen. They learnt there twenty written characters a day.[19]

It is probable that, in this commercial city, quite a large number of children received some form of elementary education— that is to say, that they were taught the rudiments of writing and how to use the abacus which was in general use for reckoning. It was only the children of the poorer families that remained illiterate. In the surrounding countryside, children collected firewood, drew water from the well, took the buffalo to water. In the town, they began at an early age to help their father in his trade or their mother in the household tasks.

The development of urban life, the growth of the middle classes, and perhaps the spread of printing (there had been two printed editions of the Classical Books since the tenth century), were factors contributing to the flourishing state of both public and private education in the towns of south-eastern China. This in turn had increased the number of candidates for the official examinations by means of which officials were recruited and new blood introduced into the ruling class. There were numerous small schools in Hangchow in which the teachers — retired officials or candidates who had been unsuccessful in the examinations—were maintained by the parents of the pupils, and, it was said, the sound of reciting aloud and of musical instruments could be heard everywhere. There were also—usually in mountain retreats—private academies, provided with good libraries, for advanced students. But since the eleventh century the State education was no longer exclusively reserved for the sons of aristocrats and officials. At the end of the eleventh century, on the initiative of a counsellor of the Emperor, prefectural and sub-prefectural schools had been opened in all the provinces. Thus Hangchow had one prefectural and two sub-prefectural schools within the enclosure of the government buildings. Furthermore, shortly after the court had moved there, three establishments for higher education which had existed at Kaifeng, the capital of Northern Sung, were set up at Hangchow: the National University, the Military Academy and the Imperial Academy. In addition, a School of Medicine had been opened.

These great colleges were surrounded by vast grounds, and consisted of numerous buildings and single pavilions used for libraries, classrooms or temples for religious ceremonies. In the National University, which recruited the largest number of students, but which can serve as model for the others, there were twenty classrooms, a staff of fifteen, and nearly 2,000 students, who lived in. The number of students, coming from all over China, had been fixed at 300 in the middle of the twelfth century; it was later increased to 1,000, and had reached 1,716 by 1270. About 1270 the School of Medicine, the least important of these colleges, had no more than 250 or 300 students and four teachers. Recruitment for all these colleges was by triennial competitive examinations.[20]

The budget for these State establishments, as well as of some private schools, was met by the revenue from land with which they had been endowed at their foundation—a practice no doubt inspired by the educational foundations of the Buddhist communities. Thus the National University, founded in 1142 at Kaifeng, after its removal to Hangchow disposed of revenues amounting to 33,600 strings of cash by the end of the thirteenth century. The students of the National University were given

free board and were very well fed. But the discipline seems to
have been comparatively strict: they had to take a monthly
examination, and a full examination twice yearly, in spring and
in autumn. When they went into the town, they all had to wear
the same uniform. Religious training, which, in the family, was
limited to teaching respect and to carrying out the ancestral cult,
and sometimes included a few fragments of Buddhist texts to be
learnt by heart, filled quite an important place in the life of the
colleges. Each college had its own presiding deities, sages and
heroes of antiquity: Mother Earth, great generals deified, the
patron of medicine, etc.; and the ceremonies in their honour, the
various rites which the students were obliged to perform, seem
to have formed an important element in the discipline of the
colleges.[21]

All instruction, as soon as it ceased to be elementary, was
orientated towards the formation of candidates suitable for the
official examinations. It was usually based on the ancient classical texts, the language of which, archaic and extremely concise,
was very different from the spoken language which was the
common parlance of that period. The students had to soak themselves in these texts and become versed both in the thoughts and
sentiments expressed there and in the manner of expressing
them: the Classics furnished them with a rich store of images
and formulas, and it was the mastery acquired in using them
that marked the true scholar. Moreover, the mechanical part of
the training was considered very important; a good student had
to know almost by heart the principal classical books and be
sufficiently acquainted with the poets, both ancient and modern,
to be able to compose poems written in their style.

Here is an exercise which reveals the very acute literary judgment of its inventor — it is true that he was one of China's
greatest poets—and gives us an idea of the kind of virtuosity
required by candidates for the examinations: Su Tung-p'o (1036-
1101) taught his sons how to write compositions with many
words and few ideas, or with many ideas but few words. But
Su Tung-p'o did not ignore the value of thought. One of his sons
asked him one day if he knew of a method for writing well. 'Let
us make,' he replied, 'a comparison: in the markets, a large
number of goods are displayed. I want them to be at my disposal.
Now there is a thing that I can employ for that purpose which is

called money. If I have money, all this merchandise will be mine. Well, in the matter of literary composition, if I first of all have ideas, all the classical and historical books will be at my disposal. The essential thing in literary composition is to have ideas.'[22]

Many of the best minds in the Sung period deplored the artificial nature of a form of education likely to produce nothing but aesthetes or dilettantes without any practical knowledge — in short, persons ill prepared for their destined rôle of administrators. From this point of view, the education received by the heir to the throne in the middle of the thirteenth century can be taken as typical. The prince, we are told, comes to make his salutations to his father the Emperor at cockcrow. He returns to his apartments at the second hour, and holds conference about the affairs of his own household, after which he goes to the reading room to study the Classics and the official histories. At the end of the afternoon, he comes before the Emperor again. Interrogated by him on the Classic he has studied that morning, he is allowed to sit down and drink tea if his replies have been satisfactory. If not, the Emperor would be annoyed and would make him explain the same passage the next day. Was this not, say later historians, to show too much care for little things, while neglecting the essentials? The economic situation of the empire and enemy pressure on the frontiers were already alarming at this time.[23]

However, in 1071, the celebrated reformer Wang An-shih, who was the person responsible for the creation of schools in the prefectures and sub-prefectures, went to war against the absurdities and defects of the system of recruitment for civil servants. If, he declared, this system was able to function at all, it was only because the examinations provided the sole means of normal access to an official career. But what could be more absurd than to force young men full of vigour to shut themselves up in their rooms and devote all their time and all their energies to composing poems and rhymed couplets! Education ought to allow more room for political philosophy and for preparation for the practical tasks of administration.

Practical questions were undoubtedly less neglected after the end of the eleventh century. Thus, the tutor of the Prince Imperial in 1193 gave him an astronomical chart, a map of China, a synoptic table of the history of China and a plan of

Suchow, at that time the finest city in China after Hangchow. He inculcated into his pupil a patriotic indignation against the Barbarians in occupation of North China, but at the same time reminded him, according to the best Confucian traditions, that virtue, that is to say self-restraint and awareness of faults, was essential.[24]

It is also true that education was not always purely literary and bookish. The doctorate of letters, which included compositions in verse and prose, was certainly the most sought after. It was the one which conferred most prestige and which opened the way to the most brilliant careers. But there were also doctorates of a more specialized or more technical kind: doctorates of philology, of history and ritual, and of law, not to mention the examinations provided for military and medical officials. And it also occurred that education in private schools, far from providing culture which was the genuine article—which is to say: based on the Classics — displayed some curious tendencies. Kiangsi people (the province to the west of Chekiang), an eleventh-century author tells us, were much addicted to lawsuits. To such an extent that they had a book written by a well-known expert in chicanery which was full of dishonest tricks. This work began with examples of slanderous writings and gave lessons in inventing them. It went on to false accusations, and ended with hints as to how to drive people on to committing misdemeanours so as to have the means of blackmailing them. This book, adds the author (although this may simply be an exaggeration?) was even taught in the village schools.[25]

One thing that is quite certain is that literature played a much less important part in the education of girls than of boys, although it was not entirely absent: literary women and women-poets were not unknown. One of the greatest poets of the Sung period, Li Ch'ing-chao (1081-1140) was a woman. There were even girl child-prodigies, such as the little girl of seven who was summoned to the court by the Empress Wu Tse-t'ien (685-704) and received the command to improvise a poem on the theme of bidding farewell to her brothers. Here it is:

> In the pavilion of separation, the leaves suddenly blew away.
> On the road of farewell, the clouds lifted all of a sudden.
> Ah! How I regret that men are not like the wild geese
> Who go on their way together.[26]

However, little girls were mainly taught spinning and embroidery: making cloth was traditionally women's work. Those destined for the gay life learnt how to sing and how to play various musical instruments. Apart from a few exceptions among lower class people, women did not usually have a trade or profession. The fact that the education they received was essentially a practical one is a facet of their complete lack of independence and of the subordinate position they held in society.

## MARRIAGE AND THE POSITION OF WOMEN

A ceremony which took place at the time of the Festival of the Dead, at the beginning of April, marked the coming of age of boys and girls. It consisted in the capping of boys in their twentieth year, and the placing of hairpins in the hair of girls of fifteen.

What was the age for getting married? In urban surroundings, even among the people, marriages did not, apparently, take place before puberty. But early marriages must have been more common in the country, where the future son-in-law was sometimes adopted in infancy by his future parents-in-law. As for young men of the upper classes and sons of wealthy merchants, who often led a very free life or remained occupied with their studies over a long period, it is probable that they did not set up house until they were about thirty. The wife was usually several years younger than her husband.[27] She was never very much younger than he, because custom frowned upon anything that might imply a confusion of generations.

Marriage was primarily conceived as a means of alliance between families. For the Emperor and his close kin it came within the sphere of politics and high diplomacy. There have been numerous Chinese princesses who in the course of history were given in marriage to barbarian rulers with whom Chinese sovereigns wanted to create ties of friendship. But it was not only in court circles that marriage was used as a political weapon: the great families found no better way of increasing their influence and prestige than recourse to judicious matrimonial alliances. In the twelfth century there was a common practice in certain regions of North China whereby a fictitious marriage between children who had died young was celebrated at the time when they would have been of marriageable age: this is proof enough that it was the families who were of first concern in the question of marriage.[28]

A curious custom among the families in the upper circles of Hangchow society shows how little they troubled to disguise their interest in match-making. It happened quite frequently that influential families in the town arranged to kidnap the candidates who had come out top of the list in the official examinations for the recruitment of officials that were held in the capital. A story is told of how one day one of these lucky candidates allowed himself to be kidnapped without putting up the least show of resistance. He was led to the house of a rich and powerful family, and into the midst of a large gathering of people. A young girl dressed in purple and gold stepped forth and, coming straight to the point, announced to him: 'I am a young girl and not too ugly. I wish to become your wife. Do you consent?' At these words the prisoner bowed very politely and replied, amidst shouts of laughter from the assembled company, that he felt it a great honour to tread the ground of such a noble house, but that he would like to be allowed to return home for a moment to discuss the matter with his wife and see what the best solution might be.[29]

Even among the common people marriage was linked with family interests. In the poorest families, its immediate purpose was of an economic nature: parents who were old and in want desired to get their daughter married so as to be supported by their son-in-law. Conversely, parents-in-law who had succeeded in choosing a daughter-in-law full of filial piety were sure of being cared for in their old age. Thus marriage often acquired the character of an old age insurance for the parents or the parents-in-law. But it did sometimes happen, particularly among the lower strata of society, that marriages reflected the inclinations of the persons concerned. Novels and stories of the Sung period sometimes have as heroine women of lower class origin who marry on their own initiative without even consulting their parents.[30] This is one indication among others of the moral freedom that existed among the poorer people in urban surroundings. But in fact unions of this kind were free liaisons rather than marriages proper. As a general rule, betrothal and marriage consisted of a long series of ceremonies and exchanges of presents the number and nature of which were fixed by custom and all of which were full of symbolic significance.

These rites, which, for obvious reasons, were much more rigorously observed by the upper classes, varied from region to region. In Hangchow everyone tried to imitate the former usages of Kaifeng, the capital of Northern Sung. However, various differences in detail are recorded, including one important feature which was at variance with Kaifeng practice: when negotiations for the marriage had been begun between the families, the betrothed were allowed to meet. If the lady destined for him was not to his choice, the fiancé was free to break off the match.

As with all important affairs, marriage demanded calling in the aid of an intermediary. These were the women who acted as go-betweens. Their costume varied according to their social standing. Thus, top-ranking go-betweens, such as mediated in the marriages of members of the high mandarinate or of the aristocracy, wore a veil over their heads and a purple jacket. Those of an inferior variety wore a cap, a yellow chignon-bag and a jacket or sometimes a skirt that was very wide and full, and they went about with a green umbrella. They always went about in pairs.[31] As soon as the parents had got in touch with each other, the young girl's family dispatched, via the go-betweens, a card bearing the name and date of birth of the prospective bride. This card was handed over by the family of the future bridegroom to a soothsayer, who had to decide whether the match was lucky or unlucky. If the soothsayer came to conclusions that were favourable, the families proceeded to an exchange of cards that fixed the matter: that of the future bridegroom bore a list of the official functions held by the family during the course of three generations, the taboo names (personal names of parents and grandparents which must in no event be written), the number in the order of the family held by the bridegroom (whether he was the oldest, the second, the third, etc.), his administrative functions, the hour of his birth as near as it was known, the mention, in cases where the parents were deceased, of who was the acting head of the family, and also of whether the prospective bridegroom was an adopted son, and finally a list of the property to be assigned to the son on the occasion of his marriage (ingots of gold and silver, cultivated land, houses and villas, gardens). The card sent in return by the bride's family bore her number in the order of the family and the date of her birth, as well as the details of her dowry: head ornaments, pearls, jewels of all kinds, curtain and hangings, and fields, houses and gardens set aside for the dowry.

The go-betweens decided on a lucky day for the exchange of these cards, which were presented in dishes decorated with brightly coloured cloths. The bride's family then chose another day of lucky augury for the 'ceremony of the cups'. For this occasion they called on the parents of the bridegroom at their house, except on the occasions when the latter had hired a garden or a boat on the lake. This was the moment when promises were exchanged in each other's presence. They exchanged cups of rice-wine: the bridegroom drank four and the bride replied by drinking two. This rite, it was said, was designed 'to show that the boy was strong and the girl weak'. If his future spouse pleased him, the fiancé stuck two hairpins in her chignon. If not, two pieces of brightly coloured satin were sent to the bride's family. (At Kaifeng, a kinsman made the decision for the fiancé: on being received at the home of the young lady's parents, he examined her face in the light of his knowledge of physiognomy, and on this examination depended the fate of the betrothal.[32]) If everything went well, the young man's family sent head ornaments, gold vases, brocade skirts, rice-wine and various delicacies. The bride's family replied by sending pieces of cloth, rings, two sticks, two onions, and two bowls with four red fish swimming in them. This rite was known as the 'sending in return of sticks and fishes'. Rich families, it was said, had two fishes and two sticks made in gold for this occasion.

Every annual festival was the pretext for a further exchange of presents. Finally, shortly before the marriage, the future parents-in-law sent the prospective bride what was called 'the three golds': bracelet, small chain and pendant in gold. But sometimes, among the petty tradesmen of the town, these three articles were in silver or in gilded metal. On the eve of the marriage, the day of which was fixed by a soothsayer, the bride's family gave a little exhibition of the objects of value included in the dowry: jewels, boxes, valuable vases were laid out in a room decorated with hangings. The next day, the bride called on the parents of her future husband. This was a brilliant procession in which it was customary to invite well-known 'singing-girls' to take part. Seeds, beans, cash coins and fruits were thrown in front of the door and were scrambled for by children. This custom was supposed to keep away baneful influences at the moment when the future wife entered the home of her parents-in-law for the first time. Singing-girls bearing torches in the form of lotus flowers and candles in the form of flowers went in front of the bride. One of them held a mirror and went backwards in front of the bride to guide her on her way. The bride, supported by two maids of honour, stepped out on to a carpet of green-coloured matting: it was of evil omen for her to set foot on the actual ground itself. She had to bestride a horse-saddle and a pair of scales, objects of which the symbolic significance remains obscure, and then she betook herself to a room hung with curtains, where she rested for a while. The bridal couple and the guests then came together and exchanged the customary number of cups of rice-wine.[33]

These, in the merest outline, were the rites of marriage as practised in the fashionable world in Hangchow. It goes without saying that everyone tried to imitate them, but the number and extragavance of the ceremonies varied according to the wealth and status of the families concerned.

The family alliances brought about by marriage were much more of a 'diplomatic' than of a sentimental character. Indeed, as soon as she was married, the young wife had hardly any further contact with her own family. The wedding ceremony had the immediate effect of enfolding her completely within the family of her parents-in-law: she now participated in the ancestral cult of her new family and had to demonstrate her filial piety towards the father and mother of her husband. It was only at rare intervals that she was allowed to pay a visit to her own parents and unless she had been divorced or repudiated, she never rejoined the family circle in which she had been born. The model daughter-in-law stayed on with her parents-in-law and looked after them even in the case of the premature death of her husband; she made it a point of honour to refuse all offers of remarriage that her parents or brothers might try to arrange. However this was exceptional behaviour, worthy of the highest praise; it must be supposed that ordinarily the young wife whose husband died prematurely returned to her own family.

The motives for repudiation traditionally recognized as permissible are the following—and it will be remarked that the very order in which they are regularly quoted, as well as the nature of four of them, imply that the relations of the wife with the parents of her husband are as important as, if not more important than, her conduct in the capacity of wife as such. They are: lack of filial piety towards her parents-in-law (disobedience, insults and blows), sterility (which threatens the continuity of the ancestral cult), jealousy, illnesses which prevent participation in the ancestral cult (among which epilepsy was probably included), chattering, and the misappropriation of the property of her in-laws. However, these motives were no longer valid if the wife's parents were no longer alive, if she had already worn mourning for the father or mother of her husband, or if her husband had become wealthy but was in poverty at the time of the marriage. A final remarkable fact: divorce by mutual consent was allowed, which is as much as to say that marriage was not in fact thought of as an indissoluble bond, in spite of the solemnities that accompanied it, and was not confirmed by any sanction of a religious nature.[34]

Modesty, chastity, conjugal fidelity and filial piety towards the parents-in-law were the feminine virtues most admired. These virtues were sometimes carried to heroic extremes, and provincial officials did their utmost to call attention to the most edifying cases, such as that of the daughter of a singing-girl of Lo-shan, in Szechwan, who had been put out to nurse and was brought up by a decent family and who preferred to commit suicide rather than follow the shameful profession that her mother wanted to force her into;[35] or the wife who hanged herself rather than abandon—although urged to do so by her family —a husband who was drunken, debauched, addicted to gambling, and, to put the cap on it, condemned to an ignominious punishment, which in itself would have been sufficient cause for divorce.[36] The court rewarded such heroines with official honours. This moral code for women was in fact encouraged by the State. But it was in the most remote provinces and in the country that it held most rigorous sway. Erring daughters, mothers and fiancées were thrown upon the streets without pity. One author reports that a young girl in a Kiangsi village was driven out in this way by her father and then sold as a servant in a nearby district. She ran away into the mountains and succeeded in being taken for a goddess. Like the White-haired Girl in the modern Chinese opera, she lived off the offerings of her devotees.[37] In an emergency, resort was sometimes made to abortive drugs. It was by this means that a young village girl committed abortion after having relations with a demon in human form (after which it was discovered that the demon was nothing more than the old brown dog next door).[38]

It is clear that morals were in general very strict, and hostile to the least deviation on the part of a woman. Faultless chastity before marriage was demanded of her, and, once married, faithfulness to her husband and obedience to her parents-in-law. Wealth permitting, her husband was free to acquire one or several concubines and she had to accept these rivals without betraying the least sign of jealousy. However, polygamy, as it is improperly called, since there was never more than one legal wife, seldom occurred except among the upper circles of society and perhaps also among the wealthy merchants: men of the middle classes, and even more so men of the people, were not usually rich enough to be able to keep several women.

While traditional morality was strict with regard to women, urban surroundings, and in particular those of Hangchow, had softened it considerably. Here is a very revealing instance with regard to the conduct of the ladies of that city: the women in the region of Hangchow and Suchow, says an author, are so flirtatious and so greedy that their husbands, if they are poor, cannot satisfy their demands. So many husbands prefer to shut their eyes to the behaviour of their wives and comply with their having lovers, who are called 'complementary husbands'. Some ladies have as many as four or five friends of this kind, and those who live near Buddhist monasteries sometimes have monks as lovers.[39]

But everything was a question of social milieu: such habits would not have been permitted in the upper classes. Even so, scenes of conjugal misunderstanding seem to have been rare, and, according to Marco Polo, the Chinese household in Hangchow exhibited the greatest harmony in conjugal relations. This was no doubt one of the results of the way children were brought up. 'And this familiar intimacy is free from all jealousy,' says Marco Polo, 'or suspicion of the conduct of their women. These they treat with the greatest respect, and a man who should presume to make loose proposals to a married woman would be regarded as an infamous rascal.'[40] Courteous behaviour was indeed the rule among the wealthy people of Hangchow. But the position of women varied from one social milieu to the other.

The ladies in the highest social circles and the wives of rich merchants led a life of leisure. They hardly ever appeared in public, and usually stayed confined to their apartments. Their only occupations, apart from the time spent on their toilet and on the general management of the household, were parlour games and embroidery. The wives of petty traders, on the other hand, took an active part in running the business. They kept the accounts and served the customers. Some restaurants were even managed by women on their own. There were, it is true, only a few professions open to women: they could be midwives, marriage go-betweens, nurses, and domestic servants of all kinds. But without any doubt the married woman in the middle and lower classes played an important economic rôle, for which reason her authority in the family was equal to that of her husband. Many possessed a sound business sense. They were full of initiative and good at giving advice. Their power was sometimes inclined to be tyrannical: the harpy and the shrew were not unknown.

To conclude, we must say a word about the relations between the sexes. The stories of T'ang and of Sung times provide many instances of love-at-first-sight and of passion. The *femme fatale*, capable of 'overturning a kingdom', as the Chinese expression has it, and the coquette who leads her suitors to destruction were common literary types. But whatever the circumstances, love always seems to have had something impersonal about it: it found its fullest expression in heroic fidelity between a betrothed or a married couple. There even seems to have been a lack of individuality about the Chinese beauties most admired during the Sung period. As under the T'ang (seventh to tenth century), the ideal feminine type was a very sophisticated one. Ladies of rank and singing-girls made extravagant use of head-ornaments, combs, pearl necklaces, and above all of cosmetics, powders and perfumes. One difference however may be noted between the T'ang feminine ideal and that of Sung times: it had changed from the rather stately beauty with hair piled up in an elaborate edifice above the forehead, so much admired by the Chinese of the North in the eighth century, to one who was slender, petite and dainty. This change in type of feminine beauty corresponded without a doubt to a parallel change in manners and moral customs.

Because of its luxury, its wealth, the leisure of one section of its population, and the intensity of its social life, the great city of Hangchow provided surroundings particularly favourable for promoting civility and civilized ways of living. But they also promoted promiscuity and lewdness. The scholar class was marked by an attitude of hypocritical prudishness which, far from excluding licentiousness and profligacy, on the contrary merely corroborated them.

An author at the beginning of the Mongol period tells us that men in the upper circles of society often took to depraved habits late in life. Not only, he adds, are such habits bad for the health, but they also lead to impotence. They necessitate forming ties which impede the free flow of the 'breaths'. May those who care about their health be warned![41]

Even without this testimony, one might have guessed that the concubines bought from poor families were not always exclusively intended to be a means of providing descendants for the great families. The number of courtesans, rich and poor, leads one to suppose that promiscuous affairs played a prominent rôle in the lives of the Chinese of Hangchow in the thirteenth century. And did not Marco Polo see, in the licence that reigned in China at that time, one of the main causes of the country's subjection.

'But the people of [this] land,' he says, 'were anything rather than warriors; all their delight was in women, and nought but women; and so it was above all with the King himself, for he took thought of nothing else but women, unless it were of charity to the poor. In all his dominion there were no horses;[42] nor were the people ever inured to battle or arms, or military service of any kind. Yet the province of Manzi is very strong by nature, and all the cities are encompassed by sheets of water of great depth, and more than an arblast-shot in width; so that the country never would have been lost, had the people but been soldiers. But that was just what they were not; so lost it was.'[43]

Despite the extraordinary spread of licentiousness in Hangchow, it must not be forgotten that China, like India, had a long tradition in the matter of techniques of sexual hygiene. They were founded on Taoistic concepts, and bore traces of the influence of the magical form of Buddhism known as Tantra. The Chinese techniques were a kind of hygiene of sanctification which, by means of certain disciplines, was supposed to make the attainment of 'Long Life' possible and to lead the way to immortality. Woman, in her capacity as container of female potency (yin), supplies to man elements that are indispensable for his self-realization. Hence most of the sexual practices were aimed to enable the man to preserve his potency and male principle (yang) intact, while at the same time enabling him to incorporate the mysterious powers of the female.[41] In effect, the sole result of such practices can only have been to put the nervous system out of balance.

## ILLNESS

The Chinese, both by tradition and natural aptitude, are born naturalists. Their medical knowledge was based on a mass of detailed observations and original prescriptions which today form a heritage upon which Western medicine could draw with profit, and of which Chinese doctors are even now trying to make an inventory in an attempt to integrate it into the modern science of medicine. However, in the traditional medicine of Sung times, the whole framework of these observations and prescriptions was conceived in terms of the philosophical concepts then in force; the human body was considered to be a reproduction of the cosmos, and a state of health to be simply the reflection of a state of general harmony obtaining among separate 'virtues', while illness was the sign of a disturbance of this harmony. Everything was explained in terms of correspondences of universal validity —universal, because they applied as much to the physical universe as to the human body. Theory preceded observation, and observation, even when it was original and constituted a discovery, was never followed up for its own sake, but always integrated into the theory.

Doctors in the Sung period recognized five important organs (heart, liver, spleen, lungs and kidneys) which were each related to one of the five elements or elemental properties (water, fire, wood, metal and earth). These elements had the characteristic of being produced or destroyed one by the other according to a predetermined sequence. The five essential organs were connected with the five openings of the body: the kidneys, for instance, with the ears, and the liver with the eyes. The body was a complex network of relationships, and this was why, in acupuncture, the needle was applied at points in the body which might be remote from the diseased part or organ. Health resulted from a good circulation of the 'breaths' (warm, cold, dry, moist and fiery) which circulated all through the body, and by a good balance between the female principle or principle of cold (yin) and the male principle or principle of warmth (yang).

Illness might also have its origin in an excess of the seven sentiments (joy, anger, sadness, fear, love, hate and desire). Ideas of this kind provided a basis for both diagnostic and therapeutic purposes. An examination of the face, and also of the pulse—a science in which the Chinese were past masters—enabled an experienced doctor to identify the illness immediately. A large number of different pulse-beats were noted, each of which indicated a specific ailment.

Here is how ulcers of the leg are caused, according to an author of the first half of the twelfth century. This ailment, he first of all notes, is very rare in north-west China, but very frequent in the South. Why? Because the inhabitants of South China like drinking rice-wine and eating salt fish. Now, the special virtue of the salty taste (one of the five fundamental flavours) is, that it makes the blood descend to the lower part of the body. Fish causes slight fever and tends to give rise to ulcers. As for alcohol, the yeast and the aconite which are added to it in very small quantities are poisons. These three elements (the harmful constituents of salt, fish and alcohol) enter the spleen, through which pass the two veins of the tibia, and this is how ulcers on the legs are caused.[45]

As regards methods of treatment, they consisted of massage, which was often localized over very small areas of the body (the palm of the hand or the top of the thumb, for example), of cauterizations made with artemisia, of punctures made with a silver needle at very precisely specified points in the body, and of drugs and beverages of various kinds. Surgery was at a very

elementary stage, and was hardly used except for the castration
of eunuchs and for abscesses or fractures. Acupuncture, massage
and cauterization seem to have been employed less frequently
than drugs. These medicines were usually made from plants, and
were extremely complicated in their composition. A single decoc-
tion, for instance, might contain as many as twenty-five
ingredients. Animal substances and minerals were sometimes
used in them, such as rhinoceros horn, which was a great deal
used, various kinds of jade, and crushed pearls. There were also
remedies made from insects: toad-venom (which had the same
effect as digitalis), earthworms, spiders, centipedes boiled and
reduced to powder, etc. A recipe of this kind for curing malaria
recommends the use of a fly found on a dog. 'Take one dog fly.
Remove the legs and wings. Roll it in wax so as to form a pellet
which is to be taken with cold rice-wine on the day of the attack.'
Snakeskin is also efficacious if put into the ears of the sick person
or held in the hollow of his hands.[46] A worm gathered from the
eternal snows of the mountains of Central Asia is a good cure
for 'accumulated fever': it is cold as ice and has a flavour sweet
as honey.[47]

About 1080, official medical training, which up until then had
been divided into three branches, namely: pulsology, acupuncture and the treatment of ulcers and wounds, was re-divided into
nine specialized sections. The enumeration of them shows the
high degree of specialization attained at that time by Chinese
medicine: general medicine and the main medical theories (two
sections), treatment of rheumatism and paralyses, ophthalmo-
logy, obstetrics, dentistry and laryngology, treatment of abscesses
and fractures, acupuncture and moxibustion, treatment by
means of charms and amulets.[48]

The mention made in this list of magical methods of treatment
is sufficient indication that Chinese medicine was not, either in
its theory or in its therapeutic methods, of a scientific character.
However, although there was an understanding between doctors,
healers and magicians, it was chiefly the Taoist or Buddhist
monks that specialized in exorcism, and some of them, be it
noted, had a real gift of healing. They made use of charms on
which were inscribed designs of a cabbalistic nature, or talismans
which the sick persons had to wear all the time, or magic formulas taken from the texts of the esoteric form of Buddhism known

as Tantra. For every illness, theories and remedies varied widely according to the various schools of medicine, and sick people for their part did not hesitate to try out different treatments at the same time: treatments of a magical nature were often resorted to in this event.

According to the theories in force, malaria, to take an example, could be caused by the spirits of the dead, by the local climate, by a faulty diet, by a disturbance of the equilibrium between the cold principle and the warm principle, or by a lack of harmony between the five elemental properties within the human body, or yet again by a deity known as Mother Malaria. The doctors distinguished sixteen different kinds of malaria according to the external symptoms, and they had recourse to a large number of different kinds of treatment to combat them. These included acupuncture, cauterization, massage, arsenic in small doses, drugs made from plants, drugs made from insects, and finally charms and amulets, some of which had to be swallowed. The exact moment for taking medicine was of great importance, at whatever stage the illness might be. The moment had to be chosen according to the position of the sun and according to the stages of the crisis. Taken at the wrong moment, the cure was in danger of being worse than the malady.[49]

One branch of Chinese medicine which is not mentioned in the list of specialities covered by official tuition is that of forensic medicine. Chinese justice, due to its particular bent, was firmly founded on material proof, and as a result, forensic medicine developed in China at a much earlier date than it did in the West. Hence there survives a treatise on forensic medicine for the use of the officials directly concerned which was compiled about the middle of the thirteenth century on the basis of older works of this kind. It was not until the beginning of the seventeenth century that a similar work appeared in Europe: that of Roderic de Castro. The Chinese treatise of the thirteenth century supplies model death certificates going into great detail for all parts of the body. It gives a list of the correct methods of identifying the various types of death possible (strangulation, drowning, poison, blows, etc.), and gives instructions as to the methods which, in certain cases, make it possible to distinguish between murder, suicide or accident. It also gives instructions about first-aid for persons at the point of death in cases of hanging, drowning, sunstroke, freezing to death, or undernourishment, and for people nearly dead from drowning, it recommends, among other treatments, artificial respiration.[50]

Medical teaching was organized by the State, and the list of officially-recognized drugs was drawn up under the supervision of the official doctors at the court, who were members of the School of Medicine. Thus there existed a kind of official index which tabled a list of 850 drugs, 656 of which were in practical use during the T'ang period (seventh to tenth century). It was revised at the end of the tenth century, when 133 drugs were added to the list. In actual fact, of the 983 drugs listed, only 789 were actually in current usage. Treatises on the use of these drugs were circulated at the instigation of the government. One of them, in a hundred chapters, appeared between the years 990 and 994, and another less important one in the middle of the eleventh century. About 1080 an imperial decree went out asking the most capable doctors, wherever they might be, to give information about their most effective remedies. These drugs were tried out by the School of Medicine and the methods used in preparing them were widely diffused.[51]

This clearly shows that there existed two streams of medical practice, the one private, and the other the official one which drew strength from the traditions and discoveries of the first. The teaching organized by the State was provided by the School of Medicine that had been founded in 1076. Transferred to Hangchow, this college, as we have seen, took in between 250 and 300 students around 1270.[52] Its purpose was to supply official doctors to look after the Emperor, the people belonging to the court, and upper class people in general. The common people, on the other hand, went to private doctors, who usually handed on their profession from father to son. In their opinion, the only good doctors were those whose family had long practised the medical profession. 'Beware of taking drugs from a doctor whose family has not been in medicine for three generations,' ran a popular saying. Most doctors were specialists. Some only looked after sick children, whose most common ailments were intestinal worms and distended stomach. Others only practised acupuncture, such as the one in Hangchow at River-street Bridge, as you go down the canal. Each one had a notice up outside his shop indicating his speciality, and sometimes vaunting his art: 'Rapid recovery assured', reads a notice which can be seen on a painting of Kaifeng dating from the beginning of the twelfth century.[53] It must be presumed that it paid to advertize, because at the Shanghai Museum there is a small printing-plate in bronze from the Sung period which apparently was used for advertizing by a practician of acupuncture. It reads, at the top: 'Acupuncture shop of Master Liu of Chi-nan', and, in the centre: 'You will recognize it by the white rabbit which serves as a sign in front of the door'.

Apart from the doctor's shops, there were in Hangchow a large number of pharmacies of various kinds: some selling medicinal plants in the raw, wholesale, others selling ready-made decoctions (these being probably the most numerous), and others nothing but herbs for curing childrens' stomach disorders, others again plants gathered exclusively in the Hangchow region. These pharmacies had, in the traditional manner, a dried calabash as sign which hung over the door. In addition to these private pharmacies there were, as we have seen, public dispensaries where drugs were sold, thanks to court subsidies, at a third of the current price. But due to dishonest management on the part of the officials and employees appointed to these establishments, they cannot have been of any help to the poor for whom they had originally been established, and it is not even certain whether the institution still survived in the Hangchow of 1270. Finally, in each prefecture there were public hospitals and homes run by the State, where the poor, the aged, the infirm and the incurable were taken in and looked after free of charge.


DEATH

At the death of a near relation, each member of the family fell into a suitable state of prostration as prescribed by custom according to the degree of kinship with the deceased. Coarse clothing was worn and all enjoyments forbidden. The funeral ceremonies were designed for the purpose of getting rid of all the impurities caused by death, while aiming at the same time to exalt the deceased by transforming him into an ancestor, which in turn raised the prestige of the family stricken with mourning. They included a ritual washing and clothing of the corpse, as well as set lamentations. The women especially were experts in wailing and weeping and beating their breasts. Every family made it a point of honour to do things properly, and indeed to make them as sumptuous as possible. Thus funerals were always an occasion for spending a lot of money, and sometimes they actually ruined poor families. The coffin, the articles required for the ceremonies, and, among other things, the paper images of carriages, horses and servants which must be burned so as to accompany the dead person into the other world, the hiring of the necessary personnel, and, above all, the plot of earth where, after consultation with a specialist in geomancy, the dead person would finally be buried, all cost a great deal of money, not to mention the entertainment of friends and relations and the banquets that were offered to them, for which certain specialist firms catered.

But in Hangchow burial was not a common custom: land was scarce and the price prohibitive. Hence cremation, which was certainly much less costly than burial, had become widespread, especially among the lower and middle classes. This practice, so contrary to traditional ways, had been increasing since the end of the tenth century in several regions of China (Hopei, Shansi and the maritime provinces of the south-east) in spite of opposition from the government. Thus an imperial decree of 963 announces that 'apart from the capital (Kaifeng) and various other places, people have recently begun to burn the dead. This practice must be forbidden, except when the body has to be transported from a distance (it was customary to be buried in one's native district) or when it is a question of Buddhist monks or foreigners'.

Another edict of 972 found it necessary to repeat this prohibition. At the beginning of the twelfth century the custom of cremation, which had grown considerably, was still frowned upon by the government and in various circles: everywhere, in fact, where Confucian traditions were most clung to. A high official, in a memorial to the Emperor, criticizes the custom as being unworthy treatment of the dead, and asks that families who cannot afford to bury their dead should be allowed to inter them in land bought by the State for that purpose.[54] This was the origin of such public cemeteries as existed in Hangchow. The following anecdote is another indication of the general disapproval felt: a funeral mound called the 'Tomb of the woman in wood' was still to be seen in 1275 outside one of the gates of Hangchow. This woman's husband had had her cremated, and her son, still a child, was so shocked that his mother did not have any 'land with pines and catalpas' (a literary designation for a grave) that he often wept about it. When he grew up, he had a wooden statue made in the likeness of his mother, clothed it, put it in a coffin, and had it buried at this spot. Afterwards he had a small hut built and bought a plot of land for the maintenance of a monk to whom he encharged the cult of the deceased (incense burnt in the morning and lamps lit at nightfall).[55]

However that may be as regards the attitude of disapproval evidenced by such special cases, cremation was more or less general in Hangchow in the thirteenth century. The city's cremation ovens were in the grounds of a Buddhist foundation called the Monastery of Awakening situated at the north-east corner of the lake. The city of Suchow, during the same period, had a similar building containing ten ovens which was also in the grounds of a Buddhist monastery. When the building was destroyed by a cyclone in 1261, the prefect of Suchow tried, doubtless in vain, to prevent its being re-built. In both cities the ashes were scattered into ponds by the monks employed at the ovens. In Fukien, on the other hand, they were placed in earthenware vases which were called urns of gold.

How is the spread of a practice so contrary to the habits and concepts of the Chinese to be explained? Economic motives—the high price of land and, particularly in Chekiang, plentiful supplies of firewood—may have favoured it, but cannot account for its origin. It is very likely that the fashion began among people in upper class circles who were zealous Buddhists, and then spread to other sections of society without much to hinder its spread, since it was a society long accustomed to Buddhist concepts and modes of thought, even if the number of families who were practising members of the faith was small. It is to be remarked that it was Buddhist monasteries that saw to the carrying out of this type of ceremony. But in addition cremation, as is indicated by the popular expression for it, seems to have been thought of as a means for seeking regeneration, a kind of transmutation of the body by fire. Buddhist monks were normally cremated, but on rare occasions a monk would submit to being burnt alive. This was an ancient practice, well attested from the fifth century onwards and surviving in Fukien until modern times. Ascetic monks who died in the flames, seated in the posture of a statue of the Buddha and reciting sacred texts, were at least assured of re-birth on a higher level of being and might even achieve the attainment of nirvana.[56]

Marco Polo seems to have attended cremations of lay persons in Hangchow. His description of them shows that they were noisy and apparently joyful ceremonies. We shall close with his eye-witness account:

'And again I tell you that they have likewise for a habit that when any great rich master dies, all the relations and friends make very great mourning, and the relations, women and men, dress themselves in hemp for mourning and go behind with the body which is carried to the place where they wish to burn him, and take with them their instruments many and different and go playing and singing idol prayers aloud. And when they come to the said place where the body must be burned they stop themselves and cause horses to be made and slaves or servants, male and women, and camels, saddles, trappings, and cloth of gold and of silk and money of gold and of silver in very great abundance. And all these things they make to be painted on sheets of paper. And when they have done this they make the great fire and burn the body with these things and say that the dead man will have all those things in the other world alive of flesh and bones and the money of gold, cloths of gold and of silk. And the burning finished, they sound all the instruments together with great cheerfulness continually singing; for they say that all the honour which they do him when he is being burned, just such another will be done him in the other world by their gods and by the idols . . . and that he is born again in the other world and begins life anew.'[57]

Once cremated or interred, the dead continued to play an important rôle in the lives of Hangchow people. Every deceased person was represented by a tablet bearing his name which was placed on the little altar set up in the main room of each house. It was never forgotten to lay offerings before these tablets, and to burn incense and light lamps for them at the time of the Festival of the Dead, on the birthday of the deceased, and at New Year. In addition, all those who had been buried were visited by their near relatives at the time of the Festival of the Dead at the beginning of April, or of the Buddhist ceremonies for the dead which were held on the 15th of the 7th moon, and also on the first day of the 10th moon. A visit was made to the graves which lay outside the ramparts on the hills surrounding the lake, the funeral mounds were swept, food was laid on them, and all the visitors prostrated themselves several times.

## NOTES AND REFERENCES

1. *T'ang lü shu i* (the T'ang Code with commentary), chap. XXII, articles 13, 11, 5, 7.
2. *Chi le pien, Shuo fu* XXVII, f. 17a-b and 21a-b.
3. W. Eberhard, *Chinese Festivals,* p. 41.
4. *Yang ku man lu* (13th c.), *Shuo fu* XXIX. Cf. *Chiang hsing tsa lu, Shuo fu* XLVII, f. 7b et seq.
5. *Hou te lu,* by Li Yüan-kang (end of 12th c.), *Shuo fu* LXXI.
6. Cf. *Sung hui yao, Hsing fa,* II (Chin-yüeh), a report to the Emperor dated the 9th day of the 5th moon of 1109, which cites numerous cases of infanticide in Fukien.
7. J. J. Matignon, *Superstition, Crime et Misère en Chine,* Paris, 1902.
8. *Kuei hsin tsa chih, Hsü* B, § 49.
9. *Sung shih,* XXIX, 5th moon of the 8th year of the reign-period Shao-hsing.
10. Y, p. 147.
11. *Sui-ch'ang tsa lu,* by Cheng Yüan-yu of the Yüan period, *Shuo fu* XLVII, f. 5a-b. This text is also in the *Ku-chung sui-pi* by Ku Yen-wu in *Hai-shan hsien-kuan ts'ung-shu,* chap. II B. Consult S. Imahori, *A study of the protective institutions for babies in the Sung period,* Hiroshima University Studies (*Literature Department*), No 8, Oct. 1955.
12. Yule, *Cathay and the Way Thither,* IV, p. 116; translation of Ibn Batuta text.
13. MLL, XX, 2, pp. 307-8.
14. *Kuei hsin tsa chih, Hou,* § 63.
15. M & P, p. 336.
16. The keeping of arms was forbidden by article 20 of chap. XVI of the T'ang Code; most articles of this Code were still in force in the 13th c.
17. Y, p. 204.
18. *Kuei hsin tsa chih, ch'ien,* § 10.

19. *Sung shih* CLVII, f. 20b in the Ch'ien-lung ed. (1739). The buildings of this primary school were in the grounds of the Imperial Academy (*chung-hsüeh*).

20. Cf. *Sung shih, ibid.*, f. 33b-34b, and MLL, XV, 1, pp. 254-6, where a long paragraph is devoted to the colleges at the capital.

21. MLL, *ibid.* See Miyazaki Ichisada, *Ajiashikenkyu*, Vol. I, pp. 365-401. The life of the students at the National University under the Sung (in Japanese).

22. *Ch'ing po tsa chih, Shuo fu* XXII.

23. L. Wieger, *Textes Historiques*, p. 1951.

24. E. Chavannes, *L'Instruction d'un Futur Empereur de Chine en 1193, Mémoires concernant l'Asie Orientale*, Vol. I, 1913.

25. *Meng ch'i pi t'an*, XXV, f. 8b in the *Chin tai pi shu* edition.

26. *I shih chi wen, Shuo fu* XXVI, f. 2a.

27. The census registers of the T'ang period found at Tun-huang show that the wife was generally two to three years younger than her husband. But naturally the difference in age might vary according to region and social stratification.

28. The *Tso meng lu*, a work of the first half of the 12th c., *Shuo fu* XXXIV, f. 8b-9a, describes the ceremony of these posthumous marriages.

29. *Yü chia chi, Shuo fu* XXXII.

30. Cf. the story of the Sung period translated under the title of 'Fifteen strings of cash' in *The Courtesan's Jewel Box*, Peking 1957.

31. *Tung ching meng hua lu*, IV, p. 30.

32. *Ibid.*

33. MLL, XX, 1, pp. 304-7.

34. On matrimonial law in China, see P. Hoang, 'Le Mariage Chinois au Point de Vue Légal', *Variétés Sinologiques*, No. 14, Shanghai, 1915.

35. *Sung shih*, CDLX, 4th biography.

36. *Ibid.*, 5th biography.

37. *Kuei hsin tsa chih, ch'ien*, § 21.

38. *I chien chih, ting*, XX, 4th anecdote.

39. *Chi le pien, Shuo fu*, XXVII.

40. Y, p. 204.

41. *Kuei hsin tsa chih, Hou A*, § 40. The *I chien chih, i*, IX, f. 7a, tells the story of a very wealthy doctor of Kaifeng, at the beginning of the 12th c., who, in his old age, acquired ten concubines and almost completely ruined his health. As for proofs of the dissolute life led by the students of the various colleges, they are innumerable.

42. The criticism is inappropriate, because the damp, low-lying territory of the Yangtze region is suitable neither for horse-breeding nor for cavalry battles.

43. Y, p. 145.

44. This very brief outline is based on R. H. van Gulik, *Erotic Color Prints of the Ming Period, with an Essay on Chinese Sex Life from the Han to the Ch'ing Dynasty*, Tokyo, 1951.

45. *Chi le pien, Shuo fu* XXVII.

46. R. Hoeppli, 'Malaria in Chinese Medicine', *Sinologica*, IV, 2, 1955.

47. *Kuei hsin tsa chih, Hsü* B, § 8.

48. Tung Tso-pin, *Ch'ing ming shang ho t'u*, Taipei, 1954, notes at the end, p. 5. On the School of Medicine, see *Sung shih* CLVII, f. 33b-34b in the Ch'ien-lung ed.

49. R. Hoeppli, *op. cit.*

50. *Sung t'i-hsing hsi yüan lu* by Sung Tz'u of the Sung period, in the *Ts'ung shu chi ch'eng*, No. 1456. This manual of forensic medicine is a compilation of earlier works, and must date from the middle of the 13th c. In its present form, containing additions from the Mongol period (1279-1368), it was until recently still in use as an official guide for doctors in the law-courts' police. On the general characteristics of Chinese medicine, see P. Huard and Ming Wong, *La Médecine Chinoise au Cours des Siècles*, Paris, 1959.

51. *Sung shih* CLVII, *loc. cit.*

52. *Ibid.*, and MLL, XV, 1, p. 256.

53. Tung Tso-pin, *op. cit.*

54. On cremation in China, see A. C. Moule, *Quinsai and Other Notes on Marco Polo*, pp. 44-51.

55. MLL, XV, 7, pp. 250-61.

56. Cf. J. Gernet, 'Les Suicides par le Feu chez les Bouddhistes Chinois', in *Mélanges de l'Institut des Hautes Etudes Chinoises de l'Université de Paris*, Vol. II, 1960, pp. 527-58.

57. M & P, p. 337.

# CHAPTER V

# THE SEASONS AND THE UNIVERSE

THE SEASONS AND DAYS OF THE YEAR: *Climate of the Hangchow region. Calendar. Working days and holidays of officials, merchants and the common people.* FESTIVALS: *Their aim. The New Year festival and the Feast of Lanterns. Spring festivals: the new wine and the new fire; the festival of the dead. An unlucky day: the 5th of the 5th moon. Autumn festivals: festival of weavers, festival of the moon and of women. The tidal bore at Hangchow in September. Festival of chrysanthemums.* RELIGION: 1. *General conceptions. Confusion of the natural and the supernatural. Western influences. Dissident cults.* 2. *The official cult. Ritualism and ostentation. An example: the sacrifices to Heaven and Earth. Hostility of the scholars to all unofficial forms of religion. Indifference to doctrine.* 3. *Family cults. Ancestors and household gods.* 4. *Popular cults and beliefs. Local deities. Mediums and visionaries. Secret societies: a Manichean sect. Pestilences, ghosts and demons. The judgment of the dead.* 5. *Buddhism and Taoism. An outworn creed. The Buddhist liturgy. Buddhist doctrine and morality. Taoism. Foreign religions.*

## THE SEASONS AND THE DAYS OF THE YEAR

THE CHANGING seasons make us aware of the passing of time. Moreover, certain abnormal climatic events stay in the memory of those who have witnessed them and serve as a landmark. For this reason, let us first of all say a word about the climate of Hangchow.

Although Hangchow is on the same latitude as Cairo, it sometimes has severe winters after the end of December. Thus, in 1186 it snowed without stopping for nearly a month and in the city the snow reached a depth of ten inches. Three years later there were further heavy falls of snow. 'The branches of the bamboos,' says a poet, 'broke with a strange sound'. In 1132 the canals and the lake froze over. Some emigrés from the North made use of their knowledge of how to make underground ice-chambers and stored ice for the summer, also teaching Hangchow people how to do this. But later, when there was no ice left for use in the imperial palace, it was brought by fast boats that travelled day and night without stopping.[1]

In spring a continuous fine drizzle covers the sun. Following upon this come the hot-weather months—July and August—and then the whole activity of the town slowed down. Poor people, in summer attire, sat out under the porticoes hoping to catch a breath of fresh air, or wandered about the city at night. The wealthy sought shelter in the coolest pavilions in their gardens. The summer, heavy and hot, is the season for downpours, but it hardly rains at all in autumn and winter, and the autumn droughts come at the worst time for the crops, just when the young rice shoots have most need of water. 'In the course of several decades,' says one author, 'I have not known a single autumn when there have not been prayers for rain.'[2]

However at almost every time of the year the air in Hangchow, as in Szechwan, is saturated with humidity, and, if a local saying is to be believed: 'As soon as it rains, it is cold. As soon as the sky clears, it is hot'.[3]

On April 9, 1231, an event occurred of which other instances could no doubt be discovered in the annals of the city. Yellow clouds laden with sand suddenly plunged the city into semi-darkness. It rained, and all the roofs of Hangchow were covered with a yellow dust which penetrated everywhere and went up the nostrils of people in the streets. Visibility was restricted to a few yards. The sun, giving no light, was 'like a metal mirror that has not yet been polished'. At night, while this strange phenomenon still continued, fire broke out in a house east of the Bridge of the Immortals and gradually spread in all directions. The next day the air was so thick with dust that it was impossible to see the glow of the fire. When, at midday, the fire was finally extinguished, a whole district in the south-east of the city—more than ten thousand houses in all—was found to have been destroyed.[4]

There were other natural events which punctuated the lives of the inhabitants of Hangchow, among them, for example, the tidal bore in September at the place where the river enters the estuary. But it was chiefly the festivals, as we shall see, that marked, in people's minds, the passing of the seasons, creating Time and giving it its rhythm throughout the twelve or thirteen moons of which each Chinese year was composed.

The calendar was actually luni-solar. The first day of the year was fixed by the court astronomers to fall on the day of the second new moon after the winter solstice. Thus the date varied from year to year. New Year's day for the years 1250 to 1276, for example, when equated with the Julian calendar, varied between January 16th at the earliest and February 13th at the latest. The year, which normally consisted of twelve moons of 30 or 29 days ('big' and 'little' moons), had only 354 days, and the difference between the lunar year and the solar year was corrected by adding seven intercalary moons during each period of ten years.[5] Thus some years contained 384 days. Each quarter corresponded to a season, equinoxes and solstices marking not the beginning, but the middle of the season. Thus the first, second and third moons were called the spring moons. But because of the intercalary moons, some seasons sometimes had four months.

The love of order and symmetry was also responsible for maintaining the very ancient custom of dividing the months into periods of ten days (two ten-day periods and one of nine days in the case of a 'little moon'), although reckoning time by the week, under the influence of occidental calendars, was not unknown.[6] With regard to the day, it was divided into twelve hours designated by a series of twelve cyclical signs. The first hour was from approximately 11 p.m. until 1 a.m. But the hours varied according to the seasons. The five hours of the night, which were called watches, and were announced in the city by beats on a drum, were longer in winter than in summer. From about one and a half hours at the summer solstice, the watches lengthened to two and a half hours in midwinter. The day was also divided, according to another system, into 100 'quarter hours', each of which was nearly equivalent to one of our quarter hours.

It was the court that fixed, printed and circulated throughout the empire the official annual calendar for each year: the Emperor was still, according to the most ancient traditions, the master and the regulator of Time. Calendars were indispensable for country people; they gave the dates of the solstices and equinoxes, and supplied detailed information for agricultural work—information which was all the more important in view of the fact that the luni-solar year was hardly ever in accord with the actual seasons. Some calendars, very popular with the common people, were in the form of almanacks which contained precise details useful for divination and geomancy: the dominant element for the day (water, fire, wood, metal, earth), lucky and unlucky days for every kind of activity (money matters, journeys, burials, building, baths, etc.), and the cyclical signs corresponding to each day.

These signs consisted of two series of written characters—ten in one series and twelve in the other—the combination of which gave sixty possible terms containing two signs. These sixty terms were used not only to designate days, but also to designate years, in continuous succession. These cyclical signs were in common usage not only among the people, but in official documents and also in historical writings, where the years are specified by reference to the reign-period. Thus, the thirtieth year of the reign-period *Shao-hsing*, designated by the cyclical signs *keng-ch'en*, corresponds to the year 1160; the third year of the reign-period *Hsien-ch'un*, designated by the cyclical signs *ting-mao*, to 1267.

The inhabitants of Hangchow were very early risers.[7]

'About four or five in the morning, when the bells of the Buddhist and Taoist monasteries have rung, hermit-monks come down from the hills surrounding the town and go about the streets of Hangchow beating their strips of iron or their wooden resonators in the form of a fish, announcing everywhere the dawn. They call out what the weather is like: 'It is cloudy', 'It is raining', 'The sky is clear'. In wind, in rain, in snow or in freezing cold, they go out just the same. They also announce any court reception to be held that day, whether a grand or a little or an ordinary audience. In this way the officials in the various government departments, the officers of the watch, and the soldiers whose names are on the list for the watch-towers, are all kept informed and hurry off to their offices or their posts. As for the monk announcers, they go round the town collecting alms on the first and the fifteenth of each month as well as on feast-days.'[8]

Imperial audiences were held at five or six o'clock in the morning. Seven o'clock was considered to be already late in the day. Drums were beaten to announce the beginning of office hours at the palace. The prefectural and sub-prefectural offices were content with the less august sound of a gong or of wooden clappers.

Government employees had to be present when the offices opened, under pain of a beating. All business was transacted in the morning and afternoon. Thus the officials had the late afternoon and the evening free. They spent their leisure hours reading, writing literary compositions, going on pleasure outings, or playing chess. But there were sometimes night watches in the offices, and the officials on duty had to write their names on a list. Under the Northern Sung (960-1127) the officials of the four imperial libraries got into the habit of not doing their watch duty under the excuse of suffering from intestinal disorders, with the result that the list for the imperial libraries was known as the 'list of stomach pains'.

The officials had the right to one day's leave at the end of each ten-day period. Apart from these days of rest, they were allowed fifty-four days regular leave per annum, divided up into short periods of seven, five or three days. These were accorded at the times of the annual festivals, such as those at the winter solstice and at the New Year, as well as on anniversaries of the death or birth of emperors. For the anniversaries of the death of his parents each official was exempted from work for one whole day. He also had the right to spend a holiday with his family every three years. The length of the holiday varied from one month to fifteen days according to the distance separating him from his family, and the time taken on the journey was not included in this. The capping of a son or the marriage of one of his children or of a near relation were also occasions for a few days' leave. The only interruption of any length of time in the career of an official was that which occurred at the time of the death of his father or of his mother: officials were then obligatorily given leave for three years, and they usually spent this enforced period of leisure in devoting themselves to their favourite pastimes: editing literary works, calligraphy, painting, etc.

Unlike the officials, merchants and ordinary people worked without pause of any kind. At dawn the shopkeepers began arranging their displays of goods, and the people from the suburbs and the surrounding country coming to sell their wares at the morning market began flowing towards the centre of Hangchow. On the Imperial Way, breakfast delicacies were sold in the early hours: fried tripe, pieces of mutton or goose, soups of various kinds, hot pancakes, steamed pancakes, iced cakes. At

the doorways of bathing establishments, pedlars offered hot
water for washing the face, inhalations, and pills for 'nourishing
the vital breath'. 'Every day,' says an inhabitant, 'from dawn
until evening, on the Imperial Way and in the adjoining streets,
there is an incessant activity of pedlars, shops and markets. This
fever suddenly ceases at the time of the evening meal. Everyone
then takes home his merchandise, shuts up shop, or packs up his
shoddy wares.'[9] The commercial activities of the city gave it, so
to speak, a sort of daily heart-beat: inwards, towards the centre,
in the morning, and outwards, towards the suburbs, in the
evening.

But many districts in Hangchow, lying off the Imperial Way,
remained animated in the evening and well beyond midnight.
Taverns and singing-girl houses were open until the fourth
drum-beat, at about two o'clock in the morning. During the
night, pole-porters took up their stand in the street of the market-
stalls, where they infused tea for sale to passers-by and people
strolling about for pleasure. There was also a nocturnal trade on
the Imperial Way, except in the vicinity of the palace, where
disturbance of any kind was to be avoided. Thus, in front of the
pleasure-grounds in the centre there was a kind of market where
crockery and various small articles were sold by lottery, just as
in the daytime. Cooked food and fruits could also be bought
there. In addition, numerous noodle shops remained open on the
main street of the city; 'the soldiers assigned to police duty do
not prevent either the common people or officials from supplying
themselves with noodles during the night'.[10] In the slaughter-
houses, activity began between three and five o'clock in the
morning in order that all animals should be slaughtered before
dawn, in time for the opening of the markets.

At the times of the great festivals, which usually lasted three
days and three nights, and especially during the Feast of Lanterns in February, on the 14th, 15th and 16th of the first moon,
the whole city stayed lit up all night long. Shows of all kinds
were in full swing. In all parts of the city there were nocturnal
markets where there were also shows and rejoicings. The
Japanese monk Jôjun thus describes one of these markets in
1072: hundreds of lamps made of green, red or white glass were
suspended from every shop front. Jade curtains were hung in the
doorways. There were women playing the flute or singing to the

accompaniment of a zither, conjurors and acrobats, dancers and musicians. Itinerant tea-vendors offered their wares at one cash a cup.[11]

For shopkeepers and artisans the only closing days when they could have a rest from their labours, apart from those resulting from special occasions such as mourning or marriage, were those of New Year's day and the day following, and the feast-day consecrated by each guild to the anniversary of its patron saint.

## FESTIVALS

Nowhere else in the world has there been such a passionate delight in festivals as in China. Nowhere else have festivals, ceremonies and minor annual rituals better been able to express the joys, aspirations and anxieties of an entire people. They not only served as a means of marking off the seasons, thus giving time its full weight and value, but they also expressed a certain understanding of life.

What was the spirit that inspired them? Many customs had a symbolical significance that we shall not attempt to elucidate here: much remains obscure, and, on examination, the avowed purpose of many forms of ritual are as often as not found to be quite different from the deep urges actually lying behind them. However, in main outline, the primary purpose of these annual festivals was to get rid of 'breaths' that had become vitiated, of pestilences and of demons, to re-create everything so that it should be new and pristine, to inaugurate a lucky period, and to open the way for beneficial influences. At the same time they offered entertainments which gave free rein to play-loving instincts, and times of merry-making during which the constraints of daily life could be forgotten.

Popular festivals common to everyone, festivals and official ceremonies at the court, and festivals organized by the religious communities, both Taoist and Buddhist, were all mixed up together. That is why they will be described here in chronological order, without distinction of any other kind, and the account will reveal many aspects of the religious life of the Chinese—in particular, of the inhabitants of Hangchow. Since the Chinese calendar was luni-solar, with the first day of the year lying anywhere between approximately January 15th and February 15th, and since festivals with dates determined by the solar calendar mingle with festivals with dates determined by the lunar calendar, we shall make an arbitrary choice of a specimen year beginning on February 1st.

The most important festivities of the whole year were those held at the New Year. In all circles of society, the preceding month was devoted to preparing for them. If it snowed during this month, this was held to be a lucky omen for the coming year, holding promise of a good harvest. The wealthy celebrated such an event by giving banquets and making snow lions which they presented to their relations and friends. Sometimes they rode on horseback to the lakeside to admire the snow-scenes there. On the 24th of the 12th moon, rich and poor alike prepared dishes of vegetables and soya beans to offer to the god of the hearth. This domestic deity was supposed to pay a visit to Heaven at the New Year in order to make his annual report on the conduct of the various members of the family. For this reason he was given special treatment on the days preceding his departure, and people even went to the length of trying to bribe him by offering him sweets. In the streets and markets dishes of rice coloured with the five colours (the colours of the four cardinal points, green, red, white and black, and yellow for the point at the centre of time and space) were auctioned.

On the 25th a porridge of red haricot beans was offered to the guardian spirits of the house, and pet dogs and cats were also given some of it. In the shops in the city there was a great deal of activity in making painted images of the door gods, paper streamers bearing the lucky characters for 'welcoming the spring', printed images of Chung K'uei, a hero of T'ang times deified as a protector against demons, and little horses out of paper. All these small articles were presented to their customers by the shopkeepers. In the same way, pharmacists made a free distribution to their customers of amulets and little bags containing ingredients efficacious in getting rid of evil influences. In the streets hawkers sold a particular kind of thistle (*atractylis lancea var. ovata*), small jujubes, and firecrackers made of sticks of bamboo filled with gunpowder. Groups of from three to five beggars, dressed as gods, went about the city beating on gongs and drums.[12] On the eve of the New Year, 'the end of the moons and the last day of the year', doorways were swept and watered, the old painted images of the door gods were taken down, images of Chung K'uei the demon-tamer hung up, peach-wood amulets nailed to the doors and red streamers fixed above them to 'welcome the spring'.

When night fell, everyone stayed indoors to sacrifice to the family ancestors and to all the guardian spirits of the house (gods of the door, of the stove, of the bed, of the courtyard, of the earth). They were offered flowers, incense and choice foods, and were asked to bring peace and health in the coming year. From the imperial palace came a procession of people all dressed up and wearing masks, and carrying gilded staffs, silvered pikes, wooden swords and green, red, white, black and yellow flags. It included a whole crowd of gods. Chasing pestilences with the sound of drums and flutes, the cortège went out through the Gate of the Eastern Flowering, and made a tour of the Pond of Dragons. The name of this rite was 'the burying of pestilences'. Like the ceremonies which took place in private houses, the aim of it was to chase away the evil influences of a year that was drawing to its close and the virtues of which were entirely exhausted.[13]

The calm which reigned in the city on New Year's day and on the 2nd and 3rd of the 1st moon was in sharp contrast to the animation of the preceding days. There were very few people in the streets, and all the shops were closed. Only a few pedlars sold by lottery dishes of cooked food, pieces of cloth, combs, flowers and toys. In every home families gathered together to celebrate. Hardly anyone went out except to go and wish relations and friends a Good New Year. Both men and women, however poor they might be, put on new clothes.

At dawn on New Year's day, as soon as the bells at the palace had stopped ringing, the Emperor burnt incense and addressed prayers to Heaven asking for a good harvest in the coming year, while the court officials, dressed in ceremonial robes, stood at the door of the temple where the sovereign was officiating. Delegates from every prefecture in the empire and foreign ambassadors came to offer him gifts.[14]

On a date that was fixed according to the solar calendar, and which corresponded to February 5th—the day of 'the establishment of spring'—an official festival was celebrated by officials of the court and of the prefectures. It was an agrarian festival. The evening before, a procession of singing-girls and of men beating drums went to the prefectural building in search of the 'spring ox'. This was a small clay animal that had to be taken to the imperial palace at dawn the next day by the prefect and the prefectural officials and employees. Ministers and court officials received that day from the Emperor head-ornaments and little streamers made of gold and silver thread which they hung on their heads. Presents of the same kind, tokens of good wishes for the New Year, were exchanged between private individuals.[15]

And indeed, the year had not yet properly begun, and it was not until the 14th, 15th and 16th of the 1st moon, when the Feast of Lanterns took place, that the beginning of the new year was celebrated in a general overflowing of gaiety and excitement. During this period of three days and three nights, which fell at the time of the full moon, the townspeople ruined themselves by the amount they spent on food and drink. There was great competition in the matter of decorations and lanterns. The doorway of every house was draped with embroideries, bead-curtains and multi-coloured lamps. All the shops, the squares, even the narrowest lanes, were lit up. The finest lanterns came from Suchow. Circular in shape, and made of glass in five different colours, they had paintings on them of landscapes, people, flowers, bamboos, birds and furry animals. The biggest were between 40 and 50 inches in diameter. The lanterns brought by sea from Fuchow, very fine also, took second place. They were of white jade, and glittered. But there were many other kinds as well, of all shapes and sizes: lanterns which turned, actuated by a thin trickle of water, displaying a roundabout of figures and small objects; lanterns with pendants of many-coloured beads from the bottom of which hung gaudy ornaments made of feathers; lanterns in the shape of slender boats with dragon prows such as were to be seen on the lake at the water-festivals; lanterns in the form of an imperial sedan-chair; lanterns which turned in the heat, with horses and horsemen on them . . . Some lanterns, decorated in gold and silver, pearls and jade, were extremely costly.[16] From north to south, over a distance of more than eleven miles, the city, seen from the surrounding heights, was like an immense bonfire.

The festival itself had every appearance of a bacchanale. Troupes of dancers, all dressed up, and of acrobats and musicians went about the city. Each one had a name, and they could be counted by the dozen. They gave shows in rich people's houses. Twenty-four families who lived near the opening of Officials' Lane and in Su-family Lane gave marionette shows: the actors had new clothes and bead-embroidered caps and wore flowers in their hair. Their waists and limbs were slender as a woman's. In the big mansions, troupes of children and young musicians played pipes and zither or sang different kinds of songs. It was impossible to move about the streets on account of all the games and shows going on in the open. A shop here or a private house there would be so magnificently decorated with lanterns of all colours that passers-by would form a crowd in the street and block the way. Everywhere could be heard the sound of pipes and drums. The round lanterns that some people carried at the end of very long staves looked from a distance like stars dancing. Young gentlemen, shouting noisily, accompanied by beautiful girls, wandered about carrying lanterns. The women wore head-ornaments in the form of butterflies. They had flowers in their hair, and their dresses were most often white, because white was a colour suitable for walks in the moonlight. There were rascals who made huge cicadas out of white paper which they called 'night butterflies'. Others made pellets of jujubes and coal-dust which burned with a bright light. Drunkenness was general. And so, when the excitement had calmed down and passers-by had become fewer, before daybreak people with small lanterns in their hands went about the squares, the streets and the lanes looking for lost property: hairpins, head-ornaments, necklaces, etc. This custom was called 'sweeping the streets'.[17]

In the imperial palace, some of the pavilions were illuminated on the evening of the 15th of the 1st moon. A scaffolding was put up which was 150 feet high and was called the 'mountain of the mountain-carrying tortoise'. It had multi-coloured lanterns hung all over it, and in the centre other lanterns made of strips of jade and placed so as to form the four characters meaning 'Ten-thousand years (to our) August Emperor'. On top of the scaffolding were official musicians, at the bottom a platform where games and shows of all kinds were performed. The palace women and over a hundred little eunuchs wearing turbans danced in a circle like marionettes. When the show was over, troupes of dancers from the town were allowed in as well as

pedlars carefully chosen out by the prefect from among those
who had the best street-cries. These people, who had all until
this moment been crowding behind one of the great gates of the
palace precincts, hurled themselves inside the palace. The palace
women scrambled to buy the wares offered by the pedlars, at
prices very much higher than they normally were. Some of these
pedlars, it was said, had made a fortune in one evening in this
way.[18]

At Kaifeng, the Northern Sung capital, the court celebrations
for the Feast of Lanterns had been rather different. A big wooden
platform was erected in front of the Pavilion of the Proclamation
of Virtues. Paintings of immortals were placed on it and statues
in five colours of two very popular Buddhist deities—Manjusrî
on his lion and Samantabhadra on his elephant—and, by means
of a cunning device, a cascade of water spouted from each of
their ten fingers. Dragons were also made, with wicker bodies
and skin of transparent green cloth. A large number of lanterns
were hidden inside, and when the contortions of these beasts
borne by invisible dancers were seen from a distance, they seemed
like real dragons flying through the air. The Emperor mounted
a pavilion in order to admire the lanterns, and near him was a
pole surmounted by the inscription: 'The Emperor shares his
pleasures with his people' (a phrase taken from a Confucian
classic), while all the spectators cried: 'Ten-thousand years!
Ten-thousand years!'[19]

On the first day of the 2nd moon it was customary for people
to give each other little green bags filled with cereal grains and
seeds of melons and other fruits. This was a way of wishing one's
friends many descendants. In the palace the women of the harem
had a battle of herbs. Officials presented works on agriculture to
the Emperor.[20]

The 8th of the 2nd moon was the anniversary of the birth of a
divinity who was the patron of numerous guilds. Shoemakers,
jewellers and hat manufacturers exhibited their chefs-d'oeuvre.[21]
Each guild organized a procession with standards and drums,
and engaged troupes of musicians and dancers. A crowd of sightseers jostled on the shores of the lake and on the dyke that
crossed the western part of the lake from north to south. For this
was the day for the jousts of the dragon-boats. There were six of

them, splendidly fitted out, decorated with flowers and brightly coloured flags. Musicians on board beat drums and gongs and played the flute. The boats faced each other in pairs, while men with pikes tried to make their opposite numbers fall into the water. Right until evening the hills and shores round the lake were thronged with sightseers. That was a day when poor men borrowed money if need be to spend on drinks and amusements, and they came with their wives and children. No one went home before getting drunk. 'This,' says one author, 'has always been the custom in this part of the country'.[22]

On the 15th there was a festival of flowers that was special to Hangchow. All the townspeople went to the gardens outside the western ramparts and in the southern suburbs to admire the rare trees and flowers there. Certain peach-trees in a garden to the south, then in full flower, were held to be the most beautiful. The prefect and the sub-prefects with all their staff had all the old men brought out to the suburbs and gave them a banquet washed down with rice-wine. Speeches were made encouraging agricultural work and weaving, and lauding the virtues of zeal and economy.

Meanwhile, in one of the biggest Taoist temples of the town there was a gathering in honour of the anniversary of the birth of Lao-tzu, the Taoist saint. Thousands of coloured lamps were lit beside his altar, and prayers said to the god asking him to give happiness to the people. The faithful from all classes came in crowds to make their devotions, a stick of incense in their hands. Grand ceremonies were also held in the Buddhist monasteries, for the 15th of the 2nd moon is the day of the entry into nirvana of the Buddha Sakyamuni. This anniversary was fêted with a profusion of streamers, flowers and fruits. The monks exhibited all their artistic treasures—calligraphy, paintings and objects of value. There was an incessant throng of visitors all day long.[23]

The most important series of festivities after the sacrifices to the household gods and the banquets at New Year, and after the excitement and frolics of the Feast of Lanterns on the 14th, 15th and 16th of the 1st moon, was the Festival of the Dead, preceded by the festival of new fire. It was fixed on the 105th day after the winter solstice, fifteen days after the spring equinox, that is to say, about April 5th. It was the only popular festival to have its date fixed according to the solar calendar. The three days preceding it were called the 'cold food' festival. All fires were extinguished, and it was only on the third day, about April 4th, that it was permitted to rekindle them. The moment came when, at the gate of one of the pavilions in the imperial palace, an official had the appointed task of producing fire by boring willow-wood with a drill. The flame, endowed with all the virtues of new fire, was used to light a large number of torches which court officials handed from one to another. The desire for renewal and purification to which this rite bears witness was also expressed in another custom: on the first day of the 'cold blood' festival, everyone fixed branches of willow above their doors, for the willow, like the peach-tree and various other plants, was supposed to keep away pestilences. All the town was suddenly full of greenery.[24]

Five days earlier the women of the imperial harem had gone to the Palace of the Restoration of Sung and to the tombs of the imperial family to place offerings. Their attendant women wore robes of purple silk, a triangular fichu, and bands of green material wound round the calves.[25]

A few days before the Festival of the Dead the new wine was celebrated. This festival was organized by the staff of the storehouses for alcoholic licquor. Courtesans and prostitutes took part in it and were classed into four categories. Their clothes and ornaments varied according to which group they belonged to. Even the poorest among them were obliged, on penalty of a fine. to get themselves some finery for the occasion, even if it meant borrowing it. Troupes of dancers and musicians were hired, and a picturesque procession went through the city. It was headed by huge banners nearly ten yards long on enormous poles each carried by four or five men. Then came drums and musicians, men in pairs carrying heavy jars of rice-wine, eight persons disguised as Taoist Immortals, and representatives of the guilds: sellers of pet fish, of sweet cakes, of noodles, of cooked food, of dwarf trees, money-changers, fishermen, hunters, etc. Groups of little boys and girls followed them, with five-stringed guitars in their hands. The procession, with men on horseback bringing up the rear, made its way to the prefecture, where the participants received from the authorities pieces of cloth, copper coins, banknotes and silver cups.[26]

On the day of the Festival of the Dead the whole population—

officials, aristocrats, merchants, common people—made a general exit from the city to gather round the lake and on the surrounding hills. There was great congestion at all the gates of the city. Some people went to the graves of their close kin, swept them, burnt sticks of incense over them, and placed offerings of food; others picnicked in the gardens at the edge of the lake to the west of the ramparts and in the southern suburbs; others again hired boats on the lake which were painted in bright colours and decorated with fine carvings, and watched the dragon-bout jousts. All stayed until nightfall to enjoy the beauty of the scenery: reflections of pink-flushed clouds on the lake, a moon that seemed to be hanging from the willow branches. Then everyone returned to the city, men of the upper classes on horseback, astride magnificent saddles, the ladies in carry-chairs, and the common people on foot.[27]

On the 28th of the 3rd moon the anniversary of the birth of 'the Holy Emperor of the Eastern Infernal Regions' was fêted in all the cities of south-east China. He was the god of destiny, and fixed the lot of every individual. Incense was offered to him, and lamps lit on his altar in a temple specially constructed for the occasion. In Hangchow itself, five temples of this kind were put up at this time in various parts of the city.[28]

The 8th of the 4th moon was the anniversary of the birth of the Buddha Sakyamuni. The faithful crowded round the shores of the lake and hired boats in order to go out on to the lake and set free into its waters 'a myriad furred, feathered and scaly animals' which they had bought alive in the markets. This rite was supposed to bestow religious merit upon those who performed it. The ceremony of bathing the statues took place in Buddhist monasteries on this day. The monks placed bronze statues on trays, poured sugared water over them, and decked them with flowers; then, tray in hand, they went round the houses of wealthy families and, in exchange for alms given them, sprinkled a spoonful of holy water on the ground.[29]

The festival of the 5th of the 5th moon was the third big festival of the year. The day on which it was held was supposed to be a particularly unlucky one. It was considered to be of ill omen if an official got appointed on the 5th of the 5th moon, and to be inadvisable to climb on to roofs or to hang out mats and bedding; and births taking place on this day were viewed with disfavour. It was the day when pestilences and evil spirits were most to be feared, the day of the malevolent animals: wasp, toad, snake, scorpion and centipede. It was therefore advisable to be provided with lucky charms. At the imperial palace, images were made from rushes and herbs representing a Taoist deity, the 'Celestial Master', taming a tiger, as well as images of insects and small animals. The townspeople gave each other amulets which they wore hung from the girdle. They bought branches of peach, willow and pomegranate, bunches of mallow, cakes, fruits and papers in the five colours (green, red, white, black and yellow) as a protection against epidemics (this was a particularly good day for the preparation of medicinal drugs). They hung above their doors tiger-heads made of artemisia and other herbs, and images of an animal deity called Pai Tse. Long ago a mythical emperor had met this beast on one of the holy mountains of China, and had learnt from it all about the demons and spirits of heaven and earth, and also been instructed how to design a talisman which protected against pestilences.

The festival was accompanied by outings on the lake, music and song. There was a parade of dragon-boats on the lake, and in the evening they were illuminated, and everyone came out to see them.[30]

On August 7th, the day of the 'establishment of autumn', an acacia was ceremonially planted in one of the courtyards of the imperial palace. A high official who had assisted in the planting then announced to the Emperor: 'Autumn has arrived', and at this juncture it was arranged that a few leaves should fall from the tree.[31]

On the evening of the 7th of the 7th moon, which was the festival of weaving, all children, from all classes of society, put on new clothes. Wealthy people gave banquets in their gardens. Indoors, pedestal tables with perfume burning on them and tables laden with fruits and rice-wines were set about for the refreshment of the guests. When night had fallen the ladies had to look at the moon and watch for the stars of the Weaving-girl and the Cowherd, two stars separated by the Milky Way which were supposed to have a once-yearly meeting on this evening. There was also a custom which ladies who wanted to become skilful embroidresses sometimes followed: they put spiders in little gold or silver boxes, and in the morning looked to see what the little creatures had woven.[32]

On the 15th of the 7th moon great Buddhist ceremonies were held in the monasteries in honour of the dead, and for the redemption of their sins, with a profusion of incense and flowers. The laity visited the graves of their close kin, swept them, and left offerings. On the markets, very busy at this time, products of the season were sold: melons, peaches, pears, jujubes, and poultry of all kinds.[33]

The mid-autumn festival, on the 15th of the 8th moon, was the festival of the moon and of women. In the moon, devoured each month by a black toad, there was a rabbit who pounded an elixir of long life at the foot of an acacia tree, the leaves and bark of which were used in the preparation of the drug. Another legend had it that it was not a rabbit, but a three-legged toad that inhabited the moon; according to yet another, there was a palace there where the queen of the moon and her attendants lived, all of an extraordinary beauty. On the evening of the 15th of the 8th month (the full moon of September), the moon is at its most brilliant. 'Moon cakes' were made, and fruit with pips was eaten symbolic of having many children. Rich people went up on to the upper storeys of their pavilions and summer-houses to admire the moonlight and drink rice-wine while listening to solos on the zither. The common people, down to the poorest, bought rice-wine, even if it meant pawning their clothes. The city was full of merry-makers that night, and the shops on the Imperial Way stayed open later than usual.[34]

One of the favourite spectacles enjoyed by the people of Hang-chow was the tidal bore which occurs where the Che river enters the estuary. In the 8th moon, during the month of September and especially about the time of the full moon, this phenomenon reached its peak of violence at the point of the river near where Hangchow was situated. The roar and the height of the waves brought a crowd of sightseers. Some days before the full moon, naval combats were held on the river, and sightseers began to appear from the 11th onwards. On the 16th, 17th and 18th almost the entire population crowded along the banks outside the eastern ramparts, and there were a great many horses and carts. All houses of more than one storey along a distance of five miles were hired by members of the imperial family and by high officials of the palace. Some poor devils, it seems, used to try at these times to swim across the river through the tremendously strong currents, holding standards of many colours in their hand. Such acts of bravado were looked upon with great disfavour by the government authorities. 'These people,' writes a governor of the city in about 1066, 'hurl a body bequeathed to them by their father and mother [and which they have no rights over] into the bottomless depths where fish and dragons live, and vie with each other in bravery. Many get drowned, and their souls are destined to remain drowned for ever. It is forbidden to soldiers and to the common people, under penalty of severe punishment, to venture into the waters of the Che river and at the time of the tidal bore.' However all prohibitions remained ineffective.[35] On September 29, 1132, there was a great crowd on the eastern ramparts. As a safety measure, a wooden parapet had been erected along the banks of the river, which were eighteen feet high, and many people had perched on it so as to see better. But at the moment of the bore the sudden rush of water, whipped up by an unexpected gust of wind, carried away the barrier as if it were a straw. Several hundred sightseers were drowned.

The 9th of the 9th moon was the festival of chrysanthemums at Hangchow. Nearly eighty different varieties were grown in the neighbourhood. Everyone bought them on that day and rooms in the taverns were transformed into bowers of chrysanthemums. The townspeople went picnicking on the hillsides, taking with them pomegranates, chestnuts, apricots, pineapples, and pies and cakes decorated with little lions or little figures made of flour scented with musk. On the markets, pork pies, mutton pies and duck pies were sold which had little flags of bright colours on them. This was the day when petals of chrysanthemum or of dogwood were floated on cups of wine; the former were said to prolong life and the latter to chase away evil influences.

During the last ten-day period of the 9th moon, mourning garments, old shoes, mats, and paper hats were sold in the city in preparation for the first day of the 10th moon, when these things were burnt in honour of the dead.[36]

There were few festivities during the 10th and 11th moons, except at the imperial palace, where the 'establishment of winter' was celebrated about November 7th, and the winter solstice about December 21st.

Certain festivals, such as the one on the 3rd of the 3rd moon, an important one in other regions of China, particularly in Szechwan, were almost entirely disregarded in Hangchow. On the other hand, the official ceremonies held at the palace and in certain large temples situated in the centre of the city were far more numerous and more elaborate than the foregoing account, necessarily limited to essential features, suggests. But it would be tiresome to go into details about these rites, which in any case only concerned court circles.[37]

RELIGION

1. *General Concepts*
Nothing could be more diversified than the religious aspects of Chinese life in the thirteenth century. Yet at the risk of over-simplification, an attempt must first and foremost be made to define the spirit which animated religious life as a whole. It must at once be admitted that it contained nothing in the nature of what we Western people of today would call religious sentiment. That is to say, that any kind of dialogue between Man and God, or mystical outpourings addressed to a personal deity, are entirely foreign to it. In so far as its specifically Chinese character is concerned, religious life seems to have been dominated by a sort of latent and unexpressed obsession: that of the possibility of cosmic disorder. That the seas might take the place of the mountains, that the seasons might no longer follow their natural sequence, that Heaven and Earth might be confounded—these were the kind of apocalyptically unnatural happenings that the ceremonies of the various cults were designed to avert.

The aim of most religious acts was either to regulate Space, to keep it literally in place—and the tutelary mountains, covered by sanctuaries both official and private, saw to this; or to regulate Time, inaugurate it, renew it—and the annual festivals helped to ensure its constant renewal; because of them, the world was never more than one year old. From any point throughout the whole of nature—mountains, hills, rivers, streams, rocks and trees—emanations could come forth which might be good or bad, propitious or unpropitious. The main purposes of ancestral graves and of the sanctuaries dedicated to ancestors, to deified historical personages, and to the innumerable deities borrowed from the Buddhist or the Taoist pantheons, seems to have been to provide a focus for good influences that would be of benefit to man, while in themselves they gave rise to beneficent emanations. The natural and the supernatural intermingled.

Each deity had a specific region which it protected: such-and-such a town, district, village or house; and its cult was a guarantee against ills of all kinds that might sweep down upon humankind: wars, floods, droughts, epidemics, fires . . . The official cult performed by the Emperor and the ordinary family cult were essentially the same. A grave in the right situation might have just as fortunate an effect on the destinies of a family as the judicious choice of a holy mountain might have on a whole region of the empire. But there were also gods for special purposes. They were called upon for protection against this or that particular scourge, or in the hope of making a fortune, or of having male descendants, or of succeeding in the official examinations . . . It was also possible to get useful information from the gods of certain sanctuaries. Candidates for the examinations slept in temples so as to have premonitory dreams; judges sometimes did the same when they felt the need for divine inspiration in order to discover who the guilty party was.

But it was local powers and local gods that were the main concern, and the most delicate problem of all was that of finding the most propitious spot for erecting a sanctuary. For any change made in the natural order of things might have grave consequences and demanded the taking of precautions. No house, no wall of a town, no temple was ever built, no grave dug, without some sort of certitude that such an act would have nothing but lucky effects. In order to choose such spots, specialists were consulted—soothsayers known as 'geomancers', who made use of the compass and of complicated tables of correspondences, and possibly of their flair as well. However, even when every precaution had been taken, the result sometimes fell short of perfection. Thus, at Ch'eng-tu, where the marking-out of the city walls had been done in accordance with indications given by the ancient method of divination by means of the shell of a tortoise, topography had also had to be taken into account. So, since the ramparts had been built on a steep hill, it was thought advisable to erect a pavilion 90 feet high 'in order to fix the North and the South'.[38] The excavation of tombs, because it disturbed nature and death, was considered to be a particularly sacrilegious act. One man who had made a habit of excavating ancient tombs in order to find antique objects (and let us remember that antiques were all the rage in the Sung period) lost his memory in his old age. He could no longer recognize even the simplest written characters.[39]

The divine was so little personalized, so *natural* as it were, that religious beliefs and practices seemed to express a lay conception of the world rather than that duality between the sacred and the profane that is so familiar to us and that seems to us essential to all religion. To know the auspicious seasons, days, orientations, places, colours, numbers and names—this was the secret for performing all actions that impinged upon the supernatural, for all things in the universe were in correspondence with each other. Portents already *were* the future, names called forth the realities they invoked. Great trouble was taken to choose propitious names and to avoid unpropitious ones. To the south of Chiu-chiang, on the shores of Lake P'u-yang, there was a mountain called the 'Peak of the Twin Swords'. The people of that region thought that the name was unlucky and that this was why the region was ravaged by wars every two hundred years. For a long time, says an author in 1177, the old men of the town had hoped that the name might be changed, but they had not been able to decide on their choice of a new one.[40] There was no distinction made between the natural or supernatural powers inherent in things and creatures, and the things and creatures themselves. Nothing would be more absurd than to describe the religious thought of the Chinese by the term 'animism'.

These were the main features of religious life in general; but they do not provide a complete picture, for since the beginning of the Christian era China had gradually become permeated by notions of moral responsibility, compassion, and a saviour god. These ideas came from the West, either by sea, or via the caravans of Central Asia. However, this contribution of new ideas made no vital change in the Chinese genius. It became amalgamated without difficulty with autochthonous practices and

beliefs: Buddhism, the great religion responsible for this enrichment, had to adapt itself to the exigencies of the Chinese way of
thinking.

Another qualification should be added to the general indications which have been given. Although the more widely practised forms of religion were limited to the cult of local deities who
ensured the prosperity of certain defined localities, there also
existed among the people sects and secret societies animated by
revolutionary and messianic hopes. These provided an aspect of
religious life in China which was outside the main tradition, and
which was 'Dionysic' and prophetic. Fasting, trance and ecstasy
were employed as a direct means of communication with the
divine. It would be wrong to suppose that the most violent and
extreme forms of religious sentiment were unknown. It all
depended on the nature of the social surroundings and on local
loyalties. For this reason it is important to distinguish between
the official cult and the various popular cults, and between the
forms taken by religion among the upper classes and those among
the common people.

2. *The Official Cult*
The official cult as observed by the Emperor, who was its principal officiant, could be described as Confucianist in so far as it
was inspired by traditional conceptions peculiar to the ruling
class. It was addressed to Heaven, Earth, and the imperial ancestors. Its purpose was to ensure the continuity of the dynasty, to
regulate Time and Space, and to give the world prosperity and
peace. In addition to the annual rites which were fixed according
to the solar calendar (the festivals for the solstices and for the
beginning of the seasons), there were also special ceremonies,
such as announcements made in the Supreme Temple (for
example, of the inauguration of a new reign-period, of the death
of a member of the imperial family, or of a public calamity), and
sacrifices to Heaven and Earth on the altar in the southern
suburbs.

One example will suffice to illustrate the characteristic features
of the cult: its ritualism, the complexity of its regulations (numbers, colours, orientations, dates, etc. were all determined with
respect to their symbolic meaning by specialists in ritual), and
the ostentation of its ceremonies. The rites of the imperial cult

were first and foremost grandiose spectacles, although these spectacles did not exclude a certain amount of religious emotion. All these traits will emerge from a description of one of the most important rites of the imperial cult—that of the sacrifices on the altar in the southern suburbs.

This altar was situated about fifteen hundred yards outside the Great Processional Gate on the southern ramparts. Its shape and dimensions had remained unaltered for several centuries. About thirty feet high, it was approached by a stairway of seventy-two steps in nine groups of eight, and was on four different levels, not including the top platform. Twelve steps led to this topmost level, which was twenty-one yards wide. On this platform there was a place for libations to the Emperor-on-High (Heaven) and two places for libations to the August Earth, as well as places for offerings made to the first emperors of the dynasty. Sixteen niches in the uppermost of the altar's four levels were used for the sacrifices to the mythical emperors of the five colours, to the planets, and to the 360 stars.[41]

It was at this altar that the Emperor performed the ordinary rites such as those on the day of the beginning of spring, which fell about February 5th, or at the winter solstice, or when prayers were made for rain in times of drought. But there was also a special ceremony held there every three years. The imperial decree announcing the date fixed for it was issued on the first day of the year, and it was held either at the winter solstice of that year, or on the first day of the following year. A day in the 5th or 6th moon was chosen on which orders were given to the official services concerned to start preparing the altar and the lustration halls. These were constructions which had a framework of wood and bamboo covered over with matting and screened with green hangings. Soldiers were given the task of levelling the surface of the Imperial Way on the stretch leading from the Supreme Temple (the temple of the imperial ancestors) north of the palace to the altar in the southern suburbs, and then covering it with fine sand. A large temporary building was erected in front of the Supreme Temple in which to place the ceremonial chariot of the Emperor; the townspeople were allowed to come and see it.

During the month before the sacrifices, in the 12th or at the end of the 11th moon, rehearsals of the ceremony were held almost every day. Three days before it, the Emperor was bidden to purify himself by fasting in the 'Hall of Great Fame'. For this he donned the 'hat of communication with Heaven', a tunic of fine silk, and various pendants. The following day, wearing a different kind of hat, he visited the 'Hall of Bright Holiness', and returned from there to the Supreme Temple and then spent the night in one of the lustration halls. At the fourth beat of the drum, just before dawn, he donned his ceremonial headgear and went to sacrifice to his ancestors. During the night, soldiers provided with torches and bearing the imperial insignia were posted on both sides of the great avenue along the whole length of the Emperor's route from the Supreme Temple right to the altar for the sacrifices to Heaven. There were so many torches that it was like daylight. High officials, members of the imperial family and of wealthy and titled families were crowded in serried ranks.

When the Emperor mounted his chariot, all lights except those lining the route were extinguished. The imperial procession, led by tame elephants, now came out through the Great Processional Gate and made its way to the altar, near which a host of standards and flags flew. The sound of the imperial guards shouting orders to each other could be heard, and the flicker of torches could be seen against the daybreak. The earth shook with the beat of drums and the solemn sound of trumpets as an immense and silent crowd stood waiting on the open space at the foot of the altar. The court musicians played the ritual music. The Emperor mounted the altar steps, which were covered with yellow gauze (yellow being the colour of the centre and of sovereignty) and sprinkled with pieces of camphor. A victim was sacrificed on the small adjacent altar to the God of the Soil, and then the Emperor, having reached the topmost platform of the altar for the sacrifices to Heaven, offered libations to Heaven, to the August Earth, and finally to his ancestors. To the last, he presented jade tablets along with the ritual wine. He read aloud what was written on these sacred tablets, which were afterwards deposited in the interior of the altar. Then he drank the 'wine of happiness', and, when all was over, he made his way to the buildings that had been erected near the altar in order to change his robes. The officials offered their congratulations. Finally he mounted a ceremonial chariot, different from the one which had brought him to the sacrificial altar. A crowd of horsemen and of people on foot, made up of people from all ranks in society, followed the procession as far as the imperial palace.[42]

This example shows how the official cult was at the same time formalistic in detail and spectacular in its general manifestation. It was a cult which was ideally suited to the requirements of the scholar-officials, who traditionally had always attached great importance to the rites, to their symbolic significance, their religious effects, and resulting psychological repercussions. They were people such as Montaigne described as being 'plus cérémonieux que dévotieux' (ceremonious rather than devout). Indeed, religion, in the eyes of the scholars, had nothing to do with satisfying the mystical leanings of individuals; its aim was to ensure the preservation of a universal order which was nothing other than the counterpart, on the supernatural level, of the political order imposed upon the world by the Emperor and his officials. This accounted for the frequent hostility on the part of the scholars towards any form of religious sentiment which deviated from what they considered to be the norm. It also accounted for the need constantly felt by the rulers to regulate all aspects of the religious life of the empire and integrate them into the framework of the official religion. The chief holy places in the provinces were carefully graded and inscribed on the list of official sacrifices below the altars and temples of the capital where the most important ceremonies of the imperial cult were performed. This was an attempt on the part of the central power to annexe to itself the power exercised by local religious centres and at the same time to maintain control over the big popular cults.

The order of importance was as follows: the altar for the sacrifices to Heaven in the southern suburbs, the temple of the imperial ancestors, the imperial god-of-the-soil altar and the altar to Prince Millet, regional deities (sacred mountains, seas and lakes), ancient Sages and deified heroes. All these deities received official titles from the Emperor, and the determination of their names, which were graded not only according to the terms employed, but also to the number of written characters of which they were composed, was one of the sovereign's most important tasks. Thus, the god of the ramparts, a popular deity, received official offerings in the event of droughts, floods and epidemics. At Hangchow, this god had his temple on one of the hills to the south of the city. He was known as 'Eternal Solidity', but had also received from the Emperor a longer and more pompous title.

This formalistic and 'administrative' conception of religion was not far from being the equivalent of a complete lack of religious belief. At least a compromise could easily be arrived at between the two, and indeed there existed a rationalist tradition among the scholars which went very far back, one of its earliest representatives being Hsün-tzu, in the third century B.C. 'If,' said this unbelieving philosopher, 'people pray for rain and get rain, why is this? I answer: There is no reason for it. If people do not pray for rain, it will nevertheless rain.'[43] But it may be noted that it was usually popular superstitions for which the scholar-officials reserved their ironical contempt. Some who were over-zealous as administrators even went to the length of demolishing local sanctuaries and cutting down sacred trees. But most of them had the sense to abstain from sacrilege of this kind for fear of the peasants' reactions.

The rationalism of the scholars was tempered with tolerance, and repressive measures were usually only directed against secret societies and against cults with political implications which threatened to be serious. As for Buddhism, which formerly, because of its influence and wealth, had aroused strong anti-clerical feelings in T'ang times and earlier, it still drew sarcastic remarks from the scholars in Sung times. Their hostility had no doubt lost some of its violence along with the decline in political and economic power of the Buddhist communities, but the intellectual antipathy remained, and their disapproval had even become accentuated on the ideological plane. As many an anecdote testifies, it was the thing, in certain upper-class circles, to be anti-Buddhist. A guest of the celebrated eleventh-century writer Ou-yang Hsiu, having just learnt that one of the children in the family was called Brother Monk, expressed his astonishment. 'How,' he said jokingly to the great scholar, 'how could you have given such a name to your son, you whose feelings about Buddhism are so well known?' — 'But,' replied the other, laughing, 'is it not customary in order to protect children as they grow up [i.e. to keep off the evil eye] to give them childhood names that are despicable, such as dog, sheep, horse?'[44]

Sometimes the scoffing took a turn of arguing the matter out.

'After the death of a near relation,' says one author, 'the Buddhist laity hold funeral services every seven days until the forty-ninth day after the death. They believe that if they act in this way, the sins of the deceased will be abolished, and that if they did not, the dead would go to hell and suffer horrible tortures. Now, after death, the body decays and the spirit dissipates in the air. How, then, can the dead suffer tortures?' 'If there is neither paradise nor hell,' says another, 'then that is that. If paradise exists, then it is to be expected that good people will be re-born there. If hells exist, it is only just that bad people should be thrown into them. It therefore follows that to address prayers to the Buddha on behalf of one's deceased parents is to regard one's father and mother as scoundrels and good-for-nothings.'⁴⁵

This opposition to Buddhism on the part of the scholars was for the most part merely a matter of individual belief. In actual fact, the official cult did not scorn appealing occasionally to Buddhist deities for their support. If, from our point of view, this appears illogical, that is only because the religious sphere in the West is divided into separate doctrines with well-defined tenets and beliefs. In China, however, differences in doctrine were never of any importance. The only religious differences were differences of social context: official cult, family religion, local, regional or village cults, or professional ones in the case of the guilds; and in all these contexts, doctrine played a subordinate rôle.

The Buddhist and Taoist communities, which were in command of wealth derived from offerings and from the grants bestowed on monasteries in recognition of their official status, were commanded by the court to hold religious services on behalf of the Emperor, his ancestors, his close kin and his dynasty. 'In this vast empire' wrote, in 1326, the bishop of Zaytun (Ch'üan-chou), André de Pérouse, 'where there are people of all nations under heaven and of all sects, every single person is authorized to live according to his own sect, for they are imbued with the idea, or rather, the error, that everyone can find salvation according to his own sect.'⁴⁶ This general indifference towards doctrine was stronger still in the cults and beliefs of the people, because often a multitude of heterogeneous elements were quite indistinguishably intermingled in them.

3. *Family Cults*

The purpose of the ancestral cult was to create an intimate link between deceased parents—and in particular the most important among them, such as heads of clans and of lineages—and the events of family life such as New Year festivals, births, marriages, etc. Associated with this cult was the idea of a destiny and an individuality belonging to each family. It was a cult common to all classes of society, but which tended to become more important among families with illustrious forbears, and we have seen how that of the imperial ancestors, because of its political significance, occupied an important place in the official cult. The Emperor had his ancestral temple, the great families sanctuaries of a more modest nature, and ordinary people contented themselves with setting up a little altar in the main room of their house. On the ancestral altars were placed the tablets bearing the names of deceased parents, in which the ancestral spirits were supposed to reside. An effort was made to capture and fix these spirits at the moment of death, when, to give life to the tablets, marks were made on them with little spots of sacrificial blood, signifying the eyes and ears of the deceased. But the deceased were also still present in their graves, and at the Festival of the Dead on the 15th of the 7th moon (April 5th), and on the 1st of the 10th moon, pious kinsmen of all who had not been cremated came to sweep and water the graves of their close kin.

But the ancestors were not the only household deities. The gods of the door, of the hearth, of the bed, of the courtyard, of the well, of the earth, each received small offerings at New Year. The images of the door gods were renewed, and the god of the hearth was treated with greater respect than usual before making his journey to report in Heaven on the conduct of each member of the family. Each of these household gods had certain definite functions—for instance, the god of the bed was responsible for the fecundity of the couple—and appeal was made to them during the course of the year if need be. They were by no means all-powerful gods (for that matter, no Chinese gods were); on the contrary, they were obliging and not at all vindictive, and could be spoken to on equal terms. As well as these, there were other gods, both Chinese and Buddhist, that could be invoked on the many occasions when petty troubles or distressing events came to disturb the happiness or the tranquillity of the family: wives might be sterile, or, contrary to the wishes of the family, be unable to give birth to anything but girls; confinements were sometimes difficult; daughters of the house clumsy and unable to sew or embroider; children sickly; illness, poverty or death might visit the house. The gods to whom the family presented their offerings had no other function but to protect them against these various misfortunes.

4. *Popular Cults and Beliefs*
The household gods upon which the happiness of each family depended were not radically different from the protective deities of urban and rural communities. With them also the essential characteristics of the cult was that it was local and practised for the benefit of a group. Popular deities were innumerable: ancient sages, great poets, warrior heroes, gods with names borrowed from the Taoist pantheon, illustrious monks, great Buddhist saints and deities, gods of the soil and gods of the ramparts were worshipped in a multitude of sanctuaries and temples. Their powers even merged with those emanating from the earth and from the waters. There were certain trees, certain rocks, rivers and mountains that were supposed to have an influence on the course of the seasons, and the people also built sanctuaries in honour of these nature deities.

Sometimes local communities performed rites which were not part of an organized cult. In one place, a rock of peculiar form might be ceremonially whipped at times of prolonged rain or drought; in another, women's worn-out shoes and dead pigs might be thrown into a deep pool when its presiding spirit, a divine dragon, refused to put an end to a period of drought.[47] On the other hand, the most important deities had their feast-days which, in the country, were at the same time days when fairs were held. Theatrical representations with clowns, jugglers and musicians were held in their honour. Requests for good harvest were addressed to them, and they were appealed to, on other days of the year, when a calamity threatened the village or the district: rains or dry weather which endangered the crops, floods, epidemics, etc. This is the first aspect of popular religion that strikes one: the extraordinary proliferation of gods.

But there are other and less well-known aspects that merit attention. Local gods were sometimes associated with spiritualistic practices. Mediums, visionaries and prophets in fact abounded among the people. Holiness and the gift of prophecy were usually incarnated in the most contemptible of creatures. Madmen, idiots, beggars in rags or poverty-stricken pedlars might be the incarnation of Chinese or Buddhist deities. Others claimed at least to be inspired by the gods and could evoke the souls of the illustrious dead and predict the future by means of riddles. Not only the common people, but sometimes also people from the upper classes and even certain emperors (for the central power liked to be surrounded with mystery and did not neglect magical aid) had faith in the ravings of such visionaries. One of them, a man called Sun the fishmonger, was summoned to the court in 1125, just before the barbarian invasion, and was housed in one of the imperial apartments. One day, the Emperor, emerging tired and starving with hunger from a long ceremony, saw Sun the fishmonger seated in the doorway of a small room with a steamed pancake held in his hand. 'Have a bite,' said the prophet, putting his pancake under the Emperor's nose. Then, seeing a look of incomprehension on the face of his illustrious interlocutor: 'A day will come when you will be glad to have even a pancake like this'. The following year the barbarians took the capital by storm and led the Emperor and his suite into captivity in the Manchurian desert.[48]

However, mediums and prophets had the opportunity of employing their gifts more efficaciously within the framework of the secret societies. The state of trance could then become collective, aided by under-nourishment, alcohol, ecstatic dances, sexual practices of a magical nature, or fasts which sometimes reached a pitch of self-mutilation.

As might be expected, we are very ignorant about these secret societies. But when the government succeeded in exterminating one of them, it sometimes happened that contemporaries left some account of its organization and practices. Thus an author of the first half of the twelfth century gives us fairly precise information about a secret society of Manichean inspiration known as the Demon Worshippers that was very popular at that period.[49] The new religion arose in Fukien and spread rapidly to the prefecture of Wen-chou and along the coast of southern Chekiang, and finally affected the whole province as far as the Yangtze. The sect, directed by an individual known as the

Demon King with the aid of two assessors called the Demon Father and the Demon Mother, practised a kind of communism of ownership. New adepts were given free lodging and food, but they had to swear terrible oaths not to reveal the names of their associates and not to violate the interdicts of their sect. Contrary to the actual practices of Buddhists, the prohibitions against meat and alcohol were strictly observed, and violation of them entailed the confiscation of the property of the guilty person, half of which was assigned to those who had denounced him, and half to the officials set up by the sect in the districts where the rebellion had succeeded in ousting the imperial administrators.

Here is an instance which demonstrates the passionate ferocity with which the Demon Worshippers adhered to the tenets of their society. The patron saint of the sect had the name of Chang Chiao.[50] Hence the word *chiao*, which means 'horn', was taboo for the faithful, and nothing, not even the most frightful tortures, would have made it escape their lips. So the prefect of T'ai-chou, in Chekiang, owing to the fact that he knew about this taboo, was able to identify the Demon Worshippers in this manner: on showing them a ram's horn, he could not get them to say the forbidden word. The sect proscribed the worship of all Chinese and Buddhist deities as well as the ancestral cult, and the only gods they recognized were the sun and the moon, which they considered to be 'true Buddhas'. Their funeral ceremonies were accompanied by a curious custom. On each side of the corpse, which was dressed and capped according to the rites customary throughout China, squatted two members of the society. 'Will you have a cap in the next world?' says one. 'No,' says the other, upon which they remove the corpse's headgear. They continue in this way until the corpse is completely naked. 'What will you have in the other world?' then say the two cronies. 'You will have the sheath of a foetus,' and they wrap it up in a sack of coarse cloth. This economical funeral fashion, together with the prohibitions against meat and alcohol and against holding banquets, provided, in the opinion of members of the sect, an excellent way of getting rich.

Like Buddhism, the new religion proclaimed that life was nothing but suffering, but they maintained that death itself brought final liberation. Hence to slay one's heretical neighbour was to ensure his salvation, and those members of the sect who had many murders to their credit had some chance of becoming Buddhas.

The regular cults with their public ceremonies, and the secret societies with their doctrines of personal salvation combined with messianic revolutionary tendencies, represented two sharply distinct and almost contradictory aspects of the religious life of the people. But this by no means exhausts the question of popular beliefs. For while the deities of the local sanctuaries were, for the ordinary person, the powers, either natural or but feebly personified, that ruled over their world, which was restricted to the locality and the group living in it, on another level, no longer that of collective practices but of traditional beliefs, the whole universe was peopled by spirits, genies, demons and ghosts.

Some of these were fantastic creatures in animal or human form, others were dogs, pigs, or foxes changed into men or sometimes into women of extraordinary beauty, others again were simply ghosts who had not received offerings or whose murder had not been avenged. How were unwelcome visitors such as these to be got rid of? The sound of firecrackers, drums and gongs chased them away. One could also strike them with a stick or a sword when one saw them. They then either regained their original form or disappeared. Willow branches or peach branches or artemisia scared away demons and pestilences. A high official passing through a market town in Szechwan at the time of the weaving of hemp noted in his travel diary that the inhabitants burnt artemisia in front of their doors in order to keep away evil influences.[51] Other methods using symbols were found effective: designs of ramparts and moats, shields and halberds, designs using magic written characters. Another method advised was to place objects which demons disliked in their path—for example, white jade, for demons, being female, like the dark and have a horror of the colour white. Conversely, there were certain acts that should be avoided. For instance, in Ch'eng-tu, in Szechwan, the drum was no longer beaten to sound the evening hours during the Sung period, because formerly it was at these hours that beheadings had taken place, and to sound the hours would awake the malevolent ghosts of the criminals whose bodies had been buried in the polo field.[52]

All evil spirits who were chased away or identified by magic means usually only haunted either families or individuals. They formed a class of supernatural beings of an entirely different nature from that of the deities of the temples and local sanctuaries. Sorcerers, Taoist monks, and sometimes Buddhist monks, were the people who could exorcise these demons, either because of their knowledge of efficacious formulae, or because of the power derived from their religion.

Numerous anecdotes testify to the very widespread belief in a world of the dead and in the existence of an infernal court of justice presided over by the king of the lower regions. Some of the judges in this tribunal were former high officials, and the complex administration by which the world of the dead was ruled was a reproduction of that in the world of the living. The officials of the infernal regions had a career in the other world. They could be promoted and degraded, and they had under them a crowd of petty employees, archivists, scribes and guards. It sometimes happened that this red-tape bureaucracy made mistakes in names and figures. Thus, people whose allotted span of life had not yet run out might be summoned too soon before the infernal tribunal owing to the error of a careless scribe, and were then sent back to the world of the living. Others might escape taking their place among the dead due to the exemplary filial piety they had shown during their life or to the merit acquired by reciting the sacred texts of Buddhism or to their knowledge of magic formulae. This was how cases of total lethargy or of temporary death were explained. People who had recovered from such events had sometimes had the opportunity of stealing a glance at the lists on which was noted everyone's fate. They had found out from it how many years of life were left to them and at what age their relations and friends would die. Sometimes one of the dead with whom they were unacquainted had entrusted them with messages for parents and the information given by the shades below was found to be correct.

These descents to the lower regions and the prophetic revelations which resulted from them had provided, since T'ang times, one of the favourite themes of the various collections of 'strange and wondrous tales'.

The ordinary person lived surrounded by mysteries and supernatural beings. Marvels were part of his daily life, and anything and everything, in this world, might be a source of disquiet to him. His words and actions were circumscribed—temporarily for some things and permanently for others—by a multitude of restrictions and prohibitions. However much he might spare himself some possible misfortunes by consultation of almanacks and horoscopes and the prescriptions of geomancers, others were sure to turn up unexpectedly.

5. *Buddhism and Taoism*

In the thirteenth century the fervour had long gone out of Buddhism, but everywhere traces remained of the religious fever that China had experienced under the dynasties of North and South and under the T'ang, from the fifth to the ninth century. Almost all the important works of art of that period had been Buddhist: sanctuaries carved out of the sides of mountains, temples and towers for sacred relics, paintings, manuscript scrolls, bronze statues (sometimes covered in gold), stone statues, steles. In one of the gorges of the river Min in Szechwan the traveller still sees soaring up in front of him, at a point where a strong current sweeps his boat along, a colossal image of the divine Maitreya, carved out of the rock at the beginning of the eighth century. It is 324 feet high, has a head 30 yards in circumference, each eye measures 18 feet across, and it is surrounded by a wooden construction with thirteen storeys.[53]

In Hangchow itself traces of the great period of Buddhism were not lacking, and there were still 57 Buddhist monasteries, large and small, within the ramparts, and 31 convents for nuns outside the city. Most of the Buddhist foundations, which amounted to a total of 385 in the two sub-prefectures centred in the town, were either situated within the urban area or near it; there were only 185 of them in the seven other districts belonging to the prefecture of Hangchow.[54] The big monasteries endowed with official status were obliged to carry out ceremonies on behalf of the court. All of them performed the rites demanded of them by the faithful—usually funeral rites. The liturgy consisted of intoned recitation of sacred texts, Indian chants, and offerings of fruits, flowers and incense made to the Buddhas. There were lighted lamps at the foot of the statues. On festive days, the finest paintings and manuscripts possessed by the monastery were exhibited for the admiration of visitors.

Streamers were hung in the great hall where rose, sometimes to a height of 30 feet, the cross-legged statues of the Buddhas with their smile, at once enigmatic and peaceful, which is the very image of the most perfect ataraxy. The most important festivals were those of the bathing of the statues on the 8th of the 4th moon, of the monks' return to the monasteries, where they remained confined for the summer months, on the 15th of the 4th moon, and the festival of the dead on the 15th of the 7th moon.

The whole of China had become permeated by Buddhism, but it had gone so deep that many people, even among the upper classes, were no longer conscious of it. The philosophers borrowed some of their ideas from Buddhism. They were no longer exclusively preoccupied with ethics and politics as their forerunners had been before the beginning of the Christian era, but tried to produce a philosophical system which would be a match for the Buddhist one. This need for a specifically Chinese philosophy made itself felt all the more sharply owing to the fact that Buddhism had ceased to be the main stimulus to intellectual life. Of the many Buddhist sects which were later to be perpetuated in Japan, the only one left was the school of dhyana (zen in Japanese), 'a resurgence of mystical Taoism, particularly esteemed by artists and by the scholars.'[55]

In all classes, the Confucian ethic and Buddhist morality mingled indistinguishably. There were works that enjoyed an astonishing popularity in Sung times which provided each and every person with a means of calculating his merits and demerits according to a scale which gave positive or negative values for every single action, good or bad. One of these manuals, which in principle were of Buddhist inspiration, was so popular that, according to a calculation made at the beginning of the twentieth century, its distribution surpassed that of the Bible.[56]

Let us briefly recall the essential principles of Buddhist doctrine, since it still provided numerous families among all sections of society with their articles of faith. The world is an illusion, a phantasmagoria. Life, resulting from our attachment to this unreal world, cannot be anything but a series of painful disappointments. Birth, illness, old age and death are all nothing but suffering. Only abstention from evil and the carrying out of pious acts will enable individuals, in the course of successive rebirths, to raise themselves in the hierarchy of beings and thus prepare the way for final deliverance.

To escape finally from the painful cycle of re-births a mystical revelation of the inner emptiness of this world was necessary. Religious practices (reading of sacred texts, abstinence from meat, worship of the Buddhas . . . ) and pious works (gifts to monks and to Buddhist communities, contributions to festivals, construction of sanctuaries . . . ) diminished one's stock of sins and increased one's stock of merits. A pious lay person would be re-born a human being in his or her next life, a sinner would be a dog, a pig, a demon, a shade. Intense faith or perhaps the recitation of a magic formula might save the believer at a moment of great peril. Finally, it was possible to intercede on behalf of · the dead, and this was why Buddhist monks played such an important rôle in funeral ceremonies and in the cult of the dead : even people who were not practising Buddhists were moved by filial piety to have Buddhist religious services performed for their dead.

Like Buddhism, Taoism also had its monasteries, its communal organization, its sacred texts, its gods and saints, its liturgy. In all this, it had patterned itself upon its rival. But its communities were less rich, less numerous and less powerful than the Buddhist ones. Having a more definite slant towards magic, Taoism sought to prolong earthly life by means of a complex ascetic discipline as much physical as mental, and to transform the body into a more rarified and durable entity. The Taoist monks knew the secret of drugs for attaining Long Life, and being exorcists and makers of charms and amulets, they knew how to chase away demons and pestilences. But two contradictory tendencies can be distinguished among the Taoists of the twelfth and thirteenth centuries. One put the accent on the occult sciences, the other on ascetic disciplines. One of the most celebrated Taoists of the twelfth century, who was hostile to everything that smacked of magic in his religion, attempted a synthesis of the three 'doctrines' (Buddhism, Taoism and Confucianism). According to him, 'man must realize in himself the natural wholeness which he has from Heaven by controlling his desires, particularly his sexual desires, which attach him to Earth and pollute his celestial nature; if his celestial nature is kept whole he can be sure of attaining Long Life and will ascend to Heaven among the Immortals.'[57]

Apart from Buddhism, which, in the course of centuries, had become completely integrated into the moral and religious thought of the Chinese, there was quite a large number of other foreign religions in thirteenth-century China. Nestorianism, a Christian heresy according to which the Virgin was not the mother of God but of a man, was introduced into China from Iran in the seventh century. It had practically disappeared by the tenth century, and it was only because of the Mongol conquest that it was reintroduced. But Marco Polo was to lament the fact that Christianity was so poorly represented in Hangchow. 'There is,' he said, 'in so great a number of people no more than one church of Nestorian Christians only.'[58] This church was founded in 1279 or 1280, just after the Mongols had established themselves in South China. Manicheism, which also came from Iran, seems to have had a greater and more lasting success, although its influence was limited geographically—we have seen how, under the Sung, it inspired revolutionary sects in Fukien and Chekiang. On the other hand, Islam and Judaism, which for long were not distinguished from each other by the Chinese, never seem to have had any real influence in south-east China. They did not spread beyond the small foreign communities of Jews and, predominantly, Muslims, which existed in the big trading ports of China.[59]

## NOTES AND REFERENCES

1. Hsü I-t'ang, op. cit.
2. Ibid.
3. Chi le pien, Shuo fu XXVII, f. 4a.
4. Kuei hsin tsa chih, Hsü A, § 64.
5. The tropical year was divided among twelve signs corresponding to our signs of the zodiac. 'If the lunar months were equivalent to the solar months, the middle of each lunar month would coincide with the middle of the duodenary sign. But since the duration of the lunar month is shorter than that of the sign, the end of the lunar month comes progressively closer to the middle of the sign, and then falls behind, so that a point is reached when

a lunar month contains no sign centre at all.' This moon, containing no sign centre, 'was declared to be intercalary, and repeated the number of the previous one, thus avoiding any disturbance of the numbering of the moons'. L. de Saussure, *L'Horométrie et le Système Cosmologique des Chinois*, Neuchâtel, 1919, p. 13.

6. On the week in China, cf. an article in the *Fu-jen hsüeh-chih* of 1942.

7. Much of the information given here is taken from Lien-shang Yang, 'Schedules of Work and Rest in Imperial China', *Harvard Journal of Asiatic Studies*, XVIII, 3-4, Dec. 19;5.

8. MLL, XIII, 5, p. 241.

9. MLL, XII, 5, pp. 241-2.

10. MLL, XIII, 6, pp. 242-3.

11. *San Tendai-Godai-san ki.*

12. MLL, VI, 4, p. 181.

13. MLL, VI, 5, pp. 181-2.

14. MLL, I, 2, p. 139.

15. MLL, I, 3, p. 140.

16. *Wu lin chiu shih*, II, 10, p. 372, and 8, p. 368.

17. *Wu lin chiu shih*, II, 8, p. 371. Cf. MLL, I, 4, pp. 140-1.

18. *Wu lin chiu shih* II, 8, pp. 368-9.

19. MLL, I, 4, p. 140.

20. MLL, I, 6, p. 143.

21. *Wu lin chiu shih*, III, 3, p. 377. Among other guilds mentioned, this passage features guilds of actors, singers of various kinds, footballers, wrestlers, crossbow-men, fencers, performers of shadow-plays, conjurers, storytellers, embroiderers and hairdressers.

22. MLL, I, 7, pp. 144-5.

23. MLL, I, 8, p. 145.

24. MLL, II, 4, p. 148.

25. *Ibid.*

26. MLL, II, 5, p. 149.

27. MLL, II, 4, p. 148.

28. MLL, II, 7, p. 150.

29. *Wu lin chiu shih*, III, 5, p. 378.

30. MLL, III, 6, p. 157.

31. MLL, IV, 2, p. 159.

32. MLL, IV, 3, pp. 159-60.

33. MLL, IV, 4, p. 160.

34. MLL, IV, 6, p. 161.

35. MLL, IV, 8, pp. 162-3, and *Wu lin chiu shih*, III, 13, pp. 381-2. It looks suspiciously as if these vainglorious acts contained an echo of ancient religious rites.
36. MLL, V, 1, p. 164, and *Wu lin chiu shih*, III, 14, p. 382.
37. For a general account of the traditional Chinese festivals, see W. Eberhard, *Chinese Festivals*, New York, 1952.
38. *Ch'eng-tu ku chin chi, Shuo fu* LXII.
39. *Hsia jih chi, Shuo fu* XXVII, f. 2b.
40. *Wu ch'uan lu*, by Fan Ch'eng-ta, chap. II, f. 19b, in the *Chih-pu-tsu chai ts'ung-shu* edition.
41. *Wu lin chiu shih*, I, 3, pp. 342-3.
42. This description of the ceremony of the sacrifices at the altar of the southern suburb is taken from *Wu lin chiu shih*, I, 3, pp. 341-2.
43. *Hsün-tzu*, translated by H. H. Dubs, pp. 181-2.
44. *Fu chang lu, Shuo fu* XXVII, f. 3a.
45. *Ch'uei chien lu, Shuo fu* XXVII, f. 6a-b.
46. *Sinica Franciscana*, ed. A. van den Wyngaert, Vol. I, Florence, 1929, p. 376.
47. *Wu ch'uan lu*, chap. I. f. 15b.
48. *Chi le pien, Shuo fu* XXVII, f. 25b.
49. *Chi le pien, Shuo fu* XXVII, f. 5a-6b. This text by Chuang Che (first half of 13th c.), so important and so detailed, unfortunately escaped the attention of E. Chavannes and P. Pelliot in their study of Manicheism in China, 'Un Traité manichéen retrouvé en Chine', *Journal Asiatique*, March-April 1913. See, in particular, pp. 324-63, where texts are cited and translated which tell of Manichean sects in Fukien and Chekiang in the 11th and 12th c.
50. Chang Chiao was the leader of the Taoist rebellion of the Yellow Turbans in 184 A.D. Obviously the sect of Demon Worshippers, although their doctrines were derived from Manicheism, nevertheless borrowed certain elements from Taoism and Buddhism.
51. *Wu ch-uan lu*, chap. I, f. 13a.
52. *Hsia jih chi, Shuo fu* XXVII, f. 2b.
53. *Wu ch'uan lu*, chap. I, f. 11b.
54. MLL, XV, 4, p. 258.
55. P. Demiéville, 'La Situation religieuse en Chine au temps de Marco Polo', *Oriente Poliano*, pub. by l'Istituto Italiano per il Medio ed Estremo Oriente, Rome, 1957.
56. Lien-sheng Yang, 'The concept of "Pao" as a basis for social relations in China', in *Chinese Thought and Institutions*, ed. by J. K. Fairbank, Chicago, 1957, p. 300.
57. See P. Demiéville, *La Situation religieuse* . . . , pp. 193-236.

58. On the Nestorian church in Hangchow, see A. C. Moule, *Quinsai*, p. 36. In chap. CXLVIII of the *Livre de Marco Polo*, ed. Charignon, III, p. 148, reference is made to two Nestorian churches founded in 1278 in Chen-chiang, on the right bank of the Yangtze, below Nanking.
59. The best recent account of Chinese religions is that by R. Stein, *Les religions de la Chine*, in *l'Encyclopédie Française*, section C, chap. IV, Paris, 1957.

# CHAPTER VI

# LEISURE HOURS

EFFECTS OF URBAN LIFE: *Professionals and amateurs.* AMUSEMENTS: *Popular theatres. Street entertainments. Boxing matches. Theatrical entertainments in the home. Indoor games.* ARTS AND LETTERS: *New tendencies. Influence of printing. Broadening of horizons. Attempt at philosophical systematization. Popular literature. Collections of anecdotes. Classical poetry and poems for songs. Painting: tradition and innovation.*

## EFFECTS OF URBAN LIFE

THERE WAS an aura of magic and religion about the arts and about all forms of play: it was on religious occasions that people gave themselves up to play activities, and the aims and character of the games they played went back to very early times when magic had given them a practical or a dramatic function. Vestiges of these origins still survived in T'ang times, but the growth of the towns under the Sung resulted in a secularization of games and of the arts more complete than had been the case after earlier social changes, which removed any vestiges of magico-religious thought and content.

As the rise of new social strata in the town (rich and petty traders, the urban lower classes) made itself felt, so also new needs arose in the matter of the arts and of amusements. Many types of popular entertainers appeared, and we have seen how the 'entertainment industry' employed a considerable proportion of the common people in Hangchow. It was no longer only in aristocratic and court circles that, as had traditionally been the custom since earliest times in China, jugglers, mountebanks, musicians and storytellers exhibited their talents, but they also did so in the middle of the streets, before an audience in which merchants mingled with the common people. The repertoire, the type of entertainment and the style of the performance varied according to the audience, but at the same time there was mutual borrowing between the amusements of the upper and of the lower classes which resulted in their becoming more or less the same, and this interaction had fruitful results. The tale, the short story, the novel and the drama made their appearance, or rather received the impulse for their development which had previously been lacking. Chinese literature was enriched with new forms, and a change occurred in literary sensibility.

On the other hand, in response to the needs of a rapidly rising merchant class, the traditional and esoteric arts of the scholar class reached a wider circle. A market for works of art (paintings, calligraphy, antiques) was established simultaneously with the appearance of professional artists. This 'commercialization' of art gave rise to new aesthetic conceptions, and this, in turn, influenced those that Sung China had inherited from a distant past.

The big cities, and Hangchow more than any of them, because of the density of its population and the mixture of classes in it, had increased the opportunities for contact between different kinds of people and had intensified relations between them. Hangchow offered an endless number of meeting-places, and this provided encouragement to the formation of groups and associations. In a word, it was ideal territory for the development of enjoyments of all kinds. One of the most characteristic traits in the psychology of the town-dweller is an insatiable hankering for entertainment, a passion for every kind of amusement, for social gatherings and banquets. In the thirteenth century there existed in Hangchow a large number of societies, whether of a literary, a sporting, or a religious nature. The names they gave themselves, and no doubt their organization too, suggest that these various groups were very similar to the cult associations that enjoyed such immense popularity in China: the local associations for the sacrifices to the god of the soil, and the Buddhist associations for the carrying out of pious works. Their rules obliged each member to supply his quota towards the social gatherings and solemn banquets which were held annually, and also to contribute towards the ceremonial expenses (chiefly marriages and funerals) that might be incurred by each individual member. This kind of institution lay at the origin of those associations for mutual aid and of those groups formed to administer funds for religious, and sometimes for purely secular, purposes, which continued to exist in China right down to modern times.[1] Social gatherings on certain fixed dates and contributions towards expenses were probably among the characteristic features of the various kinds of associations that we find mentioned as having existed in Hangchow in the thirteenth century.

The most celebrated of them was the Poetry Society of the Western Lake, to which all the best scholars of Hangchow belonged, as well as all those scholars who had come from various regions to make a stay in the town. They held competitions of poetry in free or regular verse-forms or of poems composed to musical themes. The best of these efforts, says a contemporary, had a wide circulation, and were the delight of people of taste. The military officials, for their part, met together in a society for archery and cross-bow shooting, to which only expert archers could belong. There were also societies for football and polo, but no officials belonged to them; their membership was drawn from people from wealthy families that had no doubt made their fortune in trade, from young men belonging to the bourgeoisie of the city, and from the hangers-on of wealthy families.

Mention should also be made of the society formed by the puppeteers of Su-family Street, and of the numerous societies organized within the merchant or artisans' guilds which met on a fixed date in order to celebrate the anniversary of their patron saint. Other groups were of an exclusively religious nature, such as the Taoist association of the Magic Jewel, the members of which, all coming from wealthy families, met each month in order to recite a chapter of a sacred text, and also organized a grand festival on the 9th of the 1st moon, which was the anniversary of the birth of the Jade Emperor; or another Taoist association to which officials who were natives of Szechwan belonged, the object of which was the celebration of a festival which fell on the 3rd of the 2nd moon. Buddhist societies were more numerous, and masses of the faithful belonged to them. The chief one had several tens of thousand members, and its gathering was held on the 8th of the 4th moon, the anniversary of the birth of the Buddha Sakyamuni. It was then that the rite of the 'liberation of living creatures' was performed on the lake. Each member brought water-turtles, fish, shell-fish and birds which they set free on the shores or in the waters of the lake.[2]

It is assuredly not without good reason that contemporary accounts make pell-mell mention of all these associations which were formed for such widely varying purposes, for all of them were patterned on the same model and satisfied similar needs. They responded to the desires of lovers of the same art, of believers in the same faith, or of natives of the same district, to meet together and fraternize. Only a great city could have such a variety of them. It is not difficult to imagine what a great influence some of them, particularly the Poetry Society of the Western Lake, must have had on the development of arts and letters in the twelfth and thirteenth centuries.

## AMUSEMENTS

The town was full of places for social gatherings of one kind or another: the gardens outside the ramparts where the towns-people went for pleasure outings, odd spaces or street-corners where a gaping crowd collected round some acrobat, tea-houses where rich people went to take lessons in playing musical instruments,[3] boats on the lake where guests were entertained . . . But Hangchow had its places of amusement that were specifically designed as such. These were the special 'pleasure grounds', a kind of vast covered market where lessons were given in dramatic art and in singing and music, and where theatrical representations of all kinds could be seen daily. The name given to these establishments signified, according to the interpretation given by contemporaries, that they were places 'where no one stood on ceremony', that is to say, that people of all sorts and conditions could rub shoulders with each other there without bothering about the usual rites and formalities. There had already been bazaars of this kind in Kaifeng, the Northern Sung capital, at the beginning of the twelfth century. The first to be constructed in Hangchow dated from the reign-period known as the Restoration of Sung (1131-1162), and they were instituted for the soldiers garrisoned in the city, most of whom, being natives of the northern provinces, were separated from their families, and must have been at a loss to know how to fill their leisure hours.

The imperial government staffed these pleasure grounds with singing-girls and women-musicians, and to begin with, the function of these bazaars was to provide brothels for the soldiers. 'Nowadays,' writes an author in 1275, 'these establishments have become places of debauch and of perdition for society people and young men of good social standing.' At that time there were seventeen or twenty-three (different sources give different numbers) of these pleasure grounds in Hangchow, most of them outside the ramparts, near the gates of the city. Those in the suburbs were not controlled by the same branch of the administration which controlled those in the city proper, but all of them had a State official in charge.[4]

The pleasure grounds contained various instruction centres—thirteen in all—giving tuition in drama and music. Each one had its 'head' or 'director', and the artistes wore costumes which varied according to what group they belonged to and what their rank and classification were. They might wear violet and purple, red and blue, or sometimes a full skirt with yellow edging. The actors wore turbans of various shapes and colours, the musicians caps. Depending upon which section they belonged to, the musicians played the sad-sounding flute originating from Central Asia, the Chinese transverse flute, the 'great drum', a xylophone with six or nine elements as big as the palm of a hand, joined together with a leather thong, the four-stringed guitar, the guitar in the form of a long flat rectangle with three strings, pan-pipes with thirteen reeds, the body of which was made of a dried calabash, and an instrument similar to the xylophone but with plates made of metal or stone.

In other groups, various types of singing were taught, as well as dancing and dramatic art. The drama made quite a feature of short farcical scenes, acrobatic turns and satirical sketches. There were actors who imitated the peasants of Shantung and Hopei, for this type of comedy had been much in vogue at Kaifeng and was kept up in Hangchow. Other scenes were in the form of a ballet accompanied with songs and instrumental music. There were also Chinese shadow plays, in which the actors were puppets cut out of paper with articulated joints, and various other kinds of marionette theatres featuring puppets on strings pulled from above or on sticks manipulated from below, or 'live' ones played by families of actors with thin, graceful limbs. The puppeteers who worked the articulated puppets made them speak in a shrill, nasal voice.[5] Both shadows and puppets acted little scenes: stories of ghosts and marvels, crime stories, and romantic pieces in which history mingled with fiction. Storytellers were also popular. They all specialized in one or other type of story: tales of genies and demons, stories about shrewd judges who were particularly clever at resolving the most baffling cases, tales of battle in which the heroes showed superhuman strength and skill, Buddhist stories recounting episodes in former lives of the Buddha. Both plays and stories inclined at times to social satire and denounced the corrupt practices of those in power.[6]

Acrobats and jugglers were also to be seen in the pleasure grounds, but usually they gave their shows on the fringes of these places, in spaces marked off on the pavements by barriers. At the northern pleasure ground, near one of the bridges over which the Imperial Way ran, there were thirteen of such 'barriers'. But entertainers did not confine themselves to these spaces which were apparently specially reserved for them; they were to be seen at crossroads, in the squares and in the markets—anywhere, in fact, where they could collect a crowd. Sometimes they put up temporary shelters made of bamboo stakes and mats. Thus right in the middle of the streets passers-by could marvel at acrobats with their heads between their legs, tightrope walkers with poles on their shoulders from which hung jars of water full to the brim, not a drop of which was spilled as they walked their rope, men juggling with plates, bottles or large jugs, men exhibiting bears or performing ants, sword-swallowers, wrestlers or boxers. Groups of from three to five musicians went about singing and dancing while balancing on their shoulders one or two little boys and girls.[7] Storytellers and men who asked riddles also drew crowds, humorists too 'who gave absurd commentaries on the solemn Classics and demonstrated, by means of erudite word-play, that the Buddha, Lao-tzu and Confucius were women'.[8]

An author at the end of the thirteenth century gives the following description of the various curious spectacles he had seen in Hangchow in his childhood. 'Here is a man showing performing fish: he has a large lacquer bowl in front of him in which swim turtles, turbots and other fish. He beats time on a small bronze gong and calls up one of the creatures by name. It comes immediately and dances on the surface, wearing a kind of little hat on its head. When it has finished its turn, it dives down again, and the man calls another one. There is also the archery expert who sets up in front of the spectators a big wheel a yard and a half in diameter with all sorts of objects, flowers, birds and people painted on it. He announces that he is going to hit this or that object on the target, and having started it spinning rapidly, he shoots his arrows through the midst of the spectators. He hits the exact spot he has declared he will hit. He can even score a hit on the most precisely defined spots of the spinning target, such as a particular feather in a particular wing of a bird.' But apparently, adds the author, he was not able to transmit his art to anyone. Another entertainer is the snake-charmer who sits outside the Supreme Temple and who has only four fingers left. He will hold the strangest and most venomous snakes in his hand as if they were nothing but eels. If a snake remains hidden in its basket and lends a deaf ear, its master blows into a little pipe, and the snake comes to him immediately. This curious person has trained several dozen different kinds of snakes, some of them very large and dangerous; he keeps them in bamboo baskets. He can do whatever he likes with them, and the practice of his craft has made him quite well off. The same author also mentions a Taoist hermit who can be met with on the banks of the river carrying on his back a creel full of shell-fish of various kinds and colours, all of them hypnotized.[9]

But it was above all at festival times, when the entire population of the town made merry in the streets and spent day and night drinking and wandering about seeking for amusement, that open-air entertainments were most numerous. When sacrifices were offered at the Sacred Palace, ceremonies performed at the altar in the southern suburbs, or imperial amnesties declared at the Gate of Elegant Rectitude, shows and games of all kinds were held all over the town. Boxing matches were held between the Left and the Right Armies of the Imperial Guard on the Emperor's birthday and when banquets were held at the court. The strongest soldiers were picked out as boxers and their names placed on a special list. It was they who preceded the imperial chariot on the occasion of the ceremonies at the altar in the southern suburbs and on other occasions when sacrifices of the official cult were performed. A hundred and twenty of them, bewhiskered and wearing caps on top of their long hair that floated round their shoulders, made a cordon on each side of the official route holding each other by the wrist. As for the boxers that were to be found in the pleasure grounds and contiguous pavement spaces, they were travelling performers who gave shows in all the towns. Coming from all the prefectures in the empire, they gathered at the Protection-of-the-kingdom monastery, on the South Peak, for the big boxing competitions that were periodically held there. The winner was awarded a flag, a silver cup, lengths of silk, a brocade robe, and a horse.[10]

Most of the performers and entertainers who exhibited their talents in the pleasure grounds or in the streets gave performances in private mansions belonging to wealthy families, and sometimes even at the court, at festival times and when banquets were held. Or at least, if the performers were not the same, the performances were similar, although more skilful perhaps, more subtle, as befitted the more exacting and elegant tastes of this type of audience, than those in the pleasure grounds and markets, although there, too, people from the upper circles often mingled with the common people for the fun of keeping low company. We saw how some people with special gifts were permanently employed in rich households: chess-players, painters of chrysanthemums, writers of literary compositions, setters of amusing riddles . . . These hangers-on were part of the household. Other artistes were hired to entertain the guests at big social gatherings: fashionable singing-girls, musicians, acrobats and conjurers.[11]

It was only the most celebrated performers that were admitted into the presence of the Emperor. A text of 1280 lists fifty-five different varieties of performers, and gives the names of 554 of them who had given shows at the court towards the end of the Sung dynasty. Let us pick out a few of the different types from this varied list (some of the terms of which are difficult to interpret), to illustrate the extraordinary degree of specialization among entertainers: tellers of obscene stories, imitators of street cries, imitators of village talk, singers specializing in six different kinds of songs, sleight-of-hand experts, flyers of kites, ball players and footballers, archers and crossbow-men.[12]

Entertainments in the streets and pleasure grounds, festivals, shows given in the homes of wealthy families—all this was still not enough to satisfy the need for amusement felt by the town-dwellers. In their spare and leisure moments they all enjoyed playing indoor games of various kinds. There was every variety of these, to suit all classes and ages. There was even sometimes a sex distinction in the playing of some games. Thus, swings provided the recreation of young society ladies. Gambling games, with cash coins sometimes used as chips, were the favourite amusement of the lower classes, in spite of official prohibitions. Thete were also children's games, but unfortunately we know nothing about them.

On the other hand, some games were played by all classes of society, such as the game of 'double-six', a kind of backgammon that seems to have been introduced into China about the third century A.D. It consisted of twenty-four pieces which were moved according to the throw of the dice. This game was the rage in Sung times, and according to a twelfth-century author, 'the rich stake their slaves, their horses . . . ; the poor play for who will stand the next round of drinks'. The dice used in Sung times were identical with the ones used by us, except that the four, which was equivalent to our ace, was painted red. This was why a game with rules similar to poker was called 'turning up the red'.[13] Mention might also be made of dominoes, of 'mahjong', and of the pack of cards in which the four kings were the mythical sovereigns of the four cardinal points, which probably appeared in China during the T'ang dynasty; and finally, among the traditional upper-class games, chess, and the 'jug' or 'narrow-neck' game. These two games had been known since before the Christian era and were for long used for purposes of divination or for trial-by-ordeal. The first is related to our chess, although the rules differ considerably; the second requires very great skill: the opponents have to throw darts into a round-bellied vase with a narrow neck by making them ricochet off the skin of a kind of drum that is placed halfway between the players and the target.

## ARTS AND LETTERS

Repercussions of the social changes and technical advance which occurred under the Sung can clearly be discerned in the various forms of literary and artistic expression of the period: poetry, tales, novels, encyclopaedias, song, instrumental music, painting. The aesthete, for whom art exists in a sphere of its own, as a universal expression of the human spirit, may dismiss such trivial material questions or merely mention them in passing without taking account of them. But would it be possible to do this in a study of daily life, for which, both from the point of view of method and as a pre-requisite for understanding the facts, precisions as to the period, the historical moment, the human relationships obtaining at the time, and the geographical environment are indispensable? A whole complex of factors contributed to the changes which occurred in theme and style, and turned arts and letters in the Sung period into specific pursuits. Professionals more and more took the place of the scholar skilled in all the arts, calligrapher, painter, prose-writer and poet all in one. The spread of printing from the tenth century onwards, the development of a book-trade, the proliferation of tales, dramatic sketches, marionette and shadow plays and of popular songs, the formation of literary societies, the growth of the trade in antiques and *objets d'art*—all these novelties could not help but affect Chinese literary and artistic sensibility.

Of these factors, clearly one of the most far-reaching in its effects was the appearance of printing. It might well be said that printing came just at the right moment in China, the moment when ever-widening sections of society sought to improve themselves by learning, or perhaps simply hoped to derive from reading the pleasure they had found in listening to tales, anecdotes and poetry. It was in fact due to the rise of the merchant class and to the rapid growth of the lower class urban population that printing, in response to the new needs that resulted, came into such general use. Social change had supplied a justifiable purpose for an invention which might otherwise have passed unnoticed. Proof of this is found in the fact that the first uses to which printing was put were extremely limited. Before the eighth century wood-cut plates were used for reproducing on paper[14] charms, amulets, and small religious tracts, and, most important of all, for making holy images for distribution; the mere fact that large numbers of these could be reproduced was held by the Buddhists to have astonishing religious efficacy.

The technique of printing, which began in monastic communities, both Buddhist and Taoist, was later developed by the laity during the ninth and tenth centuries in the two regions with the greatest density of population: the lower Yangtze, and western Szechwan, where almanacks, astrological works and rudimentary dictionaries circulated among the people. However, between 932 and 953, an edition of the Confucian Classics, which so far had only been carved on stone, was officially ordered to be made in wood-block printing. Between 960 and 971 there appeared an edition of the Buddhist canon, a gigantic corpus consisting of sutras, commentaries, works on discipline and doctrinal treatises. In the middle of the tenth century attempts were made to introduce movable type, made of earthenware, tin and wood. But the overwhelming number of written characters (Chinese writing has more than seven thousand characters in common use, whereas the alphabetic notation of Romance languages, in its various forms, permits of a much more restricted number of printed signs), the cheapness of labour and the preference for good calligraphy rather than print, had the result of making the invention of movable type retard, rather than advance, the spread of printing.[15]

It is owing to the editions made in the Sung period that most of the works of that period, as well as earlier works still surviving at that time, have come down to us. These texts printed in Sung times provide us with an astonishing body of material which testifies to the extraordinary passion for learning that characterized the Chinese of the twelfth and thirteenth centuries.[16] It is a period which occupies, in the history of China, the same place as our Renaissance. The development of printing is not the only feature which justifies this comparison. In both periods there was a return to the past that was accompanied, in the spheres of art, of literature and of thought, by a general sense of renewal. While T'ang scholars had been content to explain the commentaries made in Han times (206 B.C. - A.D. 220), now the Classics were re-interpreted and given new commentaries. A new philosophy came to the aid of the commentators, and the thought of the ancient philosophers was explained in terms of hsing (the nature of things and of beings) and li (the order immanent in everything).

Archaeological discoveries aroused the passions of art-experts and art-lovers. Some of the antique bronzes and jades brought to light in the reign of Hui-tsung (1101-1125) in the vicinity of An-yang, in Honan, dated from the end of the second millenium B.C. and were contemporary with the bone and tortoise-shell inscriptions discovered from 1899 onwards in the same region. Catalogues, encyclopaedias and treatises appeared which dealt with a wide variety of topics: monographs on curious rocks, on jades, on coins, on inks, on bamboos, on plum-trees, on li-chees, on oranges,[17] on mushrooms, on different varieties of flowers, on fishes and crabs; treatises on painting and calligraphy; geographical works, some of which dealt with foreign lands; historical works.

The first general and unofficial histories of China made their appearance. As a leisure occupation, some scholars compiled small works on elementary physics, or rather, collections of curious prescriptions. Notes of the following kind are found in them: 'If, in summer, hot water is poured into a well, ice is formed'. 'Centipedes detest oil.' 'Mint takes away the smell of fish.' 'If fish is cooked with [a particular kind of] dried orange, the bones are softened. Balsam seeds can also be used for this purpose.' 'When the hands are greasy, salt can be used instead of soap.' 'To get rid of callous skin on the heels, rub them with a tile which still has bits of the cloth it was moulded on adhering to it.' 'After eating garlic, chewing a mixture of raw ginger and jujubes will restore the freshness of the breath.' 'Do not put brasenia purpurea [a kind of edible water-plant] in lacquer containers: the best lacquers will not stand up to it.'[18] The making of collections and inventories, erudition, and listing of curious facts were characteristic features of the whole period.

There were several trends in philosophical speculation. The main one was a new interest in cosmology, a subject disdained by the Confucianists of antiquity and by the founder of Chinese humanism himself. Confucius (551-479 B.C.) considered that Man was the only fit topic for the reflections of a Sage. Sung cosmological theories were expressed and summarized in esoteric diagrams explaining the origin and development of the universe. They were closely linked with ethics, since Man was thought of as being in harmony with the universe. They aimed at substituting in place of Buddhist theories a purely Chinese interpretation of the entire cosmos.

It was during the twelfth century that there arose a philosopher who was to have a profound influence on the subsequent development of Chinese thought. This was Chu Hsi (1130-1200), the founder of a realist philosophy in which matter and essence, combined into one inclusive concept, were opposed to form, or, according to the Chinese expression employed by this philosopher, to the 'breath' which gives individuality to every single creature. However form and matter were not antithetic, but complementary. The universe was still conceived of as a whole, composed of alterations and of opposing principles, which however, had to collaborate if the equilibrium of the universe was to be maintained: Chinese thought rebelled against any form of dualism. In the domain of ethics, it was characteristic of his ideas that he laid stress on education and on effort. Other philosophers took the opposite point of view and founded their system on some kind of fundamental intuition similar to that of the Buddhist dhyana sect (Japanese zen) or of the Taoists of antiquity. For them, world and mind are one. But most men are not aware of this identity because of their blindness, a blindness which is not of a purely intellectual variety: it comes from egoistic thoughts and a calculating spirit. It is only to the truly 'detached' individual that intuitive understanding is given of the profound unity that exists between the universe and the creatures within it.[19]

Contemporaneous with the enlargement of the conception of the universe came an enrichment of literature through the use of new forms and the manifestation of new tendencies. It was no longer only the scholars of the upper classes, but also the 'bourgeois' and the common people who were the originators of the new creative trends in literature. The literature of the period, partly still composed in the oral tradition and, even when written, intended to be heard rather than read, made great use of the spoken language, either that of the people or that of the upper classes. The storytellers, the professional dramatists and the puppeteers for both marionette and shadow plays produced a huge repertoire of fantastic stories, Buddhist tales, short crime stories, or romantic narratives set in the past, either in the period known as the Three Kingdoms, in the third century A.D., or in later periods, such as that of the Five Dynasties (tenth century).

Some of the librettos used by the Sung storytellers have survived. One recounts the sad end of Hui-tsung, the last Emperor of northern Sung, his captivity and his death in Manchuria. Another is the forerunner of the celebrated Ming novel that tells of the journey to India of the pilgrim Hsüan-tsang in the seventh century, accompanied by the wonderful Monkey. These tales were told in colloquial language (perhaps accompanied by a light musical accompaniment), but they also included some passages in verse, which were sung, at points where poetry seemed better suited to the circumstances, as, for instance, in the description of a pretty woman or of a landscape, or if the action had reached a specially crucial moment.[20]

The taste for collections of anecdotes, very fashionable in T'ang times, became still more pronounced under the Sung. These works, to which printing gave a wide circulation, consisted of a series of brief accounts which were mostly of a strange or fantastic nature, but which were all vouchsafed for by eye-witnesses. Personal names, place-names and dates were meticulously given. Here are some specimens of this literary form:

In a village of Kiangsi a black giant more than nine feet tall entered a house, sat down without a word, and made no reply at all to questions put to him. It was impossible to get rid of him. The servants took sticks and showered him with blows. They tried to stick lances into him, but the iron crumpled without breaking the skin. They scalded him with hot water, without any result: the giant did not even seem annoyed. The master of the house then hit upon the idea of sounding the alarm by beating on his drum (all houses in this region possessed drums for assembling the villagers in cases of attack from bandits), but the drum did not make a sound. Seeing that violence had no effect, he tried persuasion. He bowed down to the ground in front of him and begged the unwanted guest to clear out. But he might as well have whistled to the wind. Finally the giant, tired no doubt of sitting, heaved himself up and started making a leisurely tour of the house, the courtyard and the covered ways. He broke the locks of all the boxes where the household treasures were kept.

Evening came and the giant was still there. When it was time to light the lamps, they would not burn. Then the entire household was seized with terror, fled to the hills and took refuge in a temple. It was arranged for Taoist ceremonies to be performed, and the monks were asked to send a petition to Heaven. After seven days the genie finally disappeared. But from that moment onwards the master of the house began to fall into a decline and he ended up in the direst poverty.[21]

Prophetic dreams are often the theme of these anecdotes:

At the time of the barbarian invasion in 1126, a peasant who had read much (which explains his historical knowledge that features later in the story) had a nightmare. He dreamt that he had been out in the fields and had met seven horsemen. One of them, dressed in white and mounted on a white horse, turned to him in anger and addressed him more or less in these words: 'In one of your former lives you were a soldier of the T'ang period and you killed me. Now that you are in my power you must expiate.' He then stretched his bow and shot him through the heart.

The man's wife tried to calm his fears: why put faith in dreams? They were nothing but fantasies, imagination! But the man's fright only increased. He rose at dawn and decided to go and visit a relative about eighteen miles away from his village. After going a long way through the brushwood, he reached the official highway where he joined a group of peasants he found there. Suddenly a troop of horsemen rode up and shouted to the peasants to stop. Our runaway hero turned and saw that there were seven horsemen and that one of them was dressed in white and rode upon a white horse: exactly the man he had seen in his dream. Panic-stricken, he crossed the road and took to flight as fast as his legs could carry him. He heard loud shouts telling him to stop, but paid no attention to them. Then the horseman in white whipped his horse, caught up with him, and when he was face to face with him, let fly an arrow which went straight through his heart. These seven horsemen were no other than Ju-chen barbarians.[22]

If belief in spirits might sometimes result in tragic mistakes, it was also at times the cause of comical misunderstandings.

When, in his youth, the minister Lu An-lao was a student at the prefectural school of Ts'ai-chou (in south-east Honan) he went out on the sly one evening with eight companions. They were on their way back, in the middle of the night, when they got caught in a heavy shower. Not having any umbrellas, and not daring to spend a night out because of the strictness of the rules at school, they entered an inn and borrowed a large piece of hempen cloth. Holding it over them by means of stakes attached to each corner, they continued on their way under this improvised shelter. Just as they were approaching the school, a soldier on guard, torch in hand, saw them from afar and challenged them. Frightened, they retreated for some distance and waited, not daring to advance any further. The soldier came back on his rounds, and then disappeared. They seized the opportunity and jumped over the wall of the school, and spent the night with beating hearts, certain that their escapade had been discovered and that they would be severely reprimanded. The next morning, the officer of the watch sent in the following report to the prefecture: 'Last night, after the second watch, at a time when it was raining hard in the town, the soldiers on guard at a certain point on their rounds suddenly saw a strange creature coming from a northerly direction. Vague in form, it was flat as a mat in its upper part and like men walking in its lower part. It had about twenty or thirty legs. It approached the wall of the school, and then suddenly disappeared.' From the prefect down to the pettiest of employees no one could identify this animal which became the subject of interminable discussions in the neighbourhood. Many people decided that this must be a miraculous phenomenon of some kind, and put it to the administration that it would be wise to perform ceremonies of exorcism in each quarter of the town for three days and three nights, for which an image of the beast should be made so that sacrifices could be offered to it.[23]

The majority of anecdotes in these collections are about ghosts, genies and demons. Some, however, are of a more realistic character, such as the following:

In the 7th moon of the year 1150 a boat coming from the high seas put in at a little port in the province of Fukien. It had a crew of only three men and one woman, and carried a cargo of several thousand pounds of sandalwood. One of these men was a Chinese who was a native of Fuchow. Having formerly gone to sea, he had suffered shipwreck, and only had his life saved by a plank of wood which bore him to a large and unknown island. This Chinese liked playing the flute and always kept his flute attached to his belt. The islanders having brought him before their king, he discovered that this sovereign was also a keen musician and highly delighted to see a flute and hear it played. He detained his guest, invited him to his table, and gave him lodging. Later he even gave him one of his daughters in marriage. The shipwrecked mariner stayed thirteen years with these people, who did not understand his language but seemed to have guessed that he was Chinese. One fine day, he decided to return to his native country with his wife and two companions, and at the end of two months reached the Fukien coast. The police of the place, thinking he must be a smuggler, sent guards on board and brought him to the urban sub-prefecture of the city of Fuchow. 'It was then,' says our author, 'that I was able to see the boat. It was made of a large hollowed-out tree-trunk and only had one opening through which one could go in and out. Inside, there was a narrow recess where the woman lived. The two men were her brothers. Their clothing consisted of a loin cloth and a hair-band round their heads. They were barefooted. When they were offered something to drink, they knelt down, touched the ground with their hands as a form of salute, and quaffed their drink in one draught.' The woman had teeth as white as snow; but, adds the author, she was slightly dark-skinned.[24]

As a means of stirring to action or a means of persuasion, and as an allusive but effective form of expression, poetry was part of everyday life in China, and although it was specifically an art of the scholars, it was nevertheless held in the greatest veneration among many sections of society. In the ninth century, even before the spread of printing, copies of the works of the most celebrated poets of the time circulated in the markets and could be used as a means of payment for wine and tea. In Hangchow and in the neighbouring city of Shao-hsing, these poems had been engraved on stone so that lithographs could be made.[25] In the Sung period the old poetic forms were still cultivated: the regular poems with five or seven written characters to the line, and long descriptive poems that were both lyrical and erudite. But at the same time, the growing popularity of songs which were half popular and half erudite inspired the development of a new kind of poetry.

Poets in China were not tempted to be over-eloquent. Chinese is naturally concise and arrives at its meaning not by means of logical links, but by juxtapositions. Hence Western languages, although better suited than Chinese for exposition and argument, are not at all suited for rendering poetry of such a compact and allusive nature as is that of China. Nevertheless, since some examples must be given here, here are a few poems of the twelfth and thirteenth centuries which may help to give an idea of the poetic sensibility of the period. The title of each piece gives the theme.

*On hearing a seller of fish and vegetables shouting his wares outside the wall of my house, in the snow. His cry is so full of suffering that it is utterly unbearable.*

Crates under arm, out he has rushed, not a moment to lose,
Knee-deep in snow, with icy beard, bravely enduring the cold.
Out of the question for him to stay idling his time indoors:
Enduring cold is hard enough; enduring hunger's worse.

Another verse on the same theme:

His cry implies: the cost of rice is near its weight in gold.
It's the same cry as the frozen sparrow's or the hungry crow's.
What hardships you must have known, that life has brought you
    down to this!
If you ponder it at all: What do you think of Fate, I wonder? [26]

(Fan Ch'eng-ta, 1126-1193)

Some poems aimed at social satire, such as those of Liu K'o-chuang (1187-1269), whose plain-speaking led to his disgrace:

### Complaining of the cold

Out here on the frontier, the autumn wind is wicked,
And all us soldiers haven't got enough upon our backs.
That clothing-issue orderly—will he come or won't he?
With nights as cold as armour, it's hard to sleep a wink.
But back home at the capital the clever gents are snug enough,
The sun is high before THEIR scarlet doorways get unlatched, and
    lots and
Lots of cosy curtains keep THEM screened off from the winds and
    wilds,
While, drowned in drink, they don't CARE, if, outside, it's freezing
    cold. [27]

The barbarian invasions aroused national sentiments in some poets. Thus poems of patriotic inspiration are fairly frequent in the Chinese literature of the twelfth and thirteenth centuries.

### Written on the wall of an inn in Hangchow

Hill beyond green hill, pavilion behind pavilion—at the
West Lake, will the singing and the dancing never cease?
It's the warm wind that lulls them and beguiles them into thinking
That this place is the other one we knew in times of peace. [28]

(Lin Sheng, second half of the 12th century)

*On the banks of the Yangtze, looking out over occupied China*

Athwart this ridge where down below the rolling river runs,
My house in the clouds looks out over mile after mile of brooding
    sadness.
How bitterly I wish that mountains blocked my wandering gaze,
For northwards, far as eye can reach, our conquered land seems
    endless.[29]

(Tai Fu-ku, end of 13th century)

*On visiting the former Imperial Palace at Hangchow*

*(After the Mongol conquest)*

Like an ancient ruin, the grass grows high: gone are the guards
    and the gatekeepers.
Fallen towers and crumbling palaces desolate my soul.
Under the eaves of the long-ago hall fly in and out the swallows
But within: Silence. The chatter of cock and hen parrots is heard
    no more.[30]

(Hsieh Ao, 1249-1295)

In contrast to regular verse forms, which were written to be
read and always used the literary language, poems composed for
musical airs made great use of the colloquial language. These
poems, intended to be sung, are not easy, although they enjoyed
tremendous popularity throughout the Sung period. They are
composed in irregular metres, and are usually lyrical and descriptive, often being inspired by the same kind of ideas as painting
was, as the one quoted here will show. Impressionistic in character, they try to catch the exact feeling of a particular moment,
and to convey a sense of the passing of time, and so of the sadness
of life. The following example describes a landscape after rain, at
sunset. The observer, like the observer of a picture, becomes
double, one part of himself wandering in the immensity of nature
depicted:

After the rain the air is fresh
As I stand, quite still, in the belvedere by the riverside.
Light gleams on a distant stretch of the stream's clear waters,
And kingfisher blue jut, peak upon peak, the evening mountains.
Afar, yet distinct, is the broken-down bridge, and the half-hidden
    path

That leads to the quiet fishing village,
Where, towards dusk, a plume of smoke rises.
Bathed in the glow of sunset,
With yearning heart I silently lean on the scarlet railings
My feelings all in a dark turmoil,
My senses reeling, although I have drunk no wine.
And now—infinite grief!
The evening clouds have all dispersed,
The autumn light has long since faded,
My friend is a thousand miles away, and
Ended the day. I have looked and longed in vain.[31]

(Liu Yung, 11th century)

There was no definite boundary between poetry and pictorial art. A painting was often accompanied by a poem which provided a clue to the subject and expressed the same idea in another medium. Conversely, most writers were also skilled in the use of the brush, and could write their poems in a calligraphy which had aesthetic value and which conveyed to the connoisseur whatever degree it might have of verve, imagination, order and balance. The poet was already half painter in his command of line and his visual sensibility. For these reasons, the history of painting and the history of literature in China cannot be divorced the one from the other. In the Sung period they developed along parallel lines.

Novelties such as the interior decorating industry, the rapid increase in the number of art-lovers and collectors, the rise of a new class of professional painters and calligraphers, the development of the trade in antiques and objets d'art, could not fail to have some effect, and in fact led to a basic change, during the Sung period, in the very conception of art as well as in the conditions in which art was produced. Whatever apparent continuity there may seem to be from the earliest times up until Sung and after, we may rest assured that the appearance is nothing but an illusion. Not only does investigation show that both new techniques and new styles made their appearance during the Sung period, but—and this is the important thing—artistic sensibility and the very way of seeing things altered radically. This is what one would have expected quite apart from any evidence.

Here a glance at the past is indispensable. According to an

ancient conception, only traces or memories of which still survived in the twelfth and thirteenth centuries, painting is an art
akin to magic, demanding the most minutely detailed realism in
order to make the subject as lifelike as possible. The painter is
near to being a magician : he can re-create creatures and things
by making an exact image of them, and can give them an
autonomous existence by endowing them with the breath of life.
His landscapes provide for those who contemplate them the opportunity and the means for making ecstatic excursions. The
personality of the painter as a creative artist is effaced, and the
observer becomes double, one part of himself shrunk to the
dimensions of the immense vista of Nature that is the object of
contemplation of the other part. He is carried away, and loses
himself in the landscape : he is there on that mountain path
from which he sees unrolling before him a succession of peaks
and deep valleys, the dwelling-places of Immortals; or on that
bridge there, amid the wind and the snow; he hears, on the
nearby river-bank, the shrill cry of monkeys . . . In this manner, the Chinese landscape is not viewed from a fixed point. It is
a field of vision in which the eye can wander, seeing it from
different and changing points of view. The eye travels from top
to bottom (or sometimes, in the scrolls of the Sung period, from
right to left), and each landscape has a plurality of perspectives.
While creating a supernatural world, where everything is pure
and holy, such painting also aims to give an ordered picture of
the universe : the mountains represent the positions of sovereign
and vassal; earth and sky, shadow and light, the yin and the
yang, the female and the male principles, are set against each
other, alternate with each other, and complete each other. The
thing which the artist has created is a kind of talisman, possession of which confers blessedness.

In addition, painting and calligraphy (for calligraphy uses the
same techniques, and the same brush is used for writing and for
painting) were ascetic disciplines of a religious nature, a kind of
sacred play that procured longevity—in the same way, incidentally, as did the subtle and extremely difficult art of playing on
the ancient type of zither, in which the slightest details had a
deep symbolical meaning.[32] These arts demanded an absolute
mastery of the bodily movements required for them, and indeed
a control of the body as a whole, as well as a complete identifica-

on on the part of the artist with the thing he was doing (which
accounts for painters specializing, as they still did in Sung times,
in various branches of their art: bamboos, horses, orchids, etc.).
But the inspired artist who was in complete control of his art
had to paint in a sort of trance, in a prophetic delirium that
might be stimulated by alcohol, dancing or music. Such had been
the general character of creative art in China, valid for the poet
as well as for the painter.

As it happened, this alliance between inspiration and perfect
technical mastery was re-discovered by the greatest of the Sung
painters. Their art was an all-embracing one in that it demanded
total participation, and among a small élite of true artists painting retained a far-off memory of its religious significance. But the
events of the period were not to be without influence on this
traditional conception of the nature of painting.

Among the influences to which art in the Sung period was
subjected, certainly one of the weightiest was that of the style
of painting cultivated in the official Academy of Painting at
Kaifeng which had been founded by the Emperor Hui-tsung
(1101-1126), who had also gathered together the richest collection of works of art in China. It had been possible to transfer
most of this collection to Hangchow, and the style favoured by
the Emperor Hui-tsung continued to enjoy the same prestige in
the capital of South China during the twelfth and thirteenth
centuries. The styles preferred were realistic and detailed pictures
of flowers, birds, and tame and wild animals.

The new spirit which dominated the literary world was also
perceptible in the pictorial arts, and particularly in those of the
Academy. The most humble and ordinary circumstances of daily
life became subjects for painting: herbs and vegetables, common
insects such as crickets and grasshoppers, scenes of daily life
(scholars playing at double-six, musicians making music, street
scenes, children playing, etc.), carts, bridges and ramparts, houses
and palaces. This *genre* painting, in which technique was valued
more than inspiration, and in which the decorative effect was
more important than poetic meaning, had much the widest
appeal in the twelfth and thirteenth centuries. Even outside
academic circles, it enjoyed a greater popularity than any other
style. It was to be found as frequently in the art collections of
scholar families as in the homes of *nouveau-riche* merchants,

who decorated not only their homes but also their shops with paintings à la mode and with calligraphy scrolls. Specialized professional painters of orchids were maintained as members of the household in rich families. It goes without saying that, although there may have been real masterpieces in this style of genre painting which was so much the rage at that time, a great deal of lifeless and insignificant painting was turned out to satisfy the avidity of the rich collectors and the self-conceit of the noveau-riches.

However, the passion for collecting, so common among wealthy people—and let us remember that anything might be collected, not only paintings and calligraphy, but also curious rocks, jades, antique vases, steles dating from before the Christian era . . [33] — indubitably had some salutary effects. It developed a critical sense among many cultured art-lovers. Some could point out false attributions of worthless pictures to celebrated painters, and recognize by their workmanship the works of old masters and schools of painting. In spite of the widespread practice of making copies of well-known works, the idea that each great artist had his own personality began to emerge.

The taste of the period demanded that paintings of flowers, animals and still more of landscapes, should catch and evoke the feeling of a particular moment and attempt to render the quality of the atmosphere and even, one might say, its temperature. It was precisely by its exactitude in rendering such things that a good painting could be recognized. A writer recounts the following anecdote: An art-lover had acquired an old painting representing peonies and a cat. However, he was not sure if it had real value until, one day, a relative cried out on seeing the picture 'But these are peonies painted at midday precisely!—What makes you think so?—Their petals are opened out and have a matt look. Besides, the cat's pupils are like a thread: two indications to show that it is midday.'[34]

This genre painting for decorative purposes in its turn provoked a reaction. Works that were realist but without either inspiration or life were categorically condemned in certain purist circles where sensitivities were finer, and in which an entirely new style of painting developed. Here, simplification and the stripping away of all inessentials was pushed to extremes: a few lines sufficed to suggest a vast landscape with its distances lost in mist. The essential thing for the most exacting painters of the period was to seize the soul of things by an intuitive understanding similar to that of the mystic, and so be able to give spiritual depth to their landscapes. A secularization of the type of landscape represented went along with the enrichment given to it by the philosophical preoccupations of the painter—preoccupations which were the same as those that exercised the thinkers of the period. The great Sung landscape painters no longer chose as their subjects sites celebrated for being the dwelling-places of Immortals, but simply Nature in general. The proof that this new style can in part be interpreted as a reaction against commercialized forms of art lies in the horror with which the small élite of inspired painters regarded anything that might be considered vulgar.[35]

## NOTES AND REFERENCES

1. Cf. A. Smith, Village Life in China, 1899; J. Gernet, Aspects économiques du Bouddhisme . . . Saigon, 1956.
2. MLL, XIX, 4, pp. 299-300.
3. MLL, XVI, 1, p. 262.
4. Tung ching meng hua lu, V, 2, pp. 29-30; Tu ch'eng chi sheng, 7, pp. 95-8; MLL, XIX, 2, p. 298, and XX, 3, pp. 308-10; Wu lin chiu shih, VI, 2, pp. 440-1.
5. R. H. van Gulik, T'ang yin pi shih, p. 82.
6. MLL, XX, 6, pp. 312-13.
7. MLL, XX, 4, pp. 310-11.
8. L'Art de la Chine des Song, catalogue pub. by the Musée Cernuschi, Paris, 1956, R. Ruhlmann, Les Jeux et le Théatre au Temps des Song.
9. Kuei hsin tsa chih, Hou, § 34.
10. MLL, XX, 5, p. 312.
11. MLL, XIX, 5, pp. 300-1.
12. Wu lin chiu shih, IV, 2, pp. 392-408, and VI, 12, pp. 453-66.
13. R. Ruhlmann, loc. cit.
14. The invention of paper was an essential preliminary to the invention of printing. Chinese paper, in use since the 1st c. A.D., was usually made of hemp, bamboo, or the bark of a special kind of mulberry (Broussonetia papyrifera). On the paper made at Wen-

chow (south coast of Chekiang), which was one of the finest papers made in the Sung period, cf. *San-liu-hsien tsa chih, Shuo fu* XXIV, f. 7a.

15. On the history of printing in China, see P. Pelliot, *Les Débuts de l'Imprimerie en Chine*, Oeuvres posthumes, IV, Paris, 1953, and T. Carter, *The Invention of Printing in China*, 2nd ed., New York, 1955.

16. Anecdotes show that scholars in the Sung period ruined themselves buying printed books. Cf. *Fu chang lu, Shuo fu* XXXIV, f. 3b-4a.

17. A monograph on the oranges of Wenchow (Chekiang), the *Chü-lu*, by Han Yen-chih, has been translated by M. J. Hagerty in *T'oung Pao*, XXII, 1, March 1923.

18. *Wu-lei hsiang-kan*, by Su Tung-p'o, *Shuo fu* XXII.

19. M. Kaltenmark, 'Littérature Chinoise', in *Histoire des Littératures*, Vol. I, Collection de la Pléiade, Paris, 1955, pp. 1237-41. Feng Yu-lan, *A History of Chinese Philosophy*, II, pp. 434 ff.

20. M. Kaltenmark, *loc. cit.*, pp. 1235-7.

21. *I chien chih, i* 17, 4th anecdote.

22. *Ibid., chia* 1, 4th anecdote.

23. *Ibid., ping* 13, 14th anecdote.

24. *Ibid., i* 8, 9th anecdote.

25. P. Pelliot, *op. cit.*

26. *Sung shih hsüan* (anthology of poems in regular metre of the Sung period), Shanghai, 1957, p. 94.

27. *Ibid.*, pp. 104-5.

28. *Ibid.*, p. 100.

29. *Ibid.*, p. 102.

30. *Ibid.*, p. 119.

31. *T'ang Sung ming-chia tz'u hsüan*, Shanghai, 1957, p. 81. On the history of Chinese poetry in the Sung period, cf. M. Kaltenmark, *loc. cit.*, pp. 1227-35.

32. See the study by R. H. van Gulik, *The Lure of the Chinese Lute*, Tokyo, 1940.

33. On the trade in steles of the Ch'in period (end of 3rd c. B.C.) and of the Han (206 B.C. - A.D. 220) coming from the region round present-day Si-an in Shensi, cf. *Ch'ing po tsa chih, Shuo fu* XXII, f. 4a-b, and *Fu chang lu, Shuo fu* XXXIV, f 7b.

34. *Yü chia chi*, by Huang-fu Mou, *Shuo fu* XXXII.

35. For a general account of painting in China, see L. Sickman and A. Soper, *The Art and Architecture of China*.

# CHAPTER VII

## FINAL PORTRAIT

A WAY OF LIFE is subtly and inextricably bound up with ideas that belong to it, and no doubt this provides the real explanation for our interest in the details of daily life when we study the history of a people. Their habits and customs reveal to us one particular form of human experience in general, from which emerges a certain definite type of personality. It must be confessed that it is easier to sense this form of experience and the personality emerging from it than to express them in words. However, since we have come to the closing pages, perhaps we might attempt to draw a character sketch of the typical Chinese of the thirteenth century, or rather of the typical upper-class town-dweller, since this is the type we know most about. And as certain traits of his character were only touched on in passing, now is the moment to fill them in.

One thing is clear: the kind of person that has been glimpsed, in the course of this study, through an accumulation of anecdotes and petty details, is a specific product of urban life as it was lived in the great urban centres of south-east China. But simply to define him as a town-dweller is not enough. Tradition affected his behaviour just as much as period and environment, and its influence is all the weightier because it is something that is usually taken for granted. Thus, when considering the typical inhabitant of the large Chinese cities of the thirteenth century, it is possible to distinguish not only certain character traits that are peculiar to him, but also certain tendencies that seem to be permanent, being common to Chinese of all periods.

The political structure of the State as it had continued to exist in China since it was first established in the third century B.C., is perhaps not unconnected with the concepts and attitudes that most strikingly characterized the Chinese. The order that reigned in imperial China was a *moral order* which an autocratic State had been able to impose step by step, until it reached the smallest social unit: the individual family. The lack of any sharp dividing line between a man's private and his public life, between his duties to the family and his duties to the State, lay at the basis of the Chinese concept of government: morals and politics were one. Wherever there was consensus of moral opinion, respect for parents, elders and betters, wherever the individual was completely integrated into his group, there constraint was no longer necessary; and as a result, a certain amount of autonomy could be allowed to regional, village and family units.

Indeed, the immensity of the empire rendered this comparative freedom necessary, and it can be said that the Chinese succeeded in discovering a means of governing the largest number of people with the least direct intervention: the most important point was that order should reign at the level of the smallest social groupings. It would appear that this very original form of political structure had its repercussions on the Chinese concept of Man and the Universe. The order of the universe (according to this concept) was the end product of a total complex of spontaneous adaptations. Everything was a matter of example and influence, not of law. There was no law in Nature, because it was by contagious influences that Nature itself acted. This was the explanation offered for differences in temperament observed among men. The inhabitants of North China, a region dominated by the element Earth, were solid, sincere, faithful to their word, but rather slow-minded. Those of the South, on the contrary, where the element Water dominated, were lively, skilful, full of guile, but at the same time inclined to be frivolous and superficial.[1] The harmony which reigns between Man and the cosmos is a positive one. It is made up of a multitude of correspondences, and is expressed in physiological concepts, in cosmology, the arts, techniques, divination, just as much as in the rules which regulate social relations and moral conduct. Accordingly, man does not experience any kind of inner conflict. He is not midway between the animal and the divine. It is only human problems that concern him; nothing is more foreign to the Chinese genius than metaphysical anguish and anxiety.

The idea that human nature needs to be educated, that some sort of training is necessary, was no doubt generally accepted. But stress was more often laid on the benefits of being natural and of spontaneously adapting to one's environment. All men were held to be capable of good feeling, to contain the germs of that natural goodness that is to be found even among animals. In the countryside near Hangchow there was a place called the Grave-of-the-dog, and near it, a bridge called the Bridge-of-the-good-dog. In 1275 the old men of the city still told the tale of how a man whose clothing had caught fire was saved by his dog, who had the presence of mind to soak himself in water and then shake it over his master. When the dog died, the peasants buried the brave animal at this spot and also named the bridge after it in memory of his fidelity.[2] Only bad example and extremes of poverty could alter Man's natural goodness. If he suffers neither cold nor hunger and is encouraged to be good, he will act in conformity with morality.

Tolerance, and faith in human nature, both of which proceed from a firm belief in the value of social life, were the most striking moral qualities of the Chinese. But these qualities were associated with a concept of the universe as a system so well-balanced that any idea of progress was excluded. The Universe was composed of balances, not of contradictions, hence human action was not seen in the same light in imperial China as it is in the West. Whenever it ceased to be inspired by tradition, whenever it was original and independent, it was felt to be a force of disruption.

However, in contrast to the love of order, of balance and of positive values, and to the belief in the benefits of social life, there also existed tendencies of an anarchistic and mystical nature. There was another side to the Chinese temperament which was sombre, lunatic and morbid. Although very little known, it is nothing but the reverse side, the counterpart, of their manifest sociability, faith in human nature and enjoyment of life. Many facts bear witness to a pathological desire for individual annihilation. In certain religious societies, about which we have no information beyond a few passing references, the practice of black magic seems to have satisfied a sadistic taste for the macabre. Other sects were animated by a melancholy and destructive fanaticism. Mortification of the flesh was pushed to extremes, to self-mutilation and suicide. Traditional techniques of trance and possession were commonly practised. Undernourishment and sexual restraint, intended as dietetic and hygienic disciplines that would confer sanctity, resulted in temporary states of hypertension or in a permanent loss of balance of the nervous system that led to crises of mystical enthusiasm.

China was a country of visionaries, saints and prophets. But the techniques of depersonalization were much more widely practised than is usually realized. Among the lower classes they were frequently used to satisfy certain religious needs; among the scholars, to stimulate artistic inspiration. An ecstatic state of delirium was necessary for the calligrapher or the poet who was truly master of his art. Religious mysticism and aesthetic intuition: these were the two forms of Chinese irrationalism.

Urban life had the effect of modifying these tendencies. The upper-class town-dweller of the thirteenth century was a highly-strung person, and even seems, because of his extreme sensitivity to fashion and his love of display and self-dramatization, to have been rather effeminate. Unremitting pursuit of pleasure, over-indulgence in alcohol, and sexual excess drained his energy and accentuated the weaker side of his nature. Often a word or an attitude were, for him, the substitute for action. This explains his boastings and inconsequentialities. About 1275, a prefect in the region of Nanking had huge notice-boards put up along the boundaries of his administrative district. 'If the horsemen from the North arrive,' read the notice, 'I am prepared to die rather than flee.' When the Mongols got there, not a trace of this hero was to be found: he had gone into hiding. A wag then changed some of the characters on the notices so that they ended with these words: 'If I cannot conquer them, I shall flee'.[3]

The Chinese of the thirteenth century seems to have been much more sentimental and romantic than his forebears. He seems to have been consumed with a sense of the sadness of life, to have suffered from the depths of despair, which found expression in his works of art. The passing of time, failure, disgrace, the pain of parting, were frequent themes of his poetry; but he did not, as did the Chinese of T'ang times, find a counterbalance to this profound melancholy in action.

On the other hand, he showed a sense of curiosity and an enlargement of outlook unknown a few centuries earlier. His free way of life would have scandalized his T'ang forebears. Because of his courteousness, his sense of humour, and his taste for social life and the art of conversation, he is one of the subtlest and most highly cultured types of human being that Chinese civilization has ever produced. From the history of his daily life there emerges a general impression of natural self-discipline. of gaiety and of charm. He had an extraordinarily keen sense for the finer shades. Nobody, in Hangchow, would unthinkingly mention the word 'duck'. Why? When they first came to the city, the refugees from the North thought that the word was taboo for this peculiar reason: that, however hot it might be, duck soup was supposed never to give off any steam. But they soon learnt the real reason: ducks cannot produce eggs with only one drake; they require at least two or three. To mention ducks to anyone would be to pass slighting remarks about his conjugal life.[4]

The Chinese of the thirteenth century seems to have been more free and easy of manner, less stilted, than his counterpart in T'ang times. His politeness was not artificial, did not consist merely of a formal code of etiquette and prescribed behaviour; on the contrary, his entire social life, which was founded on exchanges of presents and services, was permeated by human warmth and sympathy. His kindliness was even extended to foreigners. 'They also treat foreigners who visit them for the sake of trade,' says Marco Polo, 'with great cordiality, and entertain them in the most winning manner, affording them every help and advice in their business.'[5]

He enjoyed making jokes, and there is a special kind of Chinese humour which has an inclination towards puns and word-play. It was in the Sung period that a very large number of examples of this kind of humour first appeared. It mocks without malice, and sometimes at the expense of the people of a neighbouring district; for the lively attachment that all Chinese have for their native district goes hand in hand with a humorous contempt for the customs of bordering provinces. The townspeople of Kaifeng mocked the *gaucherie* and the dialect of the peasants of Shantung and Hopei. The people in the Ch'eng-tu plains, in western Szechwan, ridiculed the inhabitants of the mountainous regions of eastern Szechwan.[6] At Shao-hsing, on the south bank of the Che river estuary, fish and firewood were scarce, in spite of the large number of lakes and rivers, and in spite of the mountainous nature of the region. Hence the saying that used to circulate in Hangchow: '[At Shao-hsing] there are mountains, but no firewood; water, but no fish; men, but no loyalty.' This saying had a way of annoying Shao-hsing people, and they became enraged as soon as they heard the first words of it.'

This Chinese whose portrait we have painted seems so human, with all his contradictions and extravagances, so close to us, so familiar, that we are almost tempted to forget everything that marks him off from us: his conception of Man and of the Universe, his aspirations, the paths his thoughts pursued, his particular kind of sensitivity—in short, all that he contains within himself of his own civilization.

## NOTES AND REFERENCES

1. *Chi le pien, Shuo fu* XXVII, f. 4a.
2. MLL, XVIII, 3, p. 290.
3. *Kuei hsin tsa chih, Hsü B,* § 31.
4. *Chi le pien, Shuo fu* XXVII, f. 19b.
5. Y, pp. 204-5. The sympathy shown to foreigners was mixed with curiosity. ' . . . whenever I have happened to visit one of their cities,' wrote the Arab traveller Ibn Batuta at the beginning of the 14th c., 'and to return to it after a while, I have always found my own likeness and those of my companions painted on the walls, or exhibited in the bazaars.' These drawings made at a moment's notice could be used, if occasion arose, for police identification. Cf. Yule and Cordier, *Cathay and the Way Thither,* IV, p. 114.
6. *Nan pu hsin shu, Shuo fu* XXVI, f. 3a-b.
7. *Chi le pien, Shuo fu* XXVII, f. 3b.

# INDEX